The How-to Guide

MW00389852

Integrating the
Common
Core in
Mathematics

For Grades K–5

Author
Linda Dacey
Contributing Author
Karen Gartland
Foreword
Gregory A. Denman

LESLEY
UNIVERSITY

 SHELL EDUCATION

Publishing Credits

Robin Erickson, *Production Director;* Lee Aucoin, *Creative Director;*
Timothy J. Bradley, *Illustration Manager;* Sara Johnson, M.S.Ed., *Editorial Director;*
Lori Nash, M.S.Ed., *Editor;* Sara Sciuto, *Assistant Editor;*
Grace Alba, *Designer;* Corinne Burton, M.A.Ed., *Publisher*

Consultant

Dana Strong, Math Consultant

Shell Education
5301 Oceanus Drive
Huntington Beach, CA 92649-1030
http://www.shelleducation.com
ISBN 978-1-4258-1197-6
© 2014 Shell Educational Publishing, Inc.

Integrating the **Common Core** in **Mathematics**

For Grades K-5

Table of Contents

Foreword

I have an expectation of the titles of educational resource books I read. They must target exactly what the content of the book will offer me as a teacher. Having read Linda Dacey's text, *The How-to Guide for Integrating the Common Core in Mathematics,* my expectations have been met with flying colors. It is a comprehensive guide, presented with clarity and example, as to how I and the teachers with whom I work can successfully integrate the rigorous demands and challenges of the Common Core Standards into their K-5 classrooms.

What Linda so effectively builds her "how-to guide" on is, first, a thorough, yet practical understanding of the applications and outcome goals of Common Core State Standards. Second, an in-depth examination of "best practices" research on math instruction. *Simply put: What works best in the classroom and why.* Finally, an appreciation of how teachers grow and students learn. She demonstrates a "boots-on-the-ground" understanding of the dynamics of 21st century math instruction.

Her book extends well beyond simply reiterating what the Standards are (we can readily procure those from the Internet) to what she presents as "unpacking a standard."

Given the Standard: *What must the student know? What will the student be able to do? How does the standard relate to other standards and critical areas? What vocabulary and symbols are important to develop? How does the knowledge develop over time? What learning targets connect to the standard? What curriculum and instruction support the learning targets? How could this standard be expressed in student-friendly language?* She then proceeds, throughout the entire book, to give teachers a showcase of specific grade level examples and tasks, illustrations, discussion points, and instructional guidelines. There is a practical and contextual application of strategies that I have yet to find with such clarity in any other professional resource. Teachers, regardless of their familiarity or previous training with CCSS, will readily see how they can effectively implement the Core's Standards for Mathematical Practices.

I am confident that Linda's text is going to become the gold standard of the implementation of the Common Core Standards in K-5 classrooms across the country. Our student learners will be the ultimate beneficiaries.

—Gregory A. Denman
Educational consultant and author of *Think it, Show it Mathematics: Strategies for Explaining Thinking*

Chapter 1

Opportunities and Challenges

 Voice from the Classroom

I first heard about these new standards from my principal. When he announced them, I found myself doing a wonderful imitation of my young daughter's new eye-rolling habit. I figured this meant there would be lots of meetings and paperwork, but no real changes to my teaching. I mean, it wasn't as if I were going to suddenly stop teaching addition and subtraction.

We started with crosswalks, looking to see how what we were teaching now mapped on to these new standards. It was challenging to understand some of the standards and I don't think this matching process helped us. We tended to see things as the same, if they seemed similar, and walked away with only a few things to change—things we would no longer teach, such as writing multiplication equations to match pictures of equal groups or repeated addition sentences. What we didn't understand was how what we saw as the same was actually different. It wasn't until the following summer when I had the opportunity to go to a local conference and learn more about these standards that I began to see them differently. I now understand that teachers need help understanding what these mean, why they are important, and how their teaching will be different.

—Second-Grade Teacher

This teacher's voice expresses what I have heard many teachers say. It's challenging to figure out what these standards mean to our teaching when they are presented to us as a list. We need time to work with others about what they mean and how we can implement them. We need to understand their purpose and to be able to make sound choices among the myriad of resources that seem to pop up online daily. Most important, we need to invest in our own learning—to take the time to read, to listen, and to talk with others about mathematics, these standards, our students, and our teaching practices.

Each of us is on our own learning trajectory about these standards. Some of us have attended numerous workshops and conferences and have coaches to help us explore ideas. Others may only have limited familiarity with the math standards, having spent time focusing on language arts. Regardless of where you are starting from, it is not a journey that ends quickly. I have been able to teach and write about these standards since they first were published, and I continue to deepen my understanding of them and what they mean to teachers and classrooms. So let's begin with a general overview of these standards.

Overview of the Standards

Demand for mathematical knowledge has increased as student performance on worldwide standardized tests continues to disappoint. In response, the National Governors Association Center for Best Practices (NGA) and the Council of Chief State School Officers (CCSSO) cooperated on the development of the Common Core State Standards, standards that were designed with the goal of creating common K–12 learning goals that would prepare students to meet expectations for career or college. In mathematics, the standards identify *Standards for Mathematical Practice* as well as content standards. As of this writing, these standards have been adopted by 45 states, something that has never happened before in the history of the United States.

These standards are intended as a set of learning outcomes, not a national curriculum. The implementation stage is where teachers' knowledge of both their craft and their students is most important. Support for these standards clearly varies at local, state, and national levels, but one thing is clear to me and hopefully to you: It is time for educators to take the lead, as we will ultimately be the key to the success of this reform effort.

We all need to:

- 🖎 understand the standards clearly,
- 🖎 gain insight into how these standards could be met within classrooms,
- 🖎 develop assessment strategies to support student success, and
- 🖎 recognize ways in which working with others and using available resources can help us to meet our goals.

This book is designed with these needs in mind. It also is written with the beliefs that all teachers want their students to succeed; that given the right circumstances, all students can succeed; and that any change comes with opportunities and challenges. To support the success of our students, we need to embrace the opportunities and find ways to address the challenges in manageable ways.

Teachers know change. No other profession has a complete change of clients every year. Every September teachers meet their new students with excitement. Yet those early days can be more tiring, too, as we establish routines and classroom expectations with a new group. The routines do get established, though, and the excitement begins to come not from the newness, but from the progress our new students are making. Just as our task is to get to know our new students and learn how to best support them, our first task here is to get to know these new standards and how to best implement them for student success.

Discussion of these standards often centers on the extent to which they provide focus, coherence, rigor, and clarity. Each attribute is considered here and returned to throughout the book.

Focus

The phrase "a mile wide and an inch deep" has often been used to describe the mathematics curriculum in the United States. Many teachers complain about the range of topics they have to *cover*, and clearly strong instruction involves much more than coverage. The Common Core provides focus on key ideas and understandings, as you cannot gain deep understanding of a great number of topics. Also, *critical areas* have been identified for each pre-secondary grade level, which provide further focus to the documents.

Coherence

Mathematical ideas need to be learned as a series of related ideas that progress across the grades, rather than through exposure in ways that do not connect one topic to the next. Too often students don't realize, for example, that the concept of division is the same, whether it is applied to whole numbers, rational numbers, or integers. Similarly, many students do not recognize that properties, such as the commutative property of addition, also apply to all types of numbers. Such generalizations are necessary to avoid students learning isolated concepts or skills that are likely to be forgotten. The Common Core provides coherence by providing standards that progress across the grade levels and that connect to one another in clear, recognizable ways.

Rigor

Teachers often feel as if education reform is just a pendulum swinging back and forth between conceptual development and skill acquisition. Similarly, curricular resources may emphasize one end of the continuum considerably more than the other. Conceptual understanding and skill development are *both* expected outcomes of the Common Core. For example, students are expected to understand the four operations and strategies used to find sums, differences, products, and quotients; reach arithmetic fluency; and apply their understandings and skills to solve problems. The Common Core also defines mathematical habits of mind (Standards for Mathematical Practices) that include rigorous terms such as persevere, precision, abstractly, and viable argument, among others.

Clarity

When learning expectations are given for grade-level spans such as 3–5, or if the language used to describe standards is imprecise, teachers remain unsure of expected outcomes. The Common Core provides specific single-grade-level standards that indicate what is to be learned when. As teachers, we need to develop a common understanding of what students need to know and how they can demonstrate that they know it. Figuring this out is often referred to as *unpacking the standards*. The standards may at first glance appear dense and challenging to comprehend as they are viewed both within and across grade levels. The progressive nature of the standards will become clear.

The Expectations Are for All Students

Before looking at specific standards, it is important to emphasize the *common* expectation of the standards. Too often we have discovered that schools in lower socio-economic areas have less rigorous standards than others with greater financial resources. This educational disparity leads to increased differences and does not match our democratic values. All students must have access to learning goals that allow for success. This is also true of students with learning challenges who are often restricted to skill development through rote procedures. "Emerging literature suggests that students with moderate and severe disabilities can learn content aligned with grade-level standards while continuing to work on basic numeracy" (Saunders et al. 2013, 24). As we think about implementing the standards, we need to address how we will meet the needs of our diverse students.

Standards for Mathematical Practice

The Standards for Mathematical Practice describe a set of proficiencies, or habits of mind, that students should develop over time. Built on the five process standards developed by the National Council of Teachers of Mathematics (NCTM 2000) and the five strands of mathematical proficiency identified in *Adding It Up* (National Research Council 2001), these eight standards (listed in Figure 1.1) have the potential to transform mathematics education in ways that would be even more significant than the content standards, as they indicate ways in which students should learn and demonstrate their knowledge of mathematics (Hull, Harbin Mills, and Balka 2012).

The goal is to have these standards integrated into all mathematical content areas in K–12 classrooms. Understanding these practice standards takes time and will be the focus of the next chapter. For now, let's consider how one mathematical task might relate to them. In third grade, students are expected to understand division's relationship to multiplication and to solve two-step problems. Figure 1.2 shows how the following task might connect to the Mathematical Practices.

Mr. Rodriquez bought a bag of 25 balloons for the party.

He used a tire pump to blow up the balloons.

He tied four balloons to his mailbox so guests could find his house.

He put the other balloons in the kitchen, dining room, and living room.

He put the same number of balloons in each room.

How many balloons did he put in each room?

Figure 1.2 Connections Between a Specific Task and the Standards for Mathematical Practices

Practice	How Practices Connect to the Task
MP1 Make sense of problems and persevere in solving them	Students can interpret the problem information. They have strategies they can use to represent the problem so that it makes sense. They try more than one approach if they get stuck.
MP2 Reason abstractly and quantitatively	Students can identify the important information in the problem statement. They can represent the information in equations, models, diagrams, or drawings.
MP3 Construct viable arguments and critique the reasoning of others	Students can explain and defend their thinking clearly and understand the explanations of others. They can identify strengths and weakness among various solutions strategies.
MP4 Model with mathematics	Students use models and equations to represent the problem. They can connect the equations $7 \times ? = 21$ and $21 \div 7 = ?$.
MP5 Use appropriate tools strategically	Students successfully use representations, mental arithmetic, and paper and pencil strategies to find a solution.
MP6 Attend to precision	Students use appropriate vocabulary, symbols, and labels to communicate their solution process.
MP7 Look for and make use of structure	Students connect the division portion of this task to multiplication by thinking *Seven times what is equal to 21?* They know that $7 \times 2 = 14$ and that $7 \times 2 + 7 = 21$, so they conclude that $7 \times 3 = 21$.
MP8 Look for and express regularity in repeated reasoning	From solving other problems, students recognize this as a two-step problem and that the division situation is one of equal shares.

According to Silver (2010, 1) "…typical classroom mathematics teaching in the United States tends not to use challenging tasks, nor to promote students' thinking about and engagement with mathematical ideas, and thus fails to help students develop understanding of the mathematics they are learning." For students to develop the habits of mind suggested by these practices, the tasks we present must be complex, especially if we want to incorporate more than one mathematical practice in a lesson or activity. Consider the following tasks. What differences in complexity do you notice among them? What mathematical practices do you think they would each tap?

☞ Find the area of this shape. (Shown only Figure A)

☞ Find the area of each shape. Explain how finding the area of Figure A could help you to find the area of Figure B. (Shown Figures A and B)

☞ You have enough fencing and a gate to make the garden shown in Figure B. If you want your garden to be as big as possible, how would you design it for the fencing you have? (Shown only Figure B)

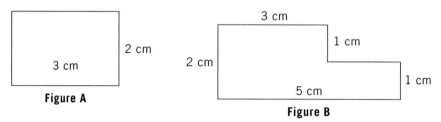

Figure A   Figure B

Content Standards

Domains, Clusters, and Standards

For grades K–8, content standards are provided for each grade level. It is helpful to understand the ways in which the standards are organized. Domains, which are large groupings of related mathematical ideas, have been specified for each grade level. The domains for the K–5 levels are summarized in Figure 1.3.

Figure 1.3 Domains Across the Grade Levels

Domains	Grade Levels					
	K	1	2	3	4	5
Counting and Cardinality (CC)	X					
Operations and Algebraic Thinking (OA)	X	X	X	X	X	X
Number and Operations in Base Ten (NBT)	X	X	X	X	X	X
Number and Operations—Fractions (NF)				X	X	X
Measurement and Data (MD)	X	X	X	X	X	X
Geometry (G)	X	X	X	X	X	X

Within these domains, related standards are organized in clusters as shown in Figure 1.4. Standards are identified by their grade level, domain, and standard number. Sometimes, they list specific standards under a broader one, for instance, 5.NF.7b is standard b, listed under standard 7 in the Number and Operations—Fractions domain at grade five.

Figure 1.4 Parts of the CCSSM Grade Level Standards

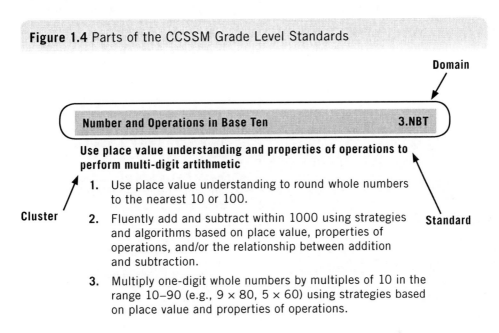

(NGA and CCSSO 2010, 5)

Critical Areas

Many of us may be so drawn to the standards themselves that we overlook the introduction section to each grade level. It is there that the critical areas for that level are identified. At grades K–5, there are two to four areas per grade. These key ideas indicate the focus of mathematical instruction for that year and help us to plan the curriculum that will allow the standards to be met. At the K–5 levels, often more than one domain is involved. The critical areas for each level are summarized in Figure 1.5. The domains that support the key idea are listed below each critical area.

Figure 1.5 Critical Areas of Instruction at Grade Levels K–5

Kindergarten	Grade 1
1. Representing and comparing whole numbers, initially with sets of objects (CC, OA, NBT, MD) 2. Describing shapes and space (G)	1. Developing understanding of addition, subtraction, and strategies for addition and subtraction within 20 (OA, NBT) 2. Developing understanding of whole number relationships and place value, including grouping in tens and ones (NBT) 3. Developing understanding of linear measurement and measuring lengths as iterating length units (MD) 4. Reasoning about attributes of, and composing and decomposing, geometric shapes (G)
Grade 2	**Grade 3**
1. Extending understanding of base-ten notation (NBT) 2. Building fluency with addition and subtraction (OA, NBT, MD) 3. Using standard units of measure (MD) 4. Describing and analyzing shapes (G, OA)	1. Developing understanding of multiplication and division and strategies for multiplication within 100 (OA, NBT, MD) 2. Developing understanding of fractional equivalence, addition and subtraction of fractions with like denominators, and multiplication of fractions by whole numbers (NF, MD) 3. Developing understanding of the structure of rectangular arrays and of area (MD, G) 4. Describing and analyzing two-dimensional shapes (G, NF)

Grade 4	Grade 5
1. Developing an understanding and fluency with multi-digit multiplication, and developing understanding of dividing to find quotients involving multi-digit dividends (OA, NBT, MD)	1. Developing fluency with addition and subtraction of fractions and developing understanding of the multiplication of fractions and of division of fractions in limited cases (unit fractions divided by whole numbers and whole numbers divided by unit fractions) (NF, MD)
2. Developing an understanding of fraction equivalence, addition and subtraction of fractions with like denominators, and multiplication of fractions by whole numbers (NF, MD)	2. Extending division to 2-digit divisors, integrating decimal fractions into the place value system and developing understanding of operations with decimals to hundredths, and developing fluency with whole number and decimal operations (OA, NBT, MD)
3. Understanding that geometric figures can be analyzed and classified based on their properties, such as having parallel sides, perpendicular sides, particular angle measures, and symmetry (MD, G)	3. Developing understanding of volume (MD, NF, G)

Summarized from the introduction sections of each grade level of the CCSS (National Governors Association 2010)

Looking closely at the critical areas gives us important perspectives on the standards. The small number of critical areas per level supports the notion that these standards are focused. At the elementary level you can see that significant attention is given to numbers and operations. Note that all but three of the 30 critical areas (describing shapes and space at kindergarten; reasoning about attributes of, and composing and decomposing, geometric shapes at grade one; and using standard units of measure at grade two) do not include a domain related to number or operations. The critical areas highlight the key ideas where several domains coalesce. In this way, these areas support focus and cohesiveness. The cohesive nature of the standards is also demonstrated with the ways in which ideas progress through the grade levels.

There are other standards in each grade level that are not part of these critical areas, and yet, they too are important. For example, in grade four, *4.NBT.4: Fluently add and subtract multi-digit whole numbers using the standard algorithm* is not connected to one of the three critical areas at that level as it is an extension of a critical area in the third grade. The standard is significant, though, as it supports the progression of the students' abilities; it is the first time the standard algorithm is stated as an expectation.

Sometimes we consider standards as a checklist. *Do I understand this one? Check. Onto the next one on the list.* We cannot meet the goals embedded in the critical areas with this way of thinking. Once we understand standards and their progressions over time, we need to think about how the domains work together to support the critical areas at that grade level.

Unpacking a Standard

A standard tells what students need to *know* and be able to *do*. To unpack a standard, we grapple with each of the following questions:

- ☞ What must the student *know*?
- ☞ What will the student be able to *do*?
- ☞ How does this standard *relate* to other standards and to the grade-level critical areas?
- ☞ What *vocabulary* and *symbols* are important to *develop*?
- ☞ How does the knowledge develop over time (*learning progression*)?
- ☞ What *learning targets* connect to the standard?
- ☞ What *curriculum* and *instruction* support the learning targets being met?
- ☞ How could this standard or its associated learning targets be *expressed* in student-friendly language?

Let's consider a specific standard in the first grade Operations and Algebraic Thinking domain.

1.OA.7 (Understand the meaning of the equal sign, and determine if equations involving addition and subtraction are true or false. For example, which of the following equations are true and which are false? $6 = 6$, $7 = 8 - 1$, $5 + 2 = 2 + 5$, $4 + 1 = 5 + 2$.) Thinking about the nouns and the verbs can be a way to begin the process. Figure 1.6, also available in Appendix A, is one way to organize the unpacking process. Here is how one teacher completed it.

Figure 1.6 Unpacking a Particular Standard

Standard	Organize by Nouns and Verbs
1.OA.7 Understand the meaning of the equal sign, and determine if equations involving addition and subtraction are true or false. For example, which of the following equations are true and which are false? 6 = 6; 7 = 8 – 1; 5 + 2 = 2 + 5; 4 + 1 = 5 + 2.	Understand • Meaning of the equal sign Determine • If equations involving addition and subtraction are true or false. For example, which of the following equations are true and which are false? 6 = 6; 7 = 8 – 1; 5 + 2 = 2 + 5; 4 + 1 = 5 + 2.
Relate to Other Standards	**Vocabulary/Symbols**
This standard is in the cluster *work with addition and subtraction equations.* I will look at each of the other standards in the cluster. It also supports the critical area *Developing understanding of addition, subtraction, and strategies for addition and subtraction within 20.*	Students must know that when they see the equal sign (=) in an equation, it means each side has the same value. An equation is only true when this is the case. *Is the same as* and *balanced* are other ways to express the relationship.
How Does This Idea Develop?	**Learning Target Examples**
Students first need lots of experience modeling addition and subtraction situations. Then, they connect these experiences to numbers and the +, –, and = symbols. Over time, they explore a variety of ways equations can be written, e.g., two numbers and an operation sign on the left and the answer on the right; the answer on the left and two numbers and an operation sign on the right; one number on each side; two numbers and an operation sign on each side. Then, they can apply their understanding of equations to decide if particular equations are true or not.	• Model an equation (true) with two numbers and an operation sign on the left and the answer on the right using the number balance (Do the same for other configurations.). • Use a number balance to show that an equation is false. • Write true and false equations.
Curriculum/Instruction	**Student-Friendly Language**
• Activities on the number balance to test and create equations • Number of the Day routine • Play concentration games that require students to match sides of equations that would be equal	*I know* what the equal sign (=) means. *I can* decide if an addition or subtraction equation is true or false.

Glossary

The Glossary is another section of the Common Core State Standards that can be forgotten if there is single focus on the specific standards. This aspect of the standards document is meant to augment the standards, in that it provides tables that summarize addition, subtraction, multiplication, and division situations as well as definitions for the terminology used throughout the standards. The tables give problem examples connected to related equations identified within the standards. The glossary can help teachers develop common definitions of the terminology used within the standards. When you read a phrase such as *tape diagram* in a standard, it may be helpful to refer to the glossary. You may find that you are familiar with this representation, but that you call it by one of the other names, such as *bar model*, provided in the definition.

Assessment

"Asking a student to understand something means asking a teacher to assess whether the student has understood it" (CCSSO 2010, 4). The new standards call upon students (and thus teachers) to deeply understand mathematics. The content progression can only be fully realized if students are able to apply what they are learning in new contexts and connect it to the next related standard(s) as a natural learning path. A variety of assessments help students know how well they understand the material and inform teachers, parents, and administrators about student progress. To be worthwhile, we must make sure that such assessments address both concepts and skills, include tasks that require higher-order thinking, and are accessible.

Formative assessments such as listening to students' conversations in the classroom or reading a child's math journal inform teachers about how to structure the next day's lesson or to determine who might need remediation or enrichment. Purposeful homework provides students with an opportunity to practice the content and to learn to persevere if they find that doing the work individually is difficult. Frequent formative assessment allows us to intervene quickly when a student lacks complete understanding. Time for assessment and intervention should become part of our planning, and we must create safe classroom environments where errors are viewed as learning in progress, not embarrassing mistakes.

Questioning techniques are also important. The manner in which we ask students questions should reflect the rigor of the standards, calling upon our students to not only respond to questions such as *What's the answer?* but also, *How do you know...?*, *What if the problem asked for....?*, or *How could you use this information if you were ...* (insert context)? (See Chapter 2 for further discussion of questioning techniques.) Coupled with the new standards, new standardized tests will be administered. At this writing, there are two major standardized testing programs being developed. States may choose between The Smarter Balanced Assessment Consortium (SBAC) tests and the Partnership for Assessment of Readiness for College and Careers (PARCC) tests to use for its statewide standardized testing. Both testing programs will require more time throughout the school year as well as a much wider use of technology for full implementation. We need to prepare our students for the particular formats and technology used to better ensure that these tests will capture what our students know.

A chapter of this book is dedicated to assessment of the new standards, including a more detailed look at these high-stakes tests, and a section on assessment is included in every chapter, but let's consider an example here. Most previous standardized tests emphasized multiple-choice questions that were simple to score. These new tests will give more attention to open-ended tasks, many of which may be in a puzzle-like format such as the example in Figure 1.7. Created for fourth graders, this problem format is easily adapted to other grade levels. To respond successfully to this task, students must compute with precision, understand the relationship between multiplication and division, and be able to explain their reasoning. In this way expectations for both the mathematical practice and content standards are addressed. We should embed similar tasks in our classroom activities.

Figure 1.7 Sample Assessment Task

Put a number in the start box.

Follow the directions.

Do this two more times.

What do you notice?

Explain why you think this happens.

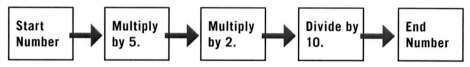

Related Documents

Though the National Governors Association Center for Best Practices and the Council of Chief State School Officers are considered the authors of the Common Core State Standards, many writers and reviewers were involved. This document is the only one that is officially approved. Drafts of *Progression Documents* provided by those identified as *The Common Core State Standards Writing Team* are available online. These can be a valuable resource for you, though many teachers find them to be challenging to read without guidance or support as they discuss complex ideas related to cognitive development and the structure of mathematics. Ideas from these documents are incorporated into this book so that more teachers will have access to the ways in which writers thought about these standards. Many states have created websites to support educators. We will consider ways to take advantage of such resources and opportunities to work with others in Chapter 10.

Next Steps

As mentioned earlier, understanding these standards and how they might connect to your classrooms is a top priority for your teaching. As the mathematical practices and assessment relate to all of the content domains, those topics are considered in the next two chapters, before we turn to each domain separately.

As you read this book, instructional scenarios are presented to model thinking and help facilitate the development of the habits of mind - not necessarily to provide the specific answer. You may want to take notes on what is new to you or about an idea that you want to explore further. Are there special projects that come to mind when you read about a particular standard that you'd like to try with your students? Is there a new model for teaching a concept that seems as though it will work well with one group of students or an individual student that you'd like to learn more about? As you are likely already being asked to teach the standards, think about what new ideas come to mind when you read about a concept or a skill described in this book that you did not understand before. Ideally, you would share the reading with a colleague or within a Professional Learning Community (PLC) so that you can discuss it together and perhaps make plans for new ideas you want to try in your classrooms. Also, note that you will see icons as you read this book. The mathematical practices icon shows where particular MP's are embedded in the mathematical tasks being explained. The classroom connections icon points out activities, lesson ideas, problems, or other classroom ideas that can be used in instruction. The following key will help you navigate through the book.

MP7
Structure

Mathematical Practices

Classroom Connections

Let's Think and Discuss

1. What was your first reaction to learning about the *Common Core State Standards*?

2. If you were given time to work with colleagues about teaching math, how would you want to spend it?

3. What opportunity does adoption of these standards give you and your students? What will be a challenge for you or your school?

Chapter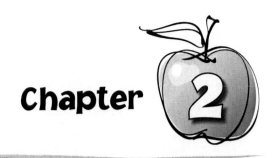

Standards for Mathematical Practice

 Voice from the Classroom

Our math coordinator helped us to understand the standards. We began in grade-level meetings where we learned about the critical areas of focus at our grade and any changes in grade-level expectations. We have worked with the content standards for a year. It is challenging sometimes because our textbooks were written before this change and we don't have money for new purchases until next year. A result, though, is that we all work together and share ideas, which has made us much stronger as a team. We were feeling pretty good about our understanding of everything until we met again for professional development with the math coordinator, this time about the mathematical practices. She began with having us read the practices and I felt totally lost. What did regularity and structure have to do with the elementary grades? You could tell everyone was getting frustrated.

Then, she had us all solve a problem in small groups. We had to record all of our work on chart paper, along with visual representation(s) and a written explanation of our thinking. At first, we were all pretty quiet, but then the noise level really picked up as we became engaged. It was amazing when we hung up our responses around the room. They were so varied and we learned so much from looking at the work of different groups.

Then, the coach brought us back to each response with more focus. For example, I remember her asking, "What evidence do you see of precise use of mathematical vocabulary?"

As we left, we knew we still had much more to learn about these practices, but we had a new vision for how mathematics could be taught. We were eager to return to our grade meetings and think about how we could teach the content standards in ways that highlighted these practices.

—Fifth-Grade Teacher

This teacher declares that she and her colleagues gained a new vision for how mathematics could be taught. Does this mean that all of our teaching strategies need to change? No! Though it does mean that we need to make sure that our students have the opportunity to meet these rigorous expectations for mathematical habits of mind, that our classrooms are places where students expect to struggle, to reason, and to share their thinking.

 Big Picture

The importance of the Standards for Mathematical Practice can be assumed from their position in the document; they are listed first. Though you may recognize aspects of these standards, their composition and definitions are new and, as of this printing, the common core writers have not provided a progression document similar to those drafted for the domains. Fortunately, educational consortia, state departments of education, individual writers, and mathematics educators have provided some worthwhile resources. (See Chapter 10.) This is one of the distinct advantages of the national involvement in the Common Core; there are numerous resources available online. You need to have a sense of what these standards are about, however, to evaluate and make good choices about these resources.

While the content standards are grade specific, the practice standards are for all students, K–12. They provide a coherent structure to the study of mathematics and establish the mathematical ways of thinking all students should develop. Like the content standards, the Standards for Mathematical Practice set criteria for learning, criteria that will be assessed. As such, it is important that we understand these standards, envision what teaching and learning looks like in classrooms that embrace them, and develop the teacher moves necessary for their development. The practice standards are referred to throughout the domain chapters. Perhaps most important, we must believe that all students are capable of meeting these goals. While listed in Chapter 1, they are repeated here in Figure 2.1 for your convenience. A listing with their definitions is provided in Appendix A.

Figure 2.1 Standards for Mathematical Practice

MP1—Make sense of problems and persevere in solving them.

MP2—Reason abstractly and quantitatively.

MP3—Construct viable arguments and critique the reasoning of others.

MP4—Model with mathematics.

MP5—Use appropriate tools strategically.

MP6—Attend to precision.

MP7—Look for and make use of structure.

MP8—Look for and express regularity in repeated reasoning.

(NGA and CCSSO 2010)

While these eight standards each have individual importance, authors of the Common Core have suggested a related structure (Figure 2.2) within them. *MP1 Make sense of problems and persevere in solving them* as well as *MP6 Attend to precision* are identified as overarching standards. The remaining six standards are coupled within three areas of focus: reasoning and explaining thinking, modeling and using tools, and seeing structure and generalizing.

Figure 2.2 Grouping of the Practice Standards

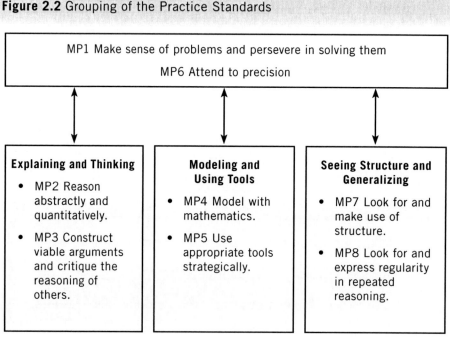

MP1 Make sense of problems and persevere in solving them

MP6 Attend to precision

Explaining and Thinking
- MP2 Reason abstractly and quantitatively.
- MP3 Construct viable arguments and critique the reasoning of others.

Modeling and Using Tools
- MP4 Model with mathematics.
- MP5 Use appropriate tools strategically.

Seeing Structure and Generalizing
- MP7 Look for and make use of structure.
- MP8 Look for and express regularity in repeated reasoning.

Adapted from McCallum Blog Post (2011)

Standards for content are closely related to standards for mathematical practice. Words such as *understand*, *apply*, *explain*, and *create* within the content standards suggest reliance on the practice standards. Interweaving the Content Standards with the Standards for Mathematical Practice will help our students view mathematics as engaging and meaningful (Parker and Novack 2012). But first, we need to understand what each of the practice standards requires of us and our students to do.

Looking Closer at Each Standard

Make Sense of Problems and Persevere in Solving Them (MP1)

This is one of the two overarching practices that should permeate our instruction. What does it mean to make sense of problems? Ideally, students will dive right into a problem, regardless of the difficulty level, and stick with it until they figure it out. If you have been teaching for any period of time, you will likely agree that this is easier said than done. Many students have a good deal of difficulty with problems that involve any type of challenge and often, as soon as they have read the problem, willingly state, "I don't know how to do this problem." Rather than pondering it even for a moment, they move right away on to the next one. Research has shown that when students are not able to draw upon a strategy that they have used before or when the lesson moves from being computation-based to problem-solving oriented, many make no attempt to solve the problem and other students give up easily (Colton 2010). A recent National Public Radio (NPR) news story suggested that academic struggle is seen in the United States as a sign of weakness, whereas in Asian countries, it is viewed as an opportunity to learn. These are the same Asian countries that, according to international test data, produce strong mathematics students (Siegel 2012). In the U.S., we often applaud students who are naturally good at something or are easily able to solve a problem right away, rather than encouraging students to work through the difficulty, gaining a sense of accomplishment once it is solved. For students to persist, they need to view themselves as capable, with abilities that will increase through their efforts. According to Carol Dweck, author of the groundbreaking book *Mindset: The New Psychology of Success,* a "…*growth mindset* is based on that belief that your basic qualities are things you can cultivate" (2007, 7).

So how do we help students learn how to make sense of a problem, and to realize that with effort, they can solve it?

- ☞ Choose a clear, appropriately leveled task for students, beyond their easy reach.

- ☞ Group students carefully, varying the groupings from individual to small group, as changing the independence level helps them to learn to persevere on their own or work cooperatively with others when called upon to do so.

✏ Make sure students have access to the appropriate tools and mathematics vocabulary to solve the task and have a toolbox of strategies from which to choose.

✏ Provide adequate time for students to work on problems, with extensions given if necessary in order to fully complete the task.

✏ Set high expectations and give students ample opportunities to reach their own level of success, which helps students gain self-confidence and often leads to a greater willingness to take on more challenging problems.

Reason Abstractly and Quantitatively (MP2)

When students are presented with a problem involving numbers, they must learn to make sense of the quantities provided and consider how several quantities may relate to one another. Students must learn to *decontextualize* given information, meaning to represent what is given symbolically, writing equations or, if appropriate, variable expressions. For example, consider the following problem.

Your chorus is planning a pizza party for its 60 members. You are in charge of ordering pizzas. You want each chorus member to be able to eat two to three slices of pizza. How many eight-slice pizzas should you order?

Students need to represent the situation in such a way that they can calculate the answer. They do not need to think about the pizza as they work with these numbers. Students must then *contextualize* the answer they found, that is, think about what their answer means within the given context. In this case, students must realize that they can only purchase a whole number of pizzas and will need to adjust their answer accordingly, while keeping the two to three slices per chorus member in mind.

Thinking quantitatively, also known as numeracy, entails being comfortable with numbers and being able to use math skills in everyday life. A student who is quantitatively literate is able to support an answer through clear communication and chooses an appropriate format such as words, a table, a graph or an equation (AAC&U 2010). Learning when it is acceptable to provide an estimate, that is, deciding *when is the answer close enough?*, through in-class problems as well as for real-life questions such as *How many books are on my shelves? How many cars did we pass on our trip?* provides a variety of opportunities for reasoning about numbers.

Teachers can support their students' ability to think quantitatively by providing contexts that are easily related to their everyday lives, with attention paid to their cultural differences and varied learning styles (Darling-Hammond 2012). Research has also shown that including quantitative reasoning opportunities into writing programs strengthens both their mathematics and their writing skills (Lutsky 2008). Activities involving number sense may include asking questions such as *How long would it take you to drive across the country?* Connections can also be made to topics students are exploring in other subjects, such as figuring out how many garter snakes it would take to make a length as long as a python or comparing data from a historical era being studied to that of today.

Construct Viable Arguments and Critique the Reasoning of Others (MP3)

Understanding is key to the content standards, and in the introduction to those standards, the writers of the Common Core state, "One hallmark of mathematical understanding is the ability to justify...a student who can explain the rule understands the mathematics and may have a better chance to succeed at a less familiar task..." (2010, 4). To explain how they solved a problem or to understand strategies their peers used, students must learn how to use words, diagrams, mathematical symbols, graphs, or equations to represent and describe their thinking. This process may range from simply turning and talking to their neighbors or participating in class discussions to more formal presentations or written explanations.

In groups, students are often more actively engaged in their own learning and more able to challenge each other's thinking about the strategies they are using. As students become more adept at their mathematical conversations, they learn to communicate with appropriate vocabulary and use clearer strategies to explain their thinking. While students work independently in pairs or small groups, the teacher can interact with students, collect assessment data, or meet with small groups within a scheduled rotation. Wedekind refers to these meetings as math exchanges. She defines the teacher's focus during these conversations as "...guiding student talk and mediating thinking as students share problem-solving strategies, discuss how math works, and move toward more effective and efficient strategies and greater mathematical understanding" (Wedekind 2011, 4).

As is true with the other practice standards, the more interesting and in-depth the task, the more fully this standard can be realized. Students' willingness to converse about an open-ended task such as *Bryan has 35 cents. What coins could Bryan have?* is far greater than when the tasks are simply right or wrong answers. Of course, having students sit together in a group with an interesting task does not always produce meaningful conversation on its own. Ways teachers can support mathematical discourse are suggested later in the chapter.

Students must also learn to systematically explain their thinking in writing to convince others, teachers and students, that their solution is correct. It is not uncommon for some students to resist justifying their thinking, stating, "I just know that's the answer." We need to consider such responses to determine if the task was too simple for the particular learners and he or she did just get it, or if such responses are coming from reluctant learners. The latter must be encouraged to justify their thinking in writing so that when problems get more complex, they will have gained experience justifying their thinking. It's important to remember that a student's solution process does not always have to be documented in words; creating a diagram or drawing a graph may more appropriately represent his or her thinking. A goal of this standard should be to teach students how to best communicate their thinking based on the task.

Throughout the process of discussing and writing about their thinking, students learn to listen to and read their classmates' justifications, to build on what they hear and read, and to recognize if they need to ask clarifying questions. If a solution does not seem valid, students should engage in meaningful dialogue about how to improve the work, just as they would in English language arts.

Model with Mathematics (MP4)

Real-world tasks do not come with instructions for finding a solution. Rather, we must solve problems with no clear solution paths outlined for us. We must, individually or collaboratively, determine what tools to use, identify appropriate mathematics skills and strategies to help us, and design our own solution path. Our problems do not come with a label stating, "Use an array to solve this problem" or, "If you need help, look on page 52." We must give students opportunities to address similarly open-ended tasks.

Different from the typical textbook word problem, tasks promoting modeling involve contexts that students are interested in, such as:

- We are going to organize the blocks by shape in the block area. Which ones should go together? How should we label them?

- As the pipes are fixed in our school, we are temporarily not allowed to drink the water in our school's water fountains. If we are going to have bottled water delivered to our school for you to drink, how many bottles of water do you think we should have delivered each week?

- If your family won $1,000 for a family vacation during spring break, how do you think it should be spent?

- The principal has agreed to let you set up an aquarium in the front hallway of the school. How many fish do you think should be purchased for a 20-gallon tank?

These questions, and others like them, allow for multiple entry points as students engage in the processes of gathering appropriate data and considering a variety of solution strategies. Often, such problems result in multiple strategies and solutions. Learning to model a real-world task encourages students to consider how useful mathematics can be to help them solve problems in their daily lives.

You may also wish to engage students in projects that promote the use of mathematics, such as those that embody the principles of Project-Based Learning (Thomas 2000) which indicate that projects have the following characteristics:

- Are central to the curriculum.

- Encourage students to struggle with the content.

- Promote purposeful investigations.

- Are student-driven.

- Are realistic.

The ultimate intent of this standard is for students to realize that the mathematics they are learning in school may be useful to them in their daily lives, as they engage in activities in which they must consider a complicated situation and simplify it by using mathematics.

Use Appropriate Tools Strategically (MP5)

As is true for an electrician's apprentice, students must first learn to appropriately use the tools of their trade and then put them to good use. This standard requires students to build a toolbox from which they carefully make choices about which tool to use based on the task they are solving. The students themselves must learn to choose the tool without the need to ask, recognizing the power that each tool holds and that the mathematics will make more sense by using that tool (http://thinkmath.edc.org/index.php/CCSS_Mathematical_Practices). But what does a mathematical toolbox hold? The standards require a number of appropriate tools, heavily relying upon visual models such as using the number line to compare numbers (Figure 2.3), arrays to model multiplication, or tape diagrams to model relationships among numbers. These models are versatile, as they are useful for modeling mathematics at all levels. Students should learn to use the same model in varying contexts; for example, arrays can be used to model multiplication with whole numbers, rational numbers, or polynomials.

Figure 2.3 Number Line to Model Order of Numbers

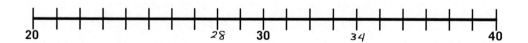

20   28   30   34   40

Other models include, but are not limited to the following:

- ➥ Manipulatives such as counters, pattern blocks, geoboards, and base ten blocks.
- ➥ Measuring tools such as rulers, balances, and protractors.
- ➥ Technological tools such as calculators, applets for making graphs, and application programs such as spreadsheets.
- ➥ Other tools such as tracing paper, graph paper, and number cubes.

As students become more adept at conceptually understanding the mathematics of the content standards, they learn to rely less on a particular tool; for example, from counting on the number line to add, they might transition to using the make-a-ten strategy. Knowing that the number line may be relied upon for reassurance, students keep it in their toolbox, in case something is forgotten or misinterpreted. Students should also know when it is more efficient to use mental math as a tool rather than paper and pencil or another tool. Using a calculator to find the answer to 52 x 50 may actually take longer than mentally using the distributive property and thinking: $50(50 + 2)$ = 2500 + 100 = 2600.

The intention of this standard is to encourage students to build their mathematics toolbox as they learn more mathematics content. Students should be able to ask themselves (http://www.weber.edu/COE/CollegePages/appropriate.html):

- ➥ Have I used the right tool for what I want to find out?
- ➥ Has the tool that I chose helped me to learn more math?
- ➥ If asked to, could I explain to someone else how to use this tool?

Attend to Precision (MP6)

As one of the two overarching practice standards, precision is something we want students to consider frequently. Prior to these standards, teachers probably thought about precision in terms of working carefully or checking work. Here we are asked to cultivate precise understanding of mathematical terms and symbols and to use them clearly when discussing a solution strategy. With a focus on mathematics vocabulary, students must engage in activities that introduce a term through a variety of experiences, through which students create their own understanding. Students may develop their vocabulary through using the following:

- Word walls

- Graphic organizers such as the Frayer model diagram shown in Figure 2.4 (Frayer, Frederick, Klausmeier 1969; Wormeli 2005)

- Math journals, including problem-solving strategies or reflections

- Concept maps

- Math dictionaries with visual models and student-created definitions

Figure 2.4 Frayer Diagram for Trapezoid

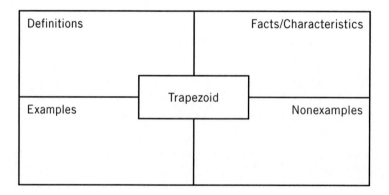

Using mathematics vocabulary appropriately gives students greater ability to communicate more clearly both in writing and when discussing their solutions (Murray 2004). Murray cautions teachers to take particular care when introducing mathematics vocabulary that may be contrary to how we use the same terms in everyday language. For example, Murray refers to the example of *odd*, which has the everyday meaning of being different from or unusual, and yet odd numbers are as common as even ones. Students will, at times, need to distinguish between various uses of the same term, just as they learn to do in their language arts classes.

As teachers encourage their students to learn appropriate use of vocabulary, they, too, must take care to precisely use mathematical terms and to provide a wide range of examples. Geometric figures must be shown in a variety of orientations and, for example, students should be asked to use their definition of prime numbers to decide if the numbers 1 or 2 are prime. Students also should experience various ways of using mathematical symbols, giving particular attention to the equal sign.

Accurate calculations, completed efficiently, with an appropriate label for the quantity, must be expressed using a level of preciseness appropriate for the situation. For example, students should learn to recognize that providing an answer to a problem about the distance from one city center to another should be given in miles, not feet. Or, when deciding how many baseballs you will need to buy based on how many students there are on the team, students must realize that they cannot purchase 6.5 baseballs and determine, based on the situation, whether to purchase 6 or 7 baseballs.

Students who attend to precision have developed, in general, a habit of mind whereby they calculate efficiently and communicate their solution strategies using appropriate vocabulary and symbols. It is expected that, as students gain expertise in the mathematics content, their ability to bring higher levels of complexity to their precision will increase as well.

Look for and Make Use of Structure (MP7)

Consider the following problem: *Describe an interesting way to find the answer to 20 x 16.*

Students who look for and make use of structure understand how to reason about the mathematics in the content standards. In actuality, learning to reason about mathematics often means to look for similarities, relationships, or patterns as they are learning. In the problem above, students who look for structure may notice that 20 may be written as 5 x 4 and 16 may be written as 4 x 4, therefore, the problem may be reconstructed as 5 x 4 x 4 x 4, or they may think of multiplying 16 x 10 + 16 x 10 and adding 160 + 160. As students determine a structure for the problem, they are making sense of the mathematics they are learning. Students recognize how ideas are related in a mathematical context, such as the relationship between the number of sides of a polygon and the number of angles. Understanding this relationship allows students to draw conclusions that may be used again when seen in other contexts.

Students learn to look for rules as they play mathematics games such as *Guess My Rule*. While interpreting the attributes of shapes in one part of a Venn diagram versus another part, they determine a category label such as *polygons with right angles* or *quadrilaterals*. Pattern finding is also a considerable component of this practice standard, as pattern recognition can often lead to the discovery of a rule or a generalization. Finding a pattern; analyzing it; and making a generalization or written rule, expression, or equation prepares students for the algebraic thinking necessary for the related content standards.

Teachers may encourage students to attempt various strategies for noticing structure, including the problem-solving strategy of solving a simpler problem (Ray 2011). When students create a simpler problem, they often notice the structure involved in the more complex one. According to Ray, over time students will recognize that if changing the numbers does not change the solution process, then it is the structure of the problem that is most important to their understanding of the mathematics.

Look for and Express Regularity in Repeated Reasoning (MP8)

A teacher is working with four students and a hundreds chart. She asks the first student to find 10 more than 28. The student steps up to the chart, points at 28 and counts to ten by ones, and announces 38 as her answer. Two more students are given examples and demonstrate a similar approach. The fourth student is asked to find 10 more than 17 and he begins to also count by ones. Then, he says, "Wait, I think there is another way," and he slides his finger down from 17 to 27. He then counts by ones to check his strategy. The other students are asked to try this approach to see if it will work for them. Two of them are quite comfortable with it, while one says, "I like counting by ones better." The teacher knows it takes a long time for students to add one ten rather than 10 ones and that they all are likely to need more exposure to this thinking, but she was pleased to see them discover this pattern.

In this situation, students are generalizing a method through repeated, similar experiences. Often students who are looking for a general method to solve a problem are looking for shortcuts, a way to make the problem easier to solve. In upper grades, students who conceptually understand the structure of the standard algorithm for whole number addition will recognize the similarity in the structure when solving a decimal addition problem. While students are paying attention to the details of how to solve the decimal problem, they are also able to see the bigger picture that the standard algorithm for addition still applies. Recognizing that the calculations are the same—like values are added together, regrouping as necessary—allows students to apply previous reasoning to this new context.

Students can be encouraged to practice this standard by asking questions such as (USD 2011):

- Does this situation look like one that you have encountered before?
- Can you explain how the solution strategy you used for this problem can be used in another problem?
- Are there situations, given a similar problem, in which this solution strategy will not work?

Recognizing patterns and generalizations in their study of mathematics, students learn to see mathematics as a cohesive whole, rather than separate unconnected parts. Knowing that they can apply a previously learned strategy in a new situation implies conceptualizing the mathematics in such a way that it is ingrained in their thinking and is useful beyond the current task.

Snapshot

Let's take a moment to consider a snapshot to get a sense of how teaching through the practice standards might look. It's the first week of school and this fourth-grade teacher knows that she wants to establish expectations, as early as possible, for what her students will do in math this year. She wants them to explore a problem that will solicit a variety of ideas so that they will have something to talk about together. She also wants to focus on the composition and decomposition of numbers and shapes as she knows they will be key to their learning how to multiply greater numbers. She displays the following tile problem as she reads the words aloud (Figure 2.5).

Figure 2.5 Tile Problem

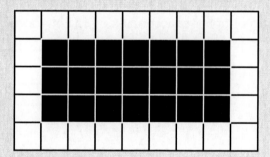

Last night I decided to make a couple of tables with tops made from black and white tiles. This drawing shows the plans I made for one of the tables. How can you figure out how many of each color tile I will need without counting all of the tiles individually? Write or draw to represent your thinking.

After reading the problem the teacher asks, "Who can tell me what you are supposed to do?" A couple of hands are raised immediately, but instead of calling on anyone right away, she says, "Anyone else have an idea?"

Satisfied that many students now have something to share, she calls on Jared, who offers, "We have to find the number of black tiles and white tiles that are needed." The teacher then asks, "Who can add on to this?" Rashi adds, "We can't just count them individually." She wants to make sure that everyone understands what that means and so she asks, "Who can use their own words to tell us what Rashi said?" No one says anything right away and then Megan replies, "We can't count them all by ones." The teacher asks if there is anything else they have to do, and Lorenzo reminds everyone that they have to write equations to show what they did.

The students are told to talk with a neighbor about a strategy for solving the problem. The teacher circulates asking questions as she does so. *Is there an equation you could write? Can you tell me more about what this equation stands for? What does your drawing show? Is there another way you could do this?* She notes that most students write that they used multiplication, either 3 x 7 or 7 x 3, to find the number of black tiles, while a few write that they counted by threes and write 3 + 3 + 3 + 3 + 3 + 3 + 3 = 21. Finding the number of white tiles without counting each of them appears to be more challenging and she notices a variety of recordings.

When she calls the larger group together, they quickly agree that there are 21 black tiles and share their equations. She asks Angela and Winston to share what they learned about the white tiles. She wants to quickly clear up the common error of counting the corner squares twice, so other students who made it can follow the rest of the lesson. She had checked with these two students and they wanted to share what they had discovered. Angela explains that they counted the top nine and the five on the side. Then they doubled these 14 and got 28 white tiles. She points to the top row and first column as she explains. Winston adds sheepishly, "Then I counted by ones to make sure we were right, but there were only 24."

We recounted twice but it was always the same. We finally realized that we were counting the corners twice." The teacher asks, "Can you show us on the tile plan what you mean?" Winston points to a corner tile and shows how it is part of the nine and part of the five. He explains that because they counted four too many, they subtracted four and writes the equation 2 x 14 − 4.

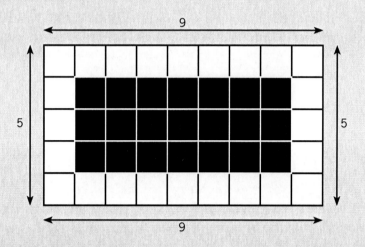

The teacher calls on Natalie to explain how the equation represents the way Angela and Winston counted.

Once students agree that there are 24 white tiles, and why this equation shows how the tiles were counted, the teacher displays five equations that could be used to represent other ways to count these tiles. A few of the equations were common among the students' recordings today and a few were on the list she made when she was planning. She tells the students they need to be detectives. They need to figure out from looking at the clues within each equation how the white tiles were counted. She gives them blank copies of the tile plan so that they can mark the white tiles to indicate how they were counted.

- $(2 \times 9) + (2 \times 3) = 24$
- $2 \times 12 = 24$
- $(2 \times 3) + (2 \times 7) + 4 = 24$
- $(5 \times 9) - (3 \times 7) = 24$
- $2 \times (9 + 3) = 24$

After independent investigation, various student volunteers demonstrate (by pointing on the tile plan) how they think the tiles were counted, based on the equation. The students are surprised that there are so many different ways to count the tiles and excited about finding them from the equations. As Monica says, "I had no idea numbers could tell us how someone did something."

The teacher is pleased with what the students accomplished. They explained their thinking, listened to each other, built on the ideas of others, made sense of the problem, modeled with mathematics, and reasoned quantitatively. Tomorrow she will ask them about a similar tile plan for a longer table. She will have the students brainstorm different ways to count and different equations they can write to represent their count. She wants them to focus on the equations themselves, how they are different and the same. She wants the students to focus on the structure and repeated reasoning involved by asking questions such as *Is there a shortcut we could use? Will this always be true? What would we change if there were one more row of black tiles?*

Teacher Strategies to Support These Standards

As we understand the practice standards more deeply, it becomes clear we must reflect on whether or not our current instructional strategies will support students becoming proficient mathematicians. We need to think about the class environment through the lens of the practice standards. We must make it clear to students that being persistent, taking risks, listening to one another carefully, analyzing errors, and debating ideas respectfully are the expected classroom norms. It is not possible for students to engage actively with, for example, sense making or critiquing the reasoning of others without these expectations. Students must also feel safe, that is, that their ideas will be listened to and respected and that sharing mistakes helps everyone to learn. Students must also expect to look to themselves for mathematical insights, rather than relying on the teacher to resolve all mathematical questions. As such, the role of teacher changes from that of *information provider* to one who chooses tasks carefully and facilitates learning based on knowledge of what students know, what they need to learn, and how they learn best.

Choosing Tasks

One of the most important choices we make as teachers is identifying the instructional tasks we will offer our students. The practice standards should have a significant influence on the tasks we choose. For example, how can we expect students to learn to persevere in solving problems if we don't provide tasks at the right level of challenge? Similarly, how can we engage students in reasoning abstractly if we do not offer tasks that require students to analyze relationships? Figure 2.6 suggests some questions to consider about the tasks we choose in relation to the Standards for Mathematical Practice. The idea is not to consider each question for each task, but rather, to focus on the questions related to the particular practice standards you plan to highlight in a lesson or activity.

Figure 2.6 Questions to Consider When Choosing Tasks

Standard for Mathematical Practice	Task Considerations
MP1 Make sense of problems and persevere in solving them	• Is the level of complexity appropriate? • Will the context of the task engage students? • Will diverse students have a way to begin? • Is the description of the tasks clear? • Are there ways I can adapt the description of the task to make it more accessible to ELL students?
MP2 Reason abstractly and quantitatively	• Does this task require students to contextualize or decontextualize mathematical ideas? • Does the task require students to make use of relationships among numbers and properties of operations?
MP3 Construct viable arguments and critique the reasoning of others	• Will the task solicit multiple approaches or opinions? • Will the task uncover incomplete understanding or misconceptions?
MP4 Model with mathematics	• Will this task solicit multiple representations? • Is the context of the task realistic?
MP5 Use appropriate tools strategically	• Does this task support use of a variety of tools or representations? • Does this task require students to choose an appropriate tool to use?
MP6 Attend to precision	• How will this task further students' understanding of mathematical terms? • Does the context suggest a level of precision required? • Will this task require students to think about appropriate labels?
MP7 Look for and make use of structure	• Will this task encourage students to note and make use of patterns? • Will this task help students uncover a mathematical structure or property?
MP8 Look for and express regularity in repeated reasoning	• Will this task help students discover a shortcut? • How might this task support the development of general methods?

Some types of tasks have been identified as particularly worthwhile. For example Barlow and McCrory (2011) suggest that tasks that stimulate disagreements are particularly appropriate as they can stimulate sense making, discussion, and reasoning. They identify three types of tasks that are likely to create opportunities for mathematical disagreements, tasks that: force students to pick a side, reveal students' misconceptions, and triggered disagreements in previous years. The following are examples of tasks that require students to take sides and that address common misconceptions:

☞ Write about why this shape is or is not a triangle.

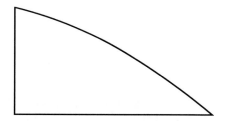

☞ Do you think Jamie's work is correct? Why or why not?

$$
\begin{array}{r}
{\scriptstyle 2 \ \ 15} \\
\cancel{3}0\cancel{5} \\
-1\,6\,8 \\
\hline
1\,4\,7
\end{array}
$$

☞ Jeri said that 1 is a prime number because it doesn't have any factors other than itself. What do you think?

As you consider your students' work, identify those errors that occur a few times. Create a similar example and ask students to "take a stand." Allow them time to debate and clarify their thinking. Sometimes you may be surprised by how deeply some misconceptions or partial understandings are held. Other times you may be delighted by how quickly erroneous thinking falls away once it is uncovered. Either way, you are engaging your students in important sense making and reasoning; you are putting them in charge of their mathematical understanding.

Letting Students Do the Work

Most of us can probably remember a time when we were taking a high-stakes test and were told to *stop working and put our pencils down*. As teachers, we need to put *our* pencils down to make sure students are doing *their* work. Too often, teachers respond to student queries by *showing* them how to complete a task or solve a problem. Even teachers committed to fostering student thinking can fall into this trap. It can be quite challenging to refrain from indicating exactly where a student made an error within a series of steps or from resolving a mathematical disagreement during a discussion, but to do so would eliminate learning opportunities for the students. We will invariably make such an error, especially when feeling the pressure of time, but our intentions to avoid doing so should be firm. We do not want to be so helpful that we lower the cognitive demand of a task (Zucker 2012). Note that the blog of well-known TED speaker Dan Meyer (dy/dan) has the motto *less helpful*.

There are other ways we can do too much of the work. For example, when we:

- ✐ **Provide too many sub-questions**, which keep students from having to make sense of a problem.

- ✐ **Provide a template** such as a coordinate graph, when students should be deciding on the tool to use.

- ✐ **Do not give wait time**, but rather just give the answer when no one responds immediately. The term wait time was coined by Mary Budd Rowe (1986) when her research established that merely waiting three seconds after posing a question increased student responses. Today, many educators recommend four to seven seconds for students to formulate their thinking. Such time may help to alleviate some of the differences between genders and support English language learners. Too often, teachers call on a quick responder or provide the answers themselves, rather than wait for a greater number of students to process their ideas.

Orchestrating Discourse

Class discussions provide opportunities for students to share their thinking and take ownership of their mathematical ideas. Such opportunities can address all of the practice standards depending on the specifics of the discourse. Interest in mathematical conversations has been growing for several years. Chapin, O'Connor, and Anderson (2009) have identified what they called five productive talk moves:

- **Revoicing** is a move that allows teachers to check to make sure that what a student has said has been heard and understood correctly. It might begin with a teacher saying, "So I think you are saying that…"

- Students also can be asked to **restate someone else's reasoning**, a move that encourages listening carefully by asking questions such as, "How would you use your own words to tell us what Erica just said?"

- Another way to focus students' attention on what others are saying, and also promote the critical analyses of the thinking of others, is the move **apply their own reasoning to someone else's.** You can encourage such responses by asking questions such as, "Do you agree with what Jasmine just said?"

- You can **prompt for further participation** through such questions as, "Who can give us another example?"

- The authors also include **wait time** (mentioned earlier) in their identified moves.

It is also important to think about which students you call on and the order in which you ask students to present their thinking. If you want a student to critique another student's thinking, you may want to first ask a student sitting on the other side of the room, as a student sitting next to him or her may be hesitant to take a different position.

Smith, Hughes, Engle, and Stein (2009) encourage us to think carefully about the students we select to present their thinking to the class and the order in which we ask them to do so. As we observe and interact with our students as they explore a task, we should note students whose work would help others to learn and understand. Some questions to consider are:

- Which students' work samples show different approaches?

- Whose work illustrates a common error or misconception that will be helpful for others to discuss?

- Whose work best illustrates a common solution strategy that most students will easily understand that I might want presented first/early?

- Whose work is concrete and might help other students better understand work presented later?

- Whose work is the most unique or efficient that I might want presented last?

- Whose work best demonstrates attention (or inattention) to precision?

Hufferd-Ackles, Fuson, and Sherin have identified four components of a math-talk learning community: questioning, explaining mathematical thinking, sources of mathematical ideas, and responsibility for learning. They describe different levels of each of these components based on the degree to which the teacher (indicating a lower, less preferred level) or students (indicating a higher, more preferred level) are taking the lead. They state, "When student thinking began to be elicited, students became more engaged and involved in classroom discourse as speakers and listeners. Their responsibility for their own learning was indicated by their desire to ask questions in class, their eagerness to go to the board to demonstrate their understanding of problems, and their volunteering to … assist struggling students" (2004, 106).

Asking Questions

Asking the right question at the right time can be immensely valuable in supporting these practice standards. Examples of questions to support discourse were identified among the talk moves, but we also need to ask questions directly related to each of the practice standards. Examples are provided in Figure 2.7.

Figure 2.7 Sample Questions to Stimulate Development of the Standards for Mathematical Practice

Standard for Mathematical Practice	Questions to Support Development
MP1 Make sense of problems and persevere in solving them	• What do you think the problem is asking you to do? • What else could you try?
MP2 Reason abstractly and quantitatively	• What would your solution mean in this context? • Are there relationships among the numbers that are useful?
MP3 Construct viable arguments and critique the reasoning of others	• Why did you choose this representation? • Can you tell me what you are doing and why?
MP4 Model with mathematics	• Is there a table or graph you could make to show this information? • Is there an equation you can write?
MP5 Use appropriate tools strategically	• Is there a representation you can make? • Is there a tool you might use?
MP6 Attend to precision	• How are you defining this term? • In this context, how important is it that the answer be exact?
MP7 Look for and make use of structure	• Have you completed other tasks similar to this one? • Do you see a pattern?
MP8 Look for and express regularity in repeated reasoning	• Can you make a generalization? • Will this method always work?

Assessment

As stated earlier in the chapter, assessment must include a focus on these standards. When you wish to focus on a particular practice standard you can translate the description of the practice into a rubric. For example, after rereading the description for *MP2 Reason abstractly and quantitatively* you could pinpoint the key behaviors students are expected to exhibit and use them to create a checklist (Figure 2.8).

Figure 2.8 Checklist for MP2

Student Name: _____ Date: _____

The student:

❏ noted or made use of numerical relationships among quantities

❏ created an equation to represent the situation

❏ checked to see if the answer made sense given the situation, or the numbers involved used properties of operations flexibly

As standardized tests will include items that require students to explain their thinking in writing, students need ample practice in doing so. Denman (2013) recommends that we familiarize students with the procedural language of such explanations, including:

👉 **What words**: *multiply to find…*

👉 **Why words**: *since, because…*

👉 **Transitional words**: *to start with, first, then, after that, second…*

👉 **Concluding words**: *therefore I know…*

Encourage students to connect phrases such as, "Because I…, I started with…" Once students have gained initial expertise for such explanations, perhaps in conjunction with their language arts instruction, students can adapt to an explanation style that fits them best, as long as completeness and clarity are maintained.

Encourage students to read and edit their explanations in pairs or small groups, as they would for any writing assignment. You can also have students reflect on their explanations by having other students try to match or actually create similar work based on what was explained.

 ## Let's Think and Discuss

1. How will you include the Standards for Mathematical Practice into your daily planning?

2. Which practice standards do you think will have the greatest impact on your teaching? Why?

3. What evidence do you expect to see that your students are mastering the habits of mind required in the practice standards?

Chapter 3

Assessment and the Common Core

 Voice from the Classroom

I like the changes within the Common Core Standards such as I want our students to understand what they are doing and to think critically. But new standardized tests make me nervous. We already pay too much attention to standardized tests and I'm afraid these tests will create even more attention, because states will be comparing themselves to one another. What worries me most is that backlash to the tests could expand and put the standards at risk.

As I find richer tasks for my students to consider, I am amazed at how much more I am learning about what they find challenging. This kind of information helps me to work with individual students. Standardized testing data is more helpful in terms of the big picture, for example, I might learn that most of my students had trouble with a particular item. It's too late for me to help those students, but I do try to look closely at the item and better understand what made it so difficult. The students I teach the following year gain from this type of feedback and reflection.

My students like to work in groups, but I have begun to require that they work independently for a few minutes before talking with others.

This requirement gives students time to gather their thoughts and, for some, to take the time they need to really understand a problem. I think it also prepares them for those assessments that do not allow for working with others.

I have begun to use some tiered lessons based on formative assessment data. I often let my students choose the level at which they want to work and they make good choices. I find that when they make choices, there is greater student engagement and independence. When they are working well, it is easier for me to have some time to work with individual students or a small group. Sometimes, just five minutes one-on-one or ten to fifteen minutes in a small group can be quite impactful when it is based on assessment data. Also, by collecting and recording more formative assessments, I can build stronger cases for students to receive help beyond which I can provide.

—First-Grade Teacher

This teacher voice reminds us how many links there are among standards, assessment, and instructional decisions. As our standards change, so must our assessment if we are to make good instructional decisions. This chapter identifies specific issues and suggestions related to assessment aimed at supporting students' success.

Big Picture

What role should assessment play in our classrooms? The National Council of Teachers of Mathematics published *Assessment Standards for School Mathematics* (1995) that asserts four purposes of assessment:

- ✏ to make instructional decisions
- ✏ to monitor our students' progress
- ✏ to evaluate students' achievement on an individual basis
- ✏ to evaluate programs

All four of these purposes remain important today. Sometimes though, it can seem as if attention is given only to the evaluation of teachers, school systems, and students based on student performance on standardized tests. Imagine what it would be like if editorials, news reports, tweets, and blogs were filled with as much attention to teachers who knew how to ask a question that gave them access to students' thinking and led to instruction that helped those learners move from a misconception to full understanding.

Assessment is not new to our classrooms. We know that we must collect evidence of learning, use such evidence to plan our instruction, and share data with parents and other stakeholders who have a right to know the success of our teaching and of student learning. We know that no one type of assessment will provide us with all that we wish to know and that important decisions must be made based on several sources of data. Yet there is new knowledge that we need. The adoption of the Common Core State Standards for Mathematics raises five new issues for educators:

- How can classroom assessment strategies help ensure that students meet grade-level content standards expected in the Common Core?

- How do we support equity through the assessment process?

- What are the implications of so called "next generation" standardized tests?

- How should we assess whether students have met the Standards for Mathematical Practice?

- How can we involve parents and students in the high-stakes testing likely to be associated with these standards?

Classroom Assessment Strategies

With all the attention given to performance on standardized tests, we can sometimes underestimate the importance of the assessment strategies within our classrooms that are conducted on a regular basis. As new standards require students to acquire both conceptual understanding and procedural fluency, we need to make sure that our assessments are attending to both types of learning. As there are expectations for students to perform at grade level, we need to find ways to uncover learning needs more quickly and to address them. As always, we must make instructional decisions based on the information we collect (Collins 2012).

Assessment decisions must be based on an understanding of how students' thinking becomes more sophisticated over time (Heritage 2008). Such learning progressions are built on research about how students learn. This is why it is important for teachers to understand the standards at their grade level as well as to recognize how they relate to standards across grade levels. Teachers must also have a deep understanding of the mathematics involved in these standards to recognize how to best assess them and how to recognize when student thinking may relate to a misconception at a later grade level.

Assessment strategies may be classified as *summative*, that is, used as assessment *of* learning, or *formative*, the assessment *for* learning. In actuality, all forms of assessment data can be used for either purpose, if that is how teachers use it. So you play a pivotal role in the assessment process and can always use data to inform your teaching.

Summative Assessment

Summative assessments are scheduled to occur after learning is assumed to have taken place and might be in the form of a completed journal or project, a performance task, or a test. They are likely to result in a grade or score that is significant in rating students' performance levels. The most familiar type of non-standardized summative assessment is the use of chapter tests or quizzes. Mathematics curricula include such tests in their materials. Some school systems require teachers to have students take these tests and report student scores to a school administrator. Zorin, Hunsader, and Thompson (2013) identify four concerns with such tests and encourage teachers to become alert to the potential difficulty of items that include:

➼ **Poor number choices** that may hide important data. For example, asking a student who may have trouble recording the regrouping of tens to hundreds to find 553 + 264. This is not a good number choice as the tens add to 11, making it difficult to conclude that the 1 ten and 10 ones were recorded appropriately.

➼ **Inappropriate contexts** for a particular mathematical task. For example, a story problem about the number of liters of water in an in-ground swimming pool that then asks students to convert the measure to milliliters, a measure that would never be used in this real-world context.

➼ **Superfluous graphics** that do not help make student learning visible. For example, including an image of graph paper next to a word problem that requires students to find 8 x 7 for its solution might be helpful to students not quite ready for the challenge or for English language learners. However, more insight into student understanding would be gained if the task required learners to explain how the given representation could be used to justify their response.

➼ **Assumptions** that must be made to respond to the task correctly. A problem that asks fourth graders to list the different perimeters a rug could have with an area of 100 square feet likely assumes that the rug is rectangular and has whole-number dimensions. Later in their study of mathematics, students will be told, sometimes fervently, that assumptions should not be made.

These tests should also be examined for their match to the Common Core State Standards. Are there some items that should be dropped because they are no longer aligned to the grade level? Is there an appropriate balance between the emphasis on procedural and conceptual learning or do some items need to be adapted? Even recently published materials need to be considered from these perspectives as we are all still learning about these expectations. And, of course, we also should be screening assessment tasks we design according to these same criteria.

Formative Assessment

The National Mathematics Advisory Panel (2008) has reported data that indicate the direct correlation between use of formative assessment and student achievement and recommends regular use of formative assessment. Formative assessment of our students is intended to give teachers and students feedback while they are learning content with hopes of improving teacher instruction and student performance (McManus 2008). Note the emphasis on both teachers and students. We need to make sure students, not just teachers, learn from formative assessment data and that such data is collected throughout the instructional process. When students are given the opportunity to analyze the results of their assessments they are often able to clear up misconceptions and further clarify their own thinking.

A position paper of the National Council of Teachers of Mathematics on Formative Assessment states that "…by applying formative strategies such as asking strategic questions, providing students with immediate feedback, and engaging students in self-reflection, teachers receive evidence of students' reasoning and misconceptions to use in adjusting instruction." (NCTM 2013, 1). Such reflection and feedback should also help students gain a better sense of where their learning stands in relationship to a standard and what, if any, actions they should take.

So what might this look like in the classroom? Here are some brief examples:

✏ A first-grade classroom is investigating sums to 20 when it becomes apparent that a few of the students do not understand the strategy of making 10. The next day the teacher implements a mini-lesson with this small group of students using 10 frames. She will show students two frames to model a sum and ask students how they might find the total without counting all of the dots. She chooses facts such as 5 + 8 with hopes that students will note the visual decomposition of the eight as five dots and three dots, and then join this row of five dots with the other similar row to make a 10 (Figure 3.1). Following several similar visual experiences, the teacher will ask the students to describe the strategy and then try other, more challenging examples.

Figure 3.1 Using the 10 Frames to Support the Make a 10 Strategy

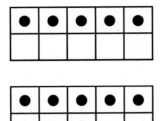

☞ A fourth-grade classroom is working on explaining their thinking in writing. The teacher has students working in groups and asks them to record their thinking on chart paper. Their responses are posted about the room and students take a gallery walk. Viewing groups are asked to post a compliment and a question to each response. This teacher believes that this group approach is a good way to begin having students assess the work of others as it can be less threatening to some students.

☞ Third-grade students have just received their quizzes back with descriptive feedback. On Shanna's quiz, the teacher wrote: *You gave a clear explanation of how you solved the first problem. What details could you add to your explanation of the second problem?* On Torry's paper she wrote: *You showed two different ways to multiply. Can you find a mistake that you made when multiplying by six?* The teacher gives students time to respond to her comments.

☞ A kindergarten teacher begins a lesson by saying, *Tell me what you know about a triangle.* She will use student responses to help her decide the language and examples of triangles she needs to highlight in the lesson.

☞ As second-grade students are measuring items in the classroom to the nearest half-inch the teacher asks questions such as: *How do you know where to place the ruler? How do you decide if something is five inches or five and a half inches long? Can you tell me how long you think this pencil is before you measure it? What makes you think so? What does this drawing on your recording sheet show?* She makes brief notes on an observation form as she listens to responses, which she will return to the next time the students are measuring lengths.

✏ A fifth-grade teacher asks students to look at the entries in their math portfolios. She asks them to choose two samples that show how their understanding of volume has increased. The students are expected to write about their choices, giving specific details about the evidence of growth in understanding.

Use of Journals

Journal writing in a mathematics class is an activity that allows students to write about a particular mathematics topic, knowing they will not be graded on what they write. Keeping the writing private, except to the teacher, gives students the opportunity to write individually and, usually, freely. There is a strong relationship between the mental journey needed to write about mathematics and the mathematics itself, as the act of writing may be used to organize and clarify thinking (Aspinwall and Aspinwall 2003). Journal entries are an excellent formative assessment tool, allowing the teacher to view what her students are thinking, sometimes before and after a class discussion. The teacher can then formulate next steps based on what all of her students are writing, not just on what a few students might say in a class discussion. The following Snapshot shows how the use of journals allows for formative assessment to be integrated into instruction.

 **Snapshot**

> The students in Ms. Ramirez's math class are quite used to writing responses to mathematics tasks as a way of expressing their initial thinking. Today, Ms. Ramirez asks her students to focus on the statement she has written on the board: *We are required to attend school for 180 days of the year.* The students know that they must take out their mathematics journals and write the statement that is on the board. They are then asked to write freely for five minutes about the mathematics that comes to mind about the statement.

Ms. Ramirez purposely chooses not to circulate around the room while they are writing. Instead, she sits at her round table in the back of the room, observing her students. She thinks that, if she circulates, this might distract her students from their writing and she wants them to feel free to write in their journals without having their teacher looking over their shoulder. She watches their enthusiasm for the writing process, observes students who may be struggling, and jots down some notes about particular students' focus on the task.

After a few minutes, the teacher announces that she would like some students to respond to the statement on the board. She records their statements on the whiteboard. Some students make new comments after listening to what other students have said. Several responses are recorded including:

- ☞ We go to school lots of days.
- ☞ There are about 30 days in a month. Since 30 x 6 = 180, we go to school for about six months.
- ☞ 180 days is less than the number of days in a year.
- ☞ Since 180 + 180 = 360 we go to school about half of the days.
- ☞ We go to school about six hours each day. Since 6 x 180 = 1,080, we are in school more than one thousand hours.

The students enjoy this conversation and everyone is able to contribute. They could talk even longer, but Ms. Ramirez wants them to note relationships among the statements. She asks students to tell how these statements are similar. One student comments that most of them include the number 180. Another student comments that many of the statements have something to do with finding another name for 180 days, like about six months. This student suggests they find the number of minutes they are in school.

At the conclusion of the whole class conversation, Ms. Ramirez asks each of the students to return to their journals to write some summary statements. Her students know that they can write any number of things in their summaries. They can write:

✏ something they learned mathematically that they didn't know before

✏ a question they have about what they have learned

✏ a comment about the discussion that they didn't get to say to the group that they wish they had

✏ anything else that comes to mind related to the discussion

Ms. Ramirez looks forward to reading students' math journals. She may just read one entry, she might make a comment or ask a question in the journal in response to something the student has written, or she might record something about what the student has written in her assessment notebook, where she keeps track of information about her students. More than once, Ms. Ramirez and a student have started a running dialogue about a particular topic in the journal. One of her students shared that he was frustrated with division and didn't see why he had to learn it. Ms. Ramirez wrote back that he should tell her his three top interests and she would help him to learn the importance of division in those areas.

Questioning for Assessment

Crowe and Stanford (2010) suggest that the power of questioning is often overshadowed by the attention given to high stakes assessment. Good questions challenge students and help teachers to uncover misconceptions (Weiss and Pasley 2004). We can probe students' understanding more deeply by asking questions such as:

✏ What more can you tell me?

✏ Can you say that another way?

- Is there something you could draw to show me what you mean?
- How do you know that you are correct?
- What does this "1" represent in your computation?
- What do you do to put numbers in order?
- How would you describe a parallelogram if you had never seen one?
- What do you know about how to use a ruler to measure?
- When would you use this if you were not in school?

Note that these questions are open-ended, and that they could be answered in a variety of ways and still be correct or partially correct. This doesn't mean you should never ask basic knowledge questions such as *What is a four-sided shape with right angles and sides of equal lengths?*, but these don't give as much insight into conceptual thinking or stimulate such thinking.

Quick questions to which a whole class responds will allow you to get a general feel for student understanding and can be as simple as, *How many fingers would you raise to show me how well you understand how to tell time if one finger is just a little, and five fingers, is quite a lot?* A quick look will allow you to assess the most common responses and identify which students are likely to need additional support or challenge. These check-in questions are often most helpful when asked at the beginning of a lesson or right after some information has been shared and you are about to assign students to individual or small-group work. Responses will allow you to adapt your lesson, help you to assign groups, or gather a small group to work with you further.

Some general "rules" about asking questions are:

- Be sure to give adequate time for students to think before accepting responses.
- Avoid yes or no questions as they do not give insight into student thinking.
- Include higher level questions rather than only questions that have one correct factual answer.
- Move away from a student when you ask a question so that the whole class feels involved.

Sometimes you may wish to pose a question and have students record their responses before answers are discussed. This allows some students to respond more thoughtfully. After the discussion, you can ask students to correct or extend their original answers. Students could also write two-sentence answers on index cards. The cards could be collected and redistributed for other students to read aloud, allowing a variety of ideas to be heard at an early stage of learning, when many might not choose to share their thinking.

Students can also be invited to pose questions themselves by suggesting, for instance, that they *write questions to show what they would like to learn about shapes* or *suggest questions that they think should be on the quiz.* You can also ask students to pose questions that they think will be helpful to their peers. Have students practice asking such questions as, *Why do you think so?* to enable good peer teaching and deeper pair shares.

Equity and Assessment

There are many equity issues associated with assessment that we need to re-examine through the goal of career and college readiness. We want to be sure that our assessment practices help our students to meet this goal and support equity. Afflerbach and Clark (2011) suggest that assessment can create barriers to learning and thus increase inequities. These authors indicate that, conversely, assessment could open avenues of support and improve positive self-identity, two factors that increase the likely success of students who are too often marginalized. The Common Core has set these standards for *all* students; our assessments must increase access to learning, not further limit it.

There are a variety of ways our classroom assessment practices can be beneficial, rather than detrimental. For example, we can:

> ✍ **Use a variety of assessment formats,** so that all learners have the opportunity to demonstrate what they know. For instance, some learners perform less well on multiple-choice assessment formats as they tend to be less contextualized (Goodwin, Ostrom, and Scott 2009). Instead of asking whether questions should be open-ended or multiple choice, we should think about which formats are best when and for which students.

- ✏ **Support student self-efficacy** by providing them opportunities to assess their own work and set their own goals.

- ✏ **Create learning environments** in which students view constructive feedback as helping them to achieve their own goals.

- ✏ **Give feedback privately** and compare student work to previous work, not to the work of other students.

- ✏ **Connect assessment tasks** to students' culture and identity by providing tasks that relate to students' interests, backgrounds, and daily lives.

- ✏ **Differentiate assessment items** to ensure access. For example, you can decrease the complexity of the non-mathematics vocabulary for English language learners.

Most importantly, we must use assessment data to provide students with additional opportunities to learn. Struggling students must be given access to additional instruction so that they can perform better. This approach is quite different from grouping students together to focus on less challenging tasks at a slower pace. Similarly, more ready students should have access to more challenging tasks so that they, too, can reach their full potential.

Standardized Testing of the Common Core State Standards

As a result of the allocation of funds from the federal Race to the Top assessment grant program, two consortia have received federal funding to create assessments: The Partnership for Assessment of Readiness for College and Career (PARCC) and the Smarter Balanced Assessment Consortium (SBAC). A national testing model allows data to be compared across students, districts, and states. Both consortia are committed to tests that better assess students' critical thinking and problem-solving skills as well as their understanding of mathematical concepts. Replacing fill-in-the-blank "bubble" tests, the PARCC and SBAC both intend to better understand students' ability to solve problems by asking questions that will require them to describe how they solved the problem as well as to provide an answer. As the mode for test taking is technology-based, the test questions can be made interactive and intentionally engaging. This is why these assessments are sometimes referred to as next generation tests. According to the Smarter Balanced website (http://www.smarterbalanced.org) the overall claim or statement of learning outcomes of the SBAC summative assessments for grades 3–8 is, "Students can demonstrate progress toward college and career readiness in mathematics." Sub-claims listed are provided below. Note the references to the Mathematical Practices within these claims.

Sub-claims of SBAC Learning Outcomes

- Students solve problems involving the major content for their grade level with connections to practices.

- Students solve problems involving the additional and supporting content for their grade level with connections to practices.

- Students express mathematical reasoning by constructing mathematical arguments and critiques.

- Students solve real-world problems engaging particularly in the modeling practice.

The PARCC consortium has articulated similar goals on its website (http://www.parccoline.org) with a strong focus on creating an assessment system that will "build a pathway to college and career-readiness for all students."

Testing Formats

Both assessments are designed to include more than one test session throughout the school year. Tests given at the beginning of the school year, while optional, are intentionally formative, providing early feedback regarding student knowledge and skills. As a result of these formative tests, teachers can learn more about their students in order to inform instruction and to gain supplemental support for their students, if necessary. Teachers are able to score the tests themselves, allowing for timely feedback. The two required end-of-year assessments are designed to first test students' ability to complete performance-based tasks where skills and concepts are applied through extended tasks. The final assessment is computer-based and will be comprised of questions that may be machine-scored. The two final assessment scores will be combined to make up the students' accountability score.

Grade-level-specific performance-level descriptors (PLDs) and achievement level descriptors (ALDs) have been created to determine what knowledge and skills must be demonstrated at a particular grade level. These PLDs and ALDs can be found in detail on the consortia websites.

The SBAC consortium has agreed to create a paper-and-pencil version of all assessments while districts are in the process of upgrading their technology, after which time all assessments will be completed online. The PARCC consortium will create paper-and-pencil tests for those students who require them as written in their Individualized Education Plans. SBAC will utilize computer adaptive testing (CAT), which bases the questions asked of students on their answers to previous questions. Students who answer a question correctly will then receive a more challenging question, while a wrong answer on a question will lead students to an easier question. While not intending to use CAT, the PARCC assessments will also be taken online for both the formative and summative assessments. Both consortia have outlined the technology requirements to allow for use of a wide variety of devices, including tablets, laptops, and desktop computers. The intention is to make the administration of the online tests as widely available to all districts as possible, within a reasonable timeframe, though some districts suggest that it is impossible for them to afford the necessary technology.

Test Questions

Prototype questions have been made available for the purpose of informing educators as to how the CCSS will be assessed using the new technology-based tests. PARCC has designated the questions to be one of three types:

Type I: Tasks assessing concepts, skills, and procedures

Type II: Tasks assessing expressing mathematical reasoning

Type III: Tasks assessing modeling/applications (http://www.parcconline.org)

The SBAC questions also focus on a variety of problem types within each assessment format described as follows:

- Selected-response items are essentially multiple-choice items, however, more than one choice may be made.

- Technology-enhanced items take advantage of the use of technology by allowing students to construct answers to questions regarding their understanding of concepts and skills through innovative responses such as drawing a picture.

- Constructed-response items act as short-answer questions intended to collect information about a student's understanding of a concept.

- Performance tasks require students to integrate meanings across standards and demonstrate depth of understanding.

So How Will Test Items Change?

First, remember that many of the items are likely to look familiar as they will be the same as traditional test items. Also, keep in mind that, over time, students' ability to succeed on tasks posed in new test formats will improve as learners and teachers become more familiar with examples and the first few rounds of testing. As our students grow accustomed to engaging in activities that require their conceptual understanding, differences in the test questions will be less noticeable. Whatever your state decides about the use of these tests, these new formats will quickly be included in published curriculum materials, so eventually many students will be exposed to new expectations on a regular basis.

Types of Responses

Both the SBAC and the PARCC tests will likely ask our students to do the following:

- Manipulate representations using technological tools

- Explain how they solved a problem, using written language

- Use or interpret representations

- Interpret the results of given data

- Identify computation results as true or false

It is likely that the technological format and the expectation of written explanations will be the greatest changes. Figure 3.2 gives an example of how an item might be transformed to take advantage of the technology platform. And of course, content changes between these and previous standards will affect the design of test questions.

Figure 3.2 Technological Test Format

Traditional task:

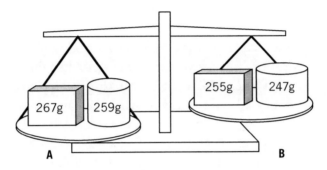

How much heavier is the total mass on side A than on side B?

Task that reflects new response possibilities:

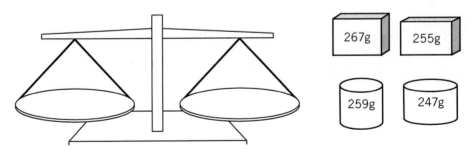

Click and drag to place all the weights on the pan scale so it will stay balanced.

Written Explanations

If your students are not currently familiar with writing mathematical explanations, this change will require considerable attention. You will want to attend to this skill from the beginning of the school year. Provide students with exemplars so they understand expectations; have students use key words such as *first, then, because,* and *so* to organize their explanations; and assign students to begin by writing their explanations in small groups or as a whole class. Use ideas from your process writing curriculum so that students expect to edit their writing for clarity and have them work in pairs to give each other feedback. Examples that require explanations are likely to be multi-step and/or have different solution paths.

Tasks requiring such explanations are likely to include a phrase such as, *show or explain how you arrived at your answer.* Your students will need to practice what it means to show and explain their thinking, rather than just arriving at an answer. Providing an explanation of what they are thinking or labeling mathematical steps for solving a multi-step problem may be a daunting task for some students. They will need practice and feedback about their responses as they learn to clearly and succinctly show their mathematical thinking. Figure 3.3 shows such an example of this change.

Figure 3.3 Comparison of Task

Traditional task:

Matt has 10 nickels.

Jeri has 3 fewer nickels than Matt.

Kyle has 5 fewer nickels than Jeri.

How many nickels does Kyle have?

Show your work.

Task that reflects newer expectations:

Together, Jeri and Matt have 15 nickels.

Kyle has 8 more nickels than Jeri.

How many nickels do Kyle, Jeri, and Matt have in all?

Show or explain how you arrived at your answer.

Embedded Representations

Particular representations such as number lines and tape diagrams are given new attention in these standards. Students are also expected to have a deep understanding of place value. Consider the task change in Figure 3.4. Note that this example includes two representations and a follow-up question.

Figure 3.4 Comparison of Task Expectation Involving Representations

Traditional task:

Write these numbers in order: 287, 302, 314, 299

Task that reflects newer expectations:

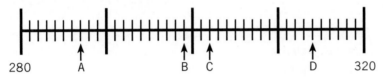

For each arrow, write the correct number: 287, 302, 314, 299

A = _____   B = _____   C = _____   D = _____

You have 289. Between which two arrows is this number?

Interpret Results

Connections to real-world applications require students to do more than compute results; learners must also understand how to apply such results in a particular situation. Figure 3.5 provides an example of an interpretation students need to make about a remainder.

Figure 3.5 Comparison of Task Expectation Involving Interpretations

Traditional task:

$27 \div 4 = \square$

Task that reflects newer expectations:

The 27 members of the Bicycle Club are driving up to the canyon where they will ride a mountain trail. Each car can take 4 members and their bikes. How many cars are needed for the trip?

Work with True/False Statements

The emphasis on properties, structure, relationships among numbers, and the use of equations supports use of true and false statements. Such examples are likely to have more than one number on each side of the equation. Figure 3.6 provides such an example. Students with conceptual understanding and familiarity with this format are likely to be able to respond more quickly than those who are not.

Figure 3.6 Comparison of Task Expectation Involving True/False Statements

Traditional task:

Write >, <, or = in the blank.

146 + 74 _____ 220

Task that reflects newer expectations:

Tell whether each statement is true or false.

321 x (25 + 6) = 321 x 25 + 321 x 6

1,456 + 736 = 1,455 + 73

New Mathematical Standards

Many of the test items will change because the standards have changed. The topic might appear at a different grade level or might no longer be given significant attention. Conversely, new ideas might be considered critical. For example, the use of equations is highlighted throughout the elementary standards. Students are expected not only to solve equations, but also to use equations to represent mathematical situations. Figure 3.7 suggests a possible related task. Note the inclusion of *times as many as,* a multiplication situation given new emphasis in fourth grade.

Figure 3.7 Comparison of Task Expectation Involving New Content

Traditional task:

Solve for ☐.

$5 \times 25 =$ ☐

Task that reflects newer expectations:

Which situation is best represented by $5 \times 25 =$ ☐ ?

  A. There are 25 markers sorted into 5 equal groups.

  B. Joey has 25 books and his mother has 4 times as many books as he has.

  C. There are 25 markers to share fairly with 5 people.

  D. There are 25 seats in a minibus and the large bus has 5 times as many seats as the minibus.

You can create additional examples by asking yourself:

☞ If I posed this question online, what different responses or ways of responding would be possible?

☞ What question stems or other scaffolding can I provide as my students learn how to explain their thinking?

☞ How might I include information shown in a representation rather than stated, or what representation might I require students to include?

☞ How might students need to interpret this computational result?

☞ How can I assess knowledge of relationships among numbers and the properties of arithmetic by embedding them in true or false questions?

☞ How are ideas among domains related?

☞ What is a new content emphasis at my grade level?

Testing Accommodations

Both SBAC and PARCC have published documents describing the accommodations that will be made available to students with learning disabilities or low cognitive ability, and English Language Learners, such as large print versions, Braille options, and tests written in several different languages. Also, two consortia have been granted awards to create alternative assessments for students with significant cognitive disabilities. Dynamic Learning Maps (DLMs) will offer two options: offering questions to students as alternative assessments through day-to-day instruction, or a summative assessment that branches based on the students' responses. The National Center and State Collaborative (NCSC) is producing a summative assessment to assess whether these students are achieving increasing higher academic outcomes.

A summary of a number of the key similarities and differences between the SBAC and PARCC assessments is outlined in Figure 3.8.

Figure 3.8 Key Similarities and Differences of the SBAC and PARCC Assessments

Similarities	Differences
• Tests are taken online except for special conditions by which a paper-pencil test may be requested	• SBAC: Adapted based on California Achievement Test (questions are asked based on students' responses to prior questions)
• Grades 3–8 will be assessed	• PARCC: Fixed form (question sets are static)
• Variety of types of items	• Retake option only available through Smarter Balanced
• Two formative components and two summative components	• Optional formative assessments offered by PARCC for grade K–2 students
• Combination of human and computerized scoring with results expected within several weeks	• SBAC: Grade 11 summative assessment
• Comparable costs at about $20–$30 per student for the summative assessments	• PARCC: High School course-based assessments

Assessment of the Standards for Mathematical Practice

As the proficiencies described in the Mathematical Practices are standards, they too, must be assessed. It seems as though high-stakes testing programs will include tasks that rely on the Mathematical Practices, but do not intend to directly measure and report the results of how well our students can apply these standards (Bill and Goldman 2012). This is not surprising, as the Standards for Mathematical Practice are what is most new about the Common Core State Standards for Mathematics. In general, educators are still discerning how such standards may look at each level. So what are some ways you can begin to access your students' achievement in relation to these practices?

- **Learn as much as you can about these practice standards**. Continue to read about them, watch videos intended to highlight them, and attend related professional development.

- **Help your students to understand the expectations** you have for them. Post them in your classroom in words that students can understand. One teacher shows her students video clips of students learning mathematics and asks the students to find evidence of a particular practice or two. For instance, students might be asked to find evidence that students use correct mathematical vocabulary (MP6) or how they connect mathematics to real-world situations (MP4). Students can also be asked to dramatize responses to a particular task demonstrating a "good" and "not so good" example of persevering in solving problems (MP1).

- **Create rubrics** for each of the practices based on the example provided in Figure 2.8 and use them to note evidence over time.

- **Be sure to ask questions** that highlight students' attention to these practices and note their responses. Possible questions include: *How could you be more precise about your description of a rhombus? Why do you think a tape diagram is the representation to use here? Do you notice any patterns in your responses that would help you to create a shortcut?*

- **Share students' work with colleagues**. Give the same task to students in a couple of classrooms at your grade level and sort the responses together based on particular practice standards. You might also want to agree to give the same task across a grade level span such as K–2 or 3–5 to collect data as to how, for example, students' justifications (MP3) become more sophisticated.

Perhaps most important, attend to whether or not students exhibit these habits of mind.

The Roles of Parents/Guardians and Students in Assessment

Parents'/Guardians' Roles

Ideally, you frequently share student assessments with parents and guardians. Sharing tasks their children completed earlier and later in the year is a wonderful way to document student learning. While this practice should continue, it is important that you also help parents/guardians understand important ways they can support assessment. They can:

- Help their children take responsibility for work completed at home by encouraging them to note when assignments are due and to create a plan for meeting that goal. Support children in the completion of their work, but do not do it for them.

- Learn about standards and assessment.

- Create a calm environment for their children at home when standardized tests are being taken at school, and anticipate children being more tired and irritable during such times.

You and your school are particularly important in helping parents and guardians understand the new tests. The 45th annual Gallup Poll, conducted in 2013, revealed that less than half of the parents of school-aged children knew that the Common Core Standards even existed (Bushaw and Lopez 2013). Without a clear understanding of the increased rigor and higher expectations for moving beyond basic skills, parents of students who have participated in field-testing of the new standardized tests have been left mystified as to why their children scored so poorly. It is incumbent upon the individual school districts and those most responsible for communicating directly with parents, (teachers) to provide explanations about how these standardized tests are different from previous state tests and why the scores have decreased. Swanson (2013) provides suggestions to teachers on how to best share information with the parent community:

- Share comparative data from across the nation to give parents a perspective as to the relative nature of the decreases.

- Provide information about their child's progress from the formative assessment results to the end-of-year summative assessment results.

- Show parents how the questions from the state assessments have changed as we have moved to SBAC or PARCC assessments. Allowing parents to see how much the questions have changed to reflect the higher expectations of the new test questions may alleviate parents' concerns about why their child has received a lower score than on past assessment tests.

- Explain to parents that the move from state standards to the Common Core State Standards will take time to adjust to and that their child's scores on the new tests will take time to adjust as well.

Students' Roles

So often when we talk about classroom assessment we think about our evaluation of the assessment data we collect. Questions understandably arise about how we will find the time to read student work, interpret it to better ensure learning, and record what we learn. Concern for our assessment responsibilities as teachers can sometimes cause us to neglect the responsibilities of students. Yet it is essential that students participate fully in this process. Here are some ways we can involve students:

- Have students reflect on their learning through exit cards, journal entries in response to feedback on tasks, or by completing rubrics. Ramdass and Zimmerman argue that self-reflection is important to student success. They state that, "Teachers can help students to hone this invaluable self-regulatory skill by giving them frequent opportunities to evaluate what they have learned or where they erred after completing a task" (2008, 41).

✏ Give students opportunities to set their own goals. For example, students needing to achieve greater fluency could identify an intermediate goal such as, "I will learn my multiplication facts to 5 x 5." As it is their goal, they are more likely to attend to it.

✏ Provide models for students that allow them to see student work samples that meet standards, which allow students to better understand expectations. Students can then give peers feedback and better self-evaluate their own work.

✏ Help students understand the learning process. Atkin, Black, and Coffey (2001) suggest that students need to understand: Where am I going? Where am I now? How can I close the gap? Teachers can do this by making goals clear, involving students in the assessment process, and having students contribute to a learning plan. Some teachers post learning expectations for a given unit and give students a copy of them as well. Midway through the unit, students might be asked to self-assess their progress on the goals by choosing a rating or drawing frowning, neutral, or smiling faces. They can then record or talk about what they will do next to continue to improve.

✏ Provide students with information about standardized tests, similar to that which you give to parents/guardians communicated in a way that students can understand.

✏ Provide students with evidence of their growth. Nothing can sabotage students' performance more than a lack of confidence. Think of students who look at a task and immediately conclude that they cannot do it. Often, with just a bit of support, they can be successful. Consider making comments such as *Hmm, just a minute ago you thought you could not succeed and now you are doing just fine. What does that tell you?*

Let's Think and Discuss

1. Think of assessment tasks you give that you find helpful. Can you identify common elements among them that might make them so?

2. Reflect on a time when you discovered particularly helpful information about student learning within a lesson. What instructional decisions did you make or what questions did you ask based on this discovery?

3. What techniques do you use to collect assessment data at the beginning or end of a lesson?

Chapter 4

Counting and Cardinality

 **Snapshot**

A kindergarten teacher likes to use menus that organize choices for students. It is December and the students are familiar with this instructional format. The students are somewhat familiar with the individual activities, but this is the first time they have been combined within a menu. There are six choices on the menu that the teacher displays on chart paper to the whole class:

✏ A picture of a book informs the students that they may choose to stay in the rug area and choose a book to read from the milk crate the teacher has filled with counting books.

✏ A picture of a number cube and a game sheet let the students know that they may choose to play Roll and Build, where they roll a number cube and build a tower that high until they have a tower for each of the numbers 1–6.

✏ A picture of two 10 frames showing the number six tells them that they may choose to play 10-Frame Match.

✏ A picture of a bag with the written numeral 8 on it lets students know that they can go to the math center to get the clear container filled with similar bags and counters. Their task is to randomly choose two bags to fill according to their numeral labels and then order the bags from least to greatest based on the number of counters they hold.

✏ A picture of a number sheet with numbers written in dotted lines shows them that they may choose to practice writing numbers.

✏ A picture of the teacher shows them that they can choose to work on one of these activities with the help of their teacher.

The teacher reviews the choices with the students. Then she says, "Those of you who would like to use the number cube, please raise your hand." She then chooses six students, in pairs, so they each have a partner and tells them to go to the table at the back of the room where they will find the materials they need. She proceeds until each group is identified and all of the students are involved in activities that relate to this domain.

Counting as well as representing and comparing numbers gets considerable attention in this kindergarten classroom throughout the year. As adults, counting is so automatic we may not recognize all the concepts and skills needed to count successfully (Dacey and Collins 2010). In fact, simple mathematical tasks are often more complex than we realize (Ginsberg and Ertle 2008).

Big Picture

The counting and cardinality domain is unique to the kindergarten level. Cardinality may be a new word to many teachers. It refers to the quantity of a set and requires the counter to recognize that the last number said while counting objects indicates the quantity of the group; that it is the answer to the question "How many are there?" It is exciting to see important developmental milestones associated with counting, such as counting on from a number other than one, getting their own focus within the Common Core State Standards. This attention to counting and cardinality gives us the opportunity to relook at this area of students' thinking in closer detail, in ways that will help ensure that each student begins with the foundation he or she needs for later success. Such a goal is significant as research suggests that kindergarten students' counting and number knowledge are predictors of calculation skills at the second-grade level (Locuniak and Jordan 2008).

This domain is organized around three clusters:

- Know number names and the count sequence
- Count to tell the number of objects
- Compare objects

Each cluster and their associated standards work together to form what we mean by counting and cardinality. Figure 4.1 summarizes what this domain specifies that kindergarten students are expected to accomplish at this level. We will consider these specific goals within the next three sections of the chapter that focus on each cluster.

Figure 4.1 Expectations within Counting and Cardinality

Task	Number Goal
Count rotely by ones and tens	1–100
Count rotely by ones from a number other than 1	2–100
Write numerals to represent a number of objects	0–20
Assign exactly one number to each object when counting	1–20
Recognize the last number in the count as the quantity	1–20
Know that counting numbers increase by 1	1–20
Count objects arranged in a row, array, or circle	1–20
Recognize that the arrangement does not change the cardinality	1–20
Produce a set with a given number of objects	1–20
Compare number of objects in two groups	1–20
Compare two written numerals	1–10

Know Number Names and the Count Sequence

In some cases, students enter kindergarten with the ability to say the number names in order, or mostly in order, to 10. This skill develops further throughout the kindergarten year, until the student can count to 100 by both ones and tens (K.CC.1). Listening to young children count to 100 tells us much about our number system. You will often hear a child drag out the number at the end of a decade, such as twenty-*niiiiiiiiiine*, as the learner tries to remember the name of the next decade. Then, usually in a much faster cadence, the child will say the numbers 31–38, like an engine building up momentum, followed by another drawn out thirty-*niiiiiiiiiine*. Listen to your students count aloud individually so that you can determine if and when they experience difficulty transitioning from one decade to another. Then, target further practice accordingly.

What makes this counting sequence so challenging, even for those students who are successful counting by tens? To older students and adults, it is clear that the familiar 0–9 pattern in the ones place applies to the tens place as well (though we don't record the 0 for natural numbers less than ten), but that is not the case at this level. Many Asian languages are consistent with their number names (Uy 2003). For instance, their name for thirteen would translate to one ten, three and fifty-seven to five tens, seven. Unfortunately, our names for two-digit numbers can obscure patterns within our counting sequence. Counting to 100, rather than perhaps 30, helps to make the counting patterns more prominent. While saying the number names in order to 100 is a rote skill, the students likely to be the first to succeed are those who recognize the structure and regularity within our number system. Our two-digit number names hide the counting patterns in the following ways:

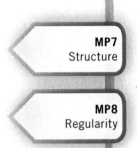

MP7
Structure

MP8
Regularity

- Eleven and twelve do not follow the regular pattern of saying something for both the tens and ones to indicate that two places are involved.

- When we say the teen numbers we identify the ones first, such as in eighteen. This never happens again after the teens.

- Unlike forty, sixty, seventy, eighty, and ninety our decade names teen, twenty, thirty, and fifty are not identical to the sound of the corresponding ones digit. If you only learned to count to 59, only the forties would sound like a familiar one-digit number.

Remember that counting to 100 by ones and tens is a standard that students must meet by the end of the kindergarten year. Much of their mathematical instruction will focus on smaller numbers. That said, students are proud of their abilities to count to what they call *really big numbers*; this is one of the reasons they often enjoy learning to count by tens. Note that when students first learn to count by tens, they may confuse counting by ones with counting by tens. That is, they may begin counting by ones, but when they reach a particular new decade, for instance, thirty, they may switch to counting by tens and say, "forty, fifty, sixty," and so forth. Saying numbers in an incorrect order is common when children are first introduced to greater numbers. Continuous exposure to rote counting throughout the year makes sense.

Over time, increase the final number until 100 is reached. Some classroom ideas include:

☞ **Use counting songs** that you can find on the Internet. When students repeatedly sing a song, they increase the likelihood that they will remember what they learned (Rinne et al. 2001).

☞ **Look for opportunities to repeat the counting sequence**, for example, while transitioning from one activity to another, waiting to enter the school building, or taking a walk.

☞ **Involve movement** as students practice the counting sequence. For example, have them copy you as you swing your arms as everyone counts from one to ten, as you wiggle your fingers as the count goes from 11 to 20, and tap your foot as everyone counts from 21 to 30.

☞ **Use games.** For example, chose a number such as 10 and have the students stand in a circle. Have students say the number names in order in a round-robin fashion. The student that says *ten* sits down, though continues to count orally with the group. The next student starts again at one and the counting continues until only one student remains standing.

While students need to master these rote counting skills, most instructional time should be spent on their integration in a contextualized task or activity. Rote practice should be a small component of students' learning and conducted in an engaging manner. Also note that students often recognize when they need practice and enjoy it when it feels like just the right time to do it. Giving students options allows them to decide what skills they want to improve.

In one kindergarten classroom, Catalia and Daniel have chosen a practice activity with a mixed up deck of 20 cards, labeled 1–20. The cards are placed face down between the two students. Catalia turns over the top card and enthusiastically announces, "It's five!" It is Daniel's job to count on from five. Not quite able to count on, he discreetly whispers, "One, two, three, four, five," and then speaks more loudly as he continues the count. Daniel turns over the next card and tells Catalia to count from nine. She repeats the nine and then continues. These students are practicing counting from a number other than one, a more sophisticated skill than counting from one (K.CC.2). Note that they are also recognizing written numerals; it is rare that counting skills are isolated (K.CC.3). You can, however, also use the activity with students who have not mastered recognition of symbols by pairing such students with those who have, or leading the class in the activity with you announcing the start numbers.

Honoring Individual Differences

Like learning how to write the letters of the alphabet and associating them with particular phonetic sounds, associating symbols with the number of objects is complex and takes time to develop. To increase the likelihood of success among diverse learners, a variety of practice opportunities should be available. Here, we limit our focus to ways to practice writing numerals, leaving the connection to collections of objects for consideration when we investigate the next cluster. Some ideas include:

- **Begin without pencils and paper.** Have students write numbers in the air or in sand, form them with dough, paint them with a brush, or make them with chenille sticks.

✏ **Support students when they first move to paper and pencil** by providing written numerals to trace, with arrows that indicate the direction of their strokes. Over time, transition to dotted lines or only part of the symbol until scaffolding is removed.

As a formative assessment task, one teacher asks students to write the numbers that they know. Note that the student represents 20 and 100 as well as the first 10 counting numbers. Several of the numerals are reversed, which is not uncommon at this early age, but is something the teacher will keep in mind when working with this student.

Count to Tell the Number of Objects

It is this cluster that focuses on counting with meaning as students make connections between numbers and quantities (K.CC.4). This connection includes the following abilities.

✏ One-to-one correspondence or the ability to say *exactly* one number name for each object being counted (K.CC.4a) is essential. Initially, children may omit objects or count objects more than once. Some students may repeatedly count the objects until they have said all of the number names they know.

✏ Stable order of our numbers, that is, the numbers are said in the same order when counting (K.CC.4a).

✏ Cardinality that requires the understanding that the last number said indicates the number of objects counted (K.CC.4b). Without this concept, students may think that the counting process is the answer.

➥ Conservation of numbers, that is, recognition that the cardinality of a group of objects does not change if the objects are rearranged (K.CC.4b). This concept allows students to count objects in any order, knowing the count will be the same. The notion of conservation is essential to the later development of flexible computation strategies and to grouping or regrouping numbers.

➥ Counting numbers increase by one, for example, five is one more than four (K.CC.4c). See Figure 4.2 for an illustration of this concept. Similar pictures are often found in counting books. Teachers who work with somewhat older students and have witnessed them compute to find 287 + 1 can attest to the fact that this idea is not as obvious as it might appear. As suggested by Van de Walle, Karp, and Bay-Williams "When children count, they don't often reflect on the way in which one number is related to another (2013, 136)."

➥ Collections of objects can be represented by corresponding written numerals. Making connections among number names, written numerals, and a group of objects connects abstract sounds and symbols to the concrete group.

MP2
Reason

MP4
Model

Figure 4.2 Representation to Show that Each Counting Number is One More

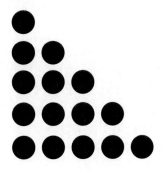

You can increase or decrease the complexity of a counting task by arranging the objects in a different manner (K.CC.5). Consider the examples in Figure 4.3. As you work with individual or small groups of students, place counters in these different arrangments. With which ones are they successful? Note that as the number of counters increases, students who have developed successful methods for keeping track may forget to use them or make minor errors as they do so.

Figure 4.3 Different Arrangements of Objects Impact Level of Challenge

| The line provides clear start and end points that help students keep track. | An array requires students to keep track of which columns or rows were counted. | With a circle, the student needs to remember which object was the first one counted to know when to stop. | When counters are scattered, the student must visualize a path to make sure each object is counted exactly once. |

Over time, students develop a conceptual understanding of why it is important to say exactly one number name for each object they are counting and develop methods for doing so. Keeping track of this process is challenging. It involves a variety of abilities such as visual memory and executive functioning. There are several ways to support students as they learn to devise their own techniques. Students can count the following:

- Beads on a string that are moved from one direction to the other as they are counted.
- Cubes that are linked as they are counted.
- Counters that move from a red plate to a blue plate as they are counted.
- Counters in a shoebox top, with a border in the middle, that move from one side of the border to the other as they are counted.

Consider this classroom example: one kindergarten teacher gathers students in the rug area and places 12 teddy bear counters in a row where they can be seen by all the students. She demonstrates counting the bears, pointing at each one as she names a number. She repeats this process, but with a different number of bears, and places them in a circle. As she models the counting process this time, she dramatizes forgetting where she started and begins to count again. She recounts, once more forgetting where she started. Then she asks, "What could I do to help me keep track of where I started?" The students suggest ideas such as keeping her finger on the first object counted, turning the first object on its side, or moving each object after it is counted. As students make suggestions, she invites them to demonstrate their ideas to the class. Next, she distributes counters to pairs of students to place in a circle. Together, the students decide the strategy they will use to keep track and then find how many objects there are.

The next day, the teacher will name a number and ask students to show that number with their counters. It is more challenging for students to produce a group of say, 15 counters, than it is to count such a group already formed (Sarama and Clements 2009). To produce a group, students must keep the goal in mind as they count (K.CC.5).

Let's step back at this point and think about what these concepts and skills might look like. Consider five-year old Selicia who is counting seven counters lined up in a row. There are no other objects on the table. She counts them correctly. When asked how many there are, she correctly responds, "Seven." The teacher places one more counter at the end of the line and Selicia counts from one to eight, identifying eight as the amount. Next, Selicia's elbow inadvertently moves a few of the counters. The teacher again asks how many there are. Selicia merely looks up and says, "Eight." Before reading further, think about Selicia's counting strengths. Then, think about what learning goals might be appropriate for her to pursue next and what tasks you might want her to consider so you could gain further information.

When counting seven or eight objects in a line, Selicia has demonstrated the ability to do the following:

- ✏ Say exactly one number name for each object (one-to-one correspondence).

- ✏ Say the number names in the correct order (stable order).

- ✏ Know that the last number of the count identifies the quantity (cardinality).

- ✏ Recognize that the number doesn't change when the objects are rearranged (conservation).

Selicia recounted to find the quantity after one more counter was added to the group. An appropriate learning goal would be the following:

- ✏ Recognize that when one more is added to a group of seven objects, the quantity is the next counting number, eight.

There are many ways these tasks could be varied to gain further information. You might wish to alter the task to determine if Selicia could do the following:

- ✏ Maintain the one-to-one correspondence when objects are arranged in an array, circle, or scattered formation.

- ✏ Demonstrate these same strengths with a greater number of counters.

- ✏ Write a number to represent the quantity.

- ✏ Recognize the cardinality of a group, without counting, when one more object is added to a group with fewer counters.

Compare Numbers

"Why does he get more?" Everyone who has spent any significant amount of time with students has heard some version of this question or of the definitive statement, "I want more!" Such comparisons likely are built on an intuitive sense of fairness or the strength of basic human needs such as hunger. These young children are not necessarily making formal comparisons; in fact, they may be using their measurement sense, rather than their number sense. For example, they might be comparing the amount of space on the plate that the raisins cover or the height of a pile of carrot sticks.

Again, while very young children exhibit some ability to make comparisons, it is a skill that develops during the kindergarten year and requires explicit attention. Ideas of same, less, and more are essential to later experience with equations and operations (K.CC.6). It is particularly important to attend to the notion of less, as learners find this concept more challenging (Van de Walle, Karp, and Bay-Williams 2013).

Initial comparisons tend to be visual; the student concludes that there are more because it looks like there are more. Matching items is usually the next approach considered. Items from two sets are lined up together in a way that establishes one-to-one correspondence. Note that students' language may still be connected to measurement ideas (Figure 4.4).

Figure 4.4 Sample Student Language for Measurement-Number Comparison

"Circles is less because they are shorter."

When objects are of very different sizes or not able to be moved, we count to compare. Also, counting is often more efficient than matching. To rely on counting requires that students recognize, for example, that eight is more than six. Note that although children are quite capable of saying these number names in order, this does not mean that they recognize that numbers said later in the sequence always represent a quantity that is greater. It is at the final stage of this progression that students can compare written numerals one through ten (K.CC.7).

Initially, students need many opportunities to form or compare collections that are less than, more than, or the same as. Possible activities include having students:

☞ Use felt boards to match common items that go together such as bat and balls.

☞ Work in pairs with one student making a set and the other student making a set that is the same (or more than or less than).

☞ Shake two boxes of counters to decide which holds less (or more) and then check their predictions by matching or counting.

You can also identify a number such as six and have students draw, stamp, or use stickers to complete the activity sheet in Figure 4.5. For some students, you may wish to show a set of six counters at the top of the page, as well as the numeral.

Figure 4.5 Activity Sample for Less, Same, and More

6		
Less	Same	More

As the students create their sets, observe the strategies they use. Do they appear to rely on visual images to create sets that are more and less, without comparing directly or counting? When using direct comparison, do they match one item in a set with exactly one item in the other set? Do they make a set of six first and then add items to make a set that is more?

After students complete the task, bring them together to discuss their thinking. Ask questions such as: *What did you do to make a group of six? What helped you to make a group that was more? What number did you show that was less? How do you know it is less?*

Honoring Individual Differences

Comparison activities can be adapted easily to meet the needs of students working on direct comparison, counting, or symbolic levels. At the practice level, the common card game of War can be played with a deck of cards that does the following:

- Shows collections of dots lined up, one beneath another, along the left or right side of the cards. This arrangement allows students to place one card on top of another to see the dots placed side by side.

- Has the face cards removed from a commercial deck leaving four sets of the numbers 1–9. Note that each card shows a collection of items (clubs, diamonds, hearts, or spades) as well as the associated written numerals.

- Contains two sets of the written numerals 0–20.

Assessment Note

These standards are developed throughout the kindergarten year with increasingly greater numbers. It can be helpful to keep a record of the students' growth by making specific observations several times during the year. The recording sheet shown in Figure 4.6 is also available in Appendix A and provides an example of such a form. You can develop an interview to assess these abilities or merely note those that are demonstrated as students work. You can also keep the form handy when you are planning, so that you can identify the standards addressed and potential performance tasks you might want to include in your plan.

Figure 4.6 Counting and Cardinality Record Sheet

Student Name:	Date	Number(s)	Comments
Rote counting by ones			
Rote counting by 10's			
Rote count by ones from a number other than one			
Write numbers to represent a number of objects			
Assign exactly one number name to each object in a set			
Know that the last number in the count tells the quantity			
Says the number names in the correct order			
Recognize that the counting numbers increase by one			
Count objects arranged in a row, array, or circle			
Recognize changing the arrangement does not change the quantity			
Produce a set with a given number of objects			
Match or count to compare two groups			
Compare two written numerals			

When students are engaged in familiar activities, some teachers find they can sit at a table and invite students to stop by for a quick assessment task. Examples include:

- ✏ How high do you think you can count? Please show me.
- ✏ When counting, what number do you say just after 24?
- ✏ How many counters do you see?
- ✏ Show me a group of 12 counters.
- ✏ Make a group with fewer counters than this group has.
- ✏ If you have 5 counters and I have 7 counters, who has more?

 Voice from the Classroom

I am so grateful to the consideration the Common Core has given to counting and cardinality. Someone really paid attention to the fact that this is such important work in kindergarten. I have to admit that I had to look up what cardinality meant. I like the idea though, of a more formal vocabulary being applied to kindergarten math. I think it makes it seem more important, more respectable, something that cannot be ignored.

When I first read the standards in this domain, I was reminded of something that happened about 10 years ago. The team of kindergarten teachers at my school had created an interview protocol that we used with each of our students in the fall and then again in the spring. One of the tasks asked the students to count a group of 10 objects. We later found out that we were not implementing this task the same way. I was putting the collection of objects in front of the students to count. At least one of my colleagues was asking the students to take 10 objects out of a filled container. We decided to include both tasks in the individual interviews and found that creating the group was more challenging for some students than just counting them. I was so pleased that these different abilities were recognized in the standards.

When I first read the Common Core, all I could think about was that patterns were not included in the standards. How could I stop teaching patterns? I now realize that I need to let something go if I want my students to go deeper with numbers. I still have students count backwards as I think it prepares them for next year, but that is not something that takes a lot of time; it doesn't distract from the major focus of our work.

—Kindergarten Teacher

 ## Let's Think and Discuss

1. What common errors do you notice when younger students count rotely? What do you think causes those errors to be common?

2. What counting books would you recommend to others? Why?

3. The conceptual and procedural ideas in this domain are used throughout our lifetimes. What methods do you use to keep track of what you are counting? How do they differ depending on what you are counting, for example, people you invited to dinner?

Operations and Algebraic Thinking

 Snapshot

Third graders are working on the following task. To encourage conversation, the teacher has assigned them to work in pairs.

Use each number in the box in the story. Write the numbers so that the story makes sense.

1	7	3	43	4	5

Nick's mother gave him some nickels and pennies and Nick put them in rows. He made _____ rows of nickels with _____ nickels in each row. He made _____ small rows of pennies with _____ pennies in each row. There are _____ less rows of nickels than pennies. There are _____ coins in all.

(Answer: 4, 7, 5, 3, 1, 43)

Many of the students begin by guessing and checking. The teacher circulates as the students work. She notes those who multiply fluently as well as the strategies that other students use. When appropriate, she calls the students together for a discussion. After a couple of students describe how they found their answers, she asks the following questions:

- 👈 Mia said that she wrote 43 first. Why do you think someone might begin with this number?

- 👈 What could you do if you could not recall 4 x 7?

- 👈 How do the nouns help us to know where the number one must be written?

- 👈 What other answers could there be if this sentence (pointing to the third sentence) and the written numeral 1 were not in the problem?

This problem and such questions require students to reason quantitatively and to engage in mathematical discourse. Multiplication is a major focus at third grade and the array or area model of multiplication is critical to understanding that multiplication is two-dimensional; its two factors indicate different things, groups and the number in each group. This teacher has provided a way for students to apply their ability to find the products of single-digit numbers, to consider the implication of the commutative property of multiplication, and to do so in ways that connect to the mathematical practices.

MP2
Reason

MP3
Construct

Big Picture

The Operations and Algebraic Thinking domain builds on the ideas developed at the kindergarten level in Counting and Cardinality. It is within this domain that the understanding of the operations addition, subtraction, multiplication, and division are conceptually developed. Particular attention is given to:

- the kinds of problems that students can use these operations to solve

- the properties of the operations and the relationships among the operations

- strategies for finding totals, differences, products, and quotients, along with eventual basic fact fluency

Though this domain focuses on whole numbers, the goal is for students to gain a deep conceptual understanding of these operations so that ideas can later be applied to all types of numbers and variable expressions as well as to support the Expressions and Equations domain at the middle school level.

At the K–2 levels, the focus of this domain is on addition and subtraction, while multiplication and division are the focus at grades 3–5. Within the K–3 levels, each operation is introduced separately, and then students form links among them. Students are expected to represent these operations in meaningful ways, for example, by using fingers, objects, drawings, dramatizations, and then expressions or equations. Solution methods might involve strategies such as direct modeling, applying properties, using relationships among the operations, or connecting to an equivalent, but easier, example. Full basic fact fluency in addition, subtraction, multiplication, and division is expected by the end of third grade. To be fluent means to be fast and accurate. A summary of these computational expectations within this domain is provided in Figure 5.1. There is also a progression to the types of problems explored at each level, which will be illustrated in the following sections focused on these operations.

Figure 5.1 Computational Expectations in Operations & Algebraic Thinking K–3

Grade	Exploration	Fluency
Kindergarten	add and subtract within 10	add and subtract within 5
Grade 1	add and subtract within 20	add and subtract within 10
Grade 2	add and subtract within 100	add and subtract within 20
Grade 3	multiply and divide within 100	multiply and divide within 100

There are important links among this domain and others at the K–5 levels. In Number & Operations in Base Ten, students gain understanding of our place value system as well as compute with greater numbers. In Measurement and Data, students apply their understanding and skills to solving problems involving measures or using data shown in graphs, while the geometric measurement of area connects to the array or area model of multiplication.

Addition and Subtraction

Over the K–2 levels, students learn about the meaning of addition and subtraction through solving problems. According to the Progressions Document for Counting and Cardinality; K–5, Operations and Algebraic Thinking, "In each grade, the situations, representations, and methods are calibrated to be coherent and to foster growth from one grade to the next" (Common Core Standards Writing Team 2011a, 6).

Consider the following problem:

Three children are on the swings. Five more children join them. How many children are on the swings now?

Diego is representing the problem with counters. Typical of kindergarten students, Diego is able to immediately identify a set of three cubes, without having to count them one by one. This ability to recognize the cardinality of a set through perception is called subitizing (Clements 1999). To find the total, Diego creates a set of five counters, joins the two sets together, and then counts all of the eight counters. To represent his thinking, he draws the two sets separately, encircles them to show them joined, and records the numeral 8 (K.OA.1; K.OA.2).

First graders might also use counting, though over time, they are expected to *count on,* that is, to count on from the three rather than *count all.* Note that while saying the number names from a number other than one is a kindergarten standard, applying the skill to find the total of two groups is expected at the first grade. Later in the year, recall would be used as this is a fact to ten (1.OA.5).

This is just one type of addition and subtraction situation. Researchers have identified four basic structures for addition and subtraction (National Research Council 2009). In CCSS-M these four problem types are as follows:

- **Add to**: joining of two sets
- **Take from**: taking away from
- **Compare**: comparing two sets
- **Put together/take apart**: two subsets within a group such as red and yellow crayons

Traditionally, regardless of the problem type, our classrooms have focused on problems that asked only about the *result* of an addition or subtraction problem such as the swings problem discussed earlier (Van de Walle, Karp, and Bay-Williams 2013). However, every one-step addition and subtraction problem involves three numbers in the related equation, and according to the standards, any one of the numbers can be missing. Within this domain, students are expected to experience each of these problem types with any one of the three numbers unknown. See Figure 5.2 for a summary of these types of problem situations.

Figure 5.2 Addition and Subtraction Situations

	Result Unknown	Change Unknown	Start Unknown
Add To	There were five children in the pool. Three more children joined them. How many children are in the pool now?	There were five children in the pool. Some more children joined them. Now there are eight children in the pool. How many children joined the children already in the pool?	There were some children in the pool. Three more children joined them. Now, there are eight children in the pool. How many children were in the pool before more joined them?
Take From	There were eight children in the pool. Five children got out of the pool. How many children are in the pool now?	There were eight children in the pool. Some more children got out. Now there are three children in the pool. How many children got out of the pool?	There were some children in the pool. Five children got out. Now there are three children in the pool. How many children were in the pool before some got out?
	Total Unknown	**Addend Unknown**	**Both Addends Unknown**
Put Together/ Take Apart	There are five girls and three boys in the pool. How many children are in the pool?	There are eight children in the pool. Five of them are girls and the rest are boys. How many boys are in the pool? (*or* give the second addend and ask about the first one.)	There are eight children in the pool. Some of them are girls and some are boys. How many girls and how many boys could there be?
	Difference Unknown	**Bigger Unknown**	**Smaller Unknown**
Compare	There are five girls and three boys in the pool. How many more girls than boys are in the pool? (Or how many fewer boys than girls are there?)	There are two more girls than boys in the pool. There are three boys in the pool. How many girls are in the pool? (Or give the comparative statement using *fewer*.)	There are five girls in the pool. There are two fewer boys than girls in the pool. How many boys are in the pool? (Or give the comparative statement using *more*.)

(adapted from the Glossary of CCSS-M 2010 and *The National Research Council's Mathematics Learning in Early Childhood* 2009)

While single-digit numbers are used in Figure 5.2, students should continue to investigate a variety of problem situations as their skills progress to both greater and other types of numbers. Also, note the variety of equations students would create for these different situations.

MP1
Make Sense

At the kindergarten level, students explore add to and take from problems with the result unknown as well as put together/take apart situations with either the total or both addends unknown (K.OA). First and second graders work with all types of problems, though first-grade students are not expected to master:

- add to situations with the start unknown;

- take from situations with the start unknown;

- put together/take apart with one of the addends unknown, and

- compare problems with the bigger or smaller set unknown; written in language that suggests use of an incorrect operation (1.OA.1). Though second graders investigate two-step problems, we do not give them two-step problems where each step is one of these more complex situations (2.OA.1).

"Start unknown" problems can be particularly challenging as students who rely on direct modeling do not know where to begin. Consider this example from a second-grade classroom. The teacher shows the students a small paper bag. She shakes it and says, "There are some chips in this bag." She asks a student volunteer to place a few more chips in the bag, one at a time, and to count them aloud as they are included. Kareem places seven counters in the bag, counting from one to seven as he does so. Next, the teacher empties the bag and asks the students to make groups of 10 as they count all the chips. The teacher then says, "So I put some chips in the bag, Kareem put seven more chips in, and you counted a total of 45 chips." As the teacher says this, she draws a tape diagram (Figure 5.3). This is a new representation she wants to introduce in this lesson. She likes this representation because it supports the relationships between addition and subtraction, can represent a variety of situations, and can be used when any of the three numbers are missing.

Figure 5.3 Tape Diagram for ☐ + 7 = 45 or 45 − 7 = ☐

45	
?	7

As the teacher observes the students at work, she is interested in the strategies they use, for instance, whether they count back, subtract five and then two, guess and check, or write an equation. She makes notes about who she wants to share their thinking and the order in which she wants them to do so. She makes sure to include a student who used a tape diagram.

This teacher understands the importance of students gaining familiarity with several symbolic representations of the situation (Figure 5.4). In this way, students can further develop their algebraic understanding of arithmetic, that is, they can recognize relationships among operations, properties, and equivalent equations.

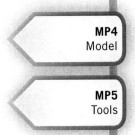

MP4
Model

MP5
Tools

Figure 5.4 Different Symbolic Representations for a Start Unknown Problem Situation.

Tape Diagram

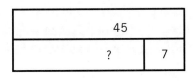

Part-Whole Number Bond

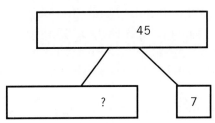

Addition: ☐ + 7 = 45

45 = ☐ + 7

Subtraction: 45 − ☐ = 7

7 = 45 − ☐

Conceptual Challenge

The meaning of the equal sign is often misunderstood (Ginsberg and Ertle 2008). When students only see the unknown isolated on one side of the equation, their experience leads them to conclude that the equal sign translates to *write the answer here*. Further, when they never see more than one number written to the right of the equal sign, they conclude that $7 = 5 + 2$ is an incorrect way to write $5 + 2 = 7$. Algebraic thinking requires students to recognize that equations may be written in a variety of formats as long as the numerical value of each side of the equation is the same. Defining "equal to" as *is the same as* is important, as is helping students become familiar with the many ways numerical relationships can be represented.

It is important to tie the various problem types with equations and to encourage multiple ways of thinking. As teachers, it is important that we make sure we model alternative recordings to broaden students' exposure to this foundation of algebraic thinking (1.OA7).

While students are solving these different types of addition and subtraction problems, their understanding of the operations increases and their computation strategies become more sophisticated. There are three steps in the learning trajectory:

- direct modeling
- counting on
- creating equivalent easier expressions

Direct Modeling

Students begin adding and subtracting with direct modeling. The counting all sequence in Figure 5.5 represents how students might use direct modeling to find 6 + 7.

Figure 5.5 Model of 6 + 7

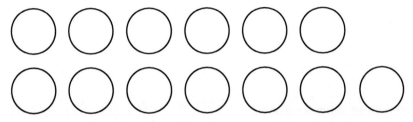

The student models each addend.

The student joins the two sets.

The student counts all of the counters to find the total.

To find 13 – 6, students might represent the 13 with counters or a drawing, remove six (or draw a line through, if drawing is used), and count what remains. This sequence is shown in Figure 5.6.

Figure 5.6 Model of 13 – 6

The student models the 13.

The student removes six of them.

The student counts to find how many remain.

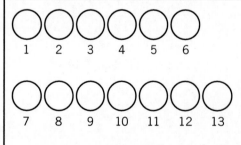

Rather than joining and recounting, the student counts on from the six.

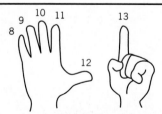

The student uses the visual image of the fingers to keep track of the six numbers said, while counting on from the seven.

Counting On

As indicated earlier, moving from *counting all* to *counting on* is an important conceptual milestone to finding totals. When students are able to count on, they are able to retain the cardinality of the first set, believe it is still the same (conservation), and count on from that number. To find 7 + 6, the student might use counters, drawings, or fingers. Over time his or her use of the strategy becomes more sophisticated and the student does not need to model the first number (Figure 5.6).

When the relationships between addition and subtraction are understood, counting on can also be used to find differences, which is helpful as counting back is more challenging than counting forward (Sarama and Clements 2009). To find 9 − 3, for example, one can count on from three, saying *four, five, six, seven, eight, nine* as a finger is identified for each number name said. This is another milestone, as using this thinking strategy requires learners to recognize that the three is part of the nine, as well as at least an intuitive understanding of the inverse relationship between addition and subtraction.

Honoring Individual Differences

It is important to realize that different family backgrounds may lead to different ways fingers are counted. Some students might hold their hands face up, while others position their hands face down while counting. Some students begin with a thumb, some with a pointer finger, and still others with a baby finger. Learn the ways your students prefer, so you can use the same approach when modeling to them.

Creating Equivalent, Easier Expressions

Over time, kindergarten students develop fluency with facts to five, and find missing addends with sums of 10 (K.OA.5; K.OA.4). Once students become fluent with sums to 10 in grade 1, they have access to one of the most important strategies, that of creating an equivalent, but easier, expression. Learning how to use known facts to find unknown facts is particularly helpful to students (Kling 2011) (1.OA.6).

For example, to find 8 + 4, a student might decompose the 4 to form 8 + 2 + 2. This making-10 strategy, together with knowing how to find a sum that is 10 more, allows a student to efficiently find sums to 20. Decomposing numbers begins in kindergarten and is reinforced in the Geometry domain as students decompose shapes (K.OA.3). Decomposing numbers to find 6 + 7, for example, the student could follow the following thinking steps:

☞ *What number do I add to 6 to find 10?*

☞ *What number plus 4 is equal to 7?*

☞ *I can add 6 + 4 + 3 to find 6 + 7.*

☞ *10 + 3 = 13, so 6 + 7 = 13.*

MP2
Reason

Students might also think about doubles and conclude that since 7 + 7 = 14, 6 + 7 = 13.

The commutative property of addition, $a + b = b + a$, also allows students to convert to an equivalent, but easier problem. For example, when finding 2 + 9, it's easier to think 9 + 2 and count up two from nine (1.OA.3). When finding the sum of 8 + 3 + 7, the associative property of addition $(a + b) + c = a + (b + c)$ allows us to add the 3 + 7 first (1.OA2; 1.OA.4).

One first-grade teacher sets up a learning station to reinforce this inverse relationship. The following activities are available at the center:

☞ In a concentration game, students match cards such as 3 + 8 = 11 with cards such as 11 – 8 = 3.

☞ Using a cup and beans, students place 10 beans in the cup. Then, they spill some beans out and decide, without looking, how many are still in the cup. They record their equations on an activity sheet with empty equation frames. ☐ + ☐ = 10

☞ Cover Up cards are folded and students must identify the covered numbers.

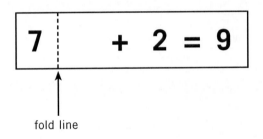

fold line

☞ Problem cards provide students with opportunities to solve word problems with the change unknown.

As different problem situations are investigated, and new strategies for finding sums and differences develop, students gain the vocabulary associated with addition and subtraction. Their understanding of these terms develops over time as shown in Figure 5.7. Within this domain they leave second grade being able to solve all of the different problem types, regardless of which number is missing, to apply strategies for finding sums and differences that will serve them well when they work with greater numbers, and to add and subtract fluently with facts to 20.

MP6
Precision

Figure 5.7 Grade-Level Vocabulary for Operations and Algebraic Thinking: Addition and Subtraction

Kindergarten	Grade 1	Grade 2
altogether	add	compose
as many as	addition	decompose
total	count on	difference
	count back	related fact
	equal to	sum
	minus	
	plus	
	subtract	
	subtraction	
	total	
	whole	

Honoring Individual Differences

Notice that the term *sum* is not used until the second grade. The word *sum* can be confusing to students because of its homonym, *some*. There are other mathematical words that have homonyms, such as *ate* and *eight*. However, *some* and *sum* can be exceptionally confusing, because both words can relate to the same context. *Some* would be associated with a *part* and *sum* with the total. While all students can find this confusing, this term can be particularly challenging for English Language Learners. Use *total* initially and be sure to write *sum* as it is first vocalized, pointing out how it is spelled differently than *some*.

Multiplication and Division

Students learn about the meaning of multiplication and division through solving problems and representing multiplication and division expressions to find products and quotients. Repeated multiplication is explored informally in second grade as students use addition to find the sum of equal groups (2.OA.4). In third grade, such equal groups would be viewed as multiplication. Array models (rows and columns) are also investigated at this level. Division may be viewed as finding the number in each equal share or finding the number of groups of equal shares. In the third grade, division does not include examples with remainders (3.OA1; 3.OA.2). In fourth grade, compare models (times as much as) are introduced and division does include remainders (4.OA.1).

MP1
Make Sense

Conceptual Challenge

Understanding that the comparative phrases *times as much as* or *times as many as* is a multiplicative relationship can be conceptually challenging (Harries and Barmby 2008). At earlier levels students making a comparison between a small tank with eight fish and a large tank of 32 fish would think additively, concluding that the large tank had 24 more fish or that the smaller tank had 24 fewer fish. Multiplicative thinking would be used to draw the conclusion that the larger tank has four times as many fish as the smaller one (The Common Core Standards Writing Team 2011a). Recognizing multiplicative relationships between two quantities is essential for later work with ratios and proportional reasoning. Use of tape diagrams can be helpful to represent a problem such as *The price of the brand-name scarf is four times as much as the scarf with the unknown brand. The price of the unknown brand scarf is $9. How much does the brand-name scarf cost?*

9

9	9	9	9

As with addition and subtraction, multiplication and division problems should be presented with all possible unknowns. The ability to find each of the missing numbers is particularly important, as finding the missing factor is the most common strategy for identifying a whole-number quotient or divisor. It is possible that you, too, think *What times six is equal to 42?* To find $42 \div 6$, third graders focus on arrays and measurement quantities, while fourth graders incorporate situations involving multiplicative comparison (3.OA.3; 4.OA.2). A summary of possible problem situations is provided in Figure 5.8. Once again, examples are all single-digit based; students should continue to explore these varied problem situations as they develop skills with greater numbers and different types of numbers. Further, the situations provided here are of countable objects. After students learn about measures, situations can involve continuous data, for instance, when compare problems involve lengths. Array situations can be specified to area once students have studied area. Compare problems can be written with fractions that indicate the relationship of the smaller quantity to that of the larger, (e.g., the shoes cost $\frac{1}{2}$ as much as the skirt). For now, it is important that you understand the differences between these problems and how they might be represented with an equation.

Figure 5.8 Multiplication and Division Situations

	Unknown Product	Group Size Unknown	Number of Groups Unknown
Equal Groups	There are four groups of chairs. There are three chairs in each group. How many chairs are there in all?	If twelve chairs are arranged in four equal groups, then how many chairs will be in each group?	If twelve chairs are arranged in three equal groups, then how many groups of chairs will there be?
	Total Unknown	**Unknown Factor**	**Unknown Factor**
Arrays	There are three rows of chairs with four chairs in each row. How many chairs are there? (array)	If twelve chairs are arranged in four equal rows, then how many chairs will be in each row? (array)	If twelve chairs are arranged in three equal rows, then how many rows of chairs will there be? (array)

	Larger Unknown	Smaller Unknown	Multiplier Unknown
Compare	There are four chairs at the front of the room. There are three times that many chairs at the back of the room. How many chairs are at the back of the room?	There are twelve chairs at the back of the room and that is three times as many chairs as there are at the front of the room. How many chairs are at the front of the room?	There are twelve chairs at the back of the room. There are four chairs at the front of the room. How many times as many chairs are there at the back as the front?

(adapted from the Glossary of CCSS-M 2010 and *The National Research Council's Mathematics Learning in Early Childhood* 2009)

While students solve multiplication and division problems, model expressions, and interpret answers, their understanding of these operations deepens. Students' computation strategies at the basic fact level become more sophisticated and culminate in fluency in both multiplication and division at the end of grade 3 (3.OA.7). The learning trajectory involves three stages:

☞ Modeling and counting all

☞ Skip counting

☞ Applying properties and the inverse relationship between multiplication and division

Modeling and Counting All

As with addition and subtraction, modeling and counting all is where students begin. It is more difficult to do this with multiplication and division, though, as the totals are so much greater and fingers rarely suffice. Drawing equal groups or arrays for an expression such as 6 x 7 is time consuming and if doing it free hand, rather than relying on a structured diagram, errors can result. See Figure 5.9 for an example.

MP4
Model

Figure 5.9 Student Example of Modeling

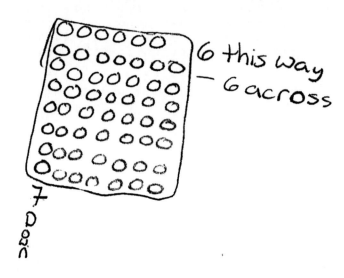

6 this way
— 6 across

7 down

MP6
Tools

Students should be encouraged to use representation methods that support their accuracy. Area models are merely arrays with objects that are contiguous and support third graders learning about areas of rectangles within the Measurement and Data domain. Students can make area arrangements with square tiles or linking cubes. They can also indicate an area on grid paper.

Initially, it is best if students make or draw a row identified by one factor and then recreate (iterate) that row until the number of rows matches the other factor. Note that replication of columns may also be used, as arrays can be viewed from either direction and do not make the distinction between number of groups and number in each group as equal group models do. Over time, students may learn to use the factors to identify the dimensions on a grid and then use these to make the associated rectangle. To do this, students must realize that corner squares are counted within each dimension (across and down to form the factors), but not when counting the total (area). See Figure 5.10.

Figure 5.10 Area Model of 7 x 6

To model 7 x 6:

The first row is identified.   The figure is then completed.

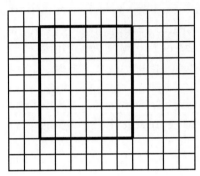

On graph paper, each dimension is identified and then the rectangle is drawn.

Area models easily show the commutative property of multiplication as the model merely needs to be turned or looked at from a different view; they also can be extended to greater numbers when appropriate.

Skip Counting

Like counting on rather than counting all in addition or subtraction, skip counting, or counting by, is more efficient in multiplication and division. Fortunately, for these older students, the cognitive challenge of adopting this strategy is not as great as it is for younger students to understand that they can count on. Further, it's use is motivated by the relatively larger numbers. Connections can be made through number lines, array models or tape diagrams. Note that the tape diagram presents a continuous, rather than discrete, model of number (e.g., it doesn't show the individual single units), and is more efficient. Examples are shown in Figure 5.11.

Figure 5.11 Representations of Skip Counting

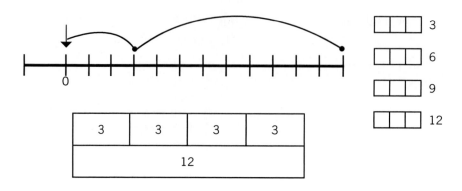

It's best to begin with counts students find familiar; counting by twos, fives, and tens is introduced within grades one and two, and so third graders can count by these numbers easily. Initially, you might give six students each a tower of five cubes. Have students place their towers, one at a time, on a tabletop, while successively counting by fives and placing the new tower directly beside the others so that an area model is formed. Record the multiplication sentence 5 x 6 = 30 or 6 x 5 = 30 to represent the situation.

As students are so familiar with counting by fives, they quickly become accustomed to counting by fives while using their fingers to keep track of the number of fives counted. A few students may prefer to look at a clock face and count by fives while focusing on the numerals on the clock. Similarly, 35 ÷ 5 can be found by counting by fives to 35, while using fingers (or some other method) to keep track of the number of fives said. With less familiar counts, addition (or subtraction) can be used. Students who are most successful are those who are facile with decomposing numbers to make a 10. For example, when counting by sixes and at 48, they can think *plus two is 50 and plus four more is 54.*

Applying Properties and the Inverse Relationship

While the previous techniques are helpful in finding products or quotients and developing meaning, they are not efficient enough for long-term use and multiplication is more than repeated addition. Over time students recall some of the easiest facts. These facts, together with properties and the relationship between multiplication and division, give access to other facts (3.OA.5).

The most valuable strategy for students to develop is that the *distributive property of multiplication*, that is, $a(b + c) = ab + ac$, allows us to decompose and compose products. This concept underpins multi-digit multiplication and division and should be established first concretely with numbers to 100 (Trent 2006).

In one third-grade classroom, the teacher has laminated strips with seven dots on them. She places two of them together and asks the students to write the total number of dots on their white boards and hold them up so she can see.

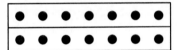 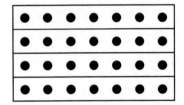

She records $2 \times 7 = 14$ and adds two more rows to the visual model. She tells students to think independently for a minute and then to share how they can find the number of dots now. Aisha shares, "I know two rows are 14 so this is 14 plus 14 or 28." The teacher records the following for students to see:

$$4 \times 7 = 2 \times 7 + 2 \times 7$$

$$4 \times 7 = 14 + 14$$

$$4 \times 7 = 28$$

She then has the students work in pairs to use this thinking to find 4×8.

The next day, she shows these students the following grid. She asks the students what they see. Their responses include lots of dots, six by eight, six times eight, and eight times six. Next, the teacher places a thin dowel stick on the diagram. She tells them to talk in partners about what they see now and how they could use it to find the total number of dots.

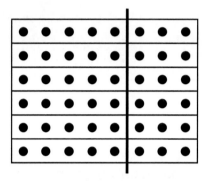

A variety of ideas are shared. One group decides that since five facts are easy, they will find 5 x 6 and 3 x 6 and add those products together to find 8 x 6. A few more examples are investigated as students' understanding that they can decompose and compose products deepens, and they learn how to find new facts based on facts they know. In the following days, this teacher has students explore arrays on paper so students can fold and explore a variety of decompositions.

Note that facts can also be related to greater facts that are known. For example, students can readily multiply by 10, so to find 9 x 6, they can think 6 x 10, or 60, and find one less six or 60 − 6 = 54. These strategies take time and must be accompanied by concrete experiences first, so that students are certain about which numbers they are decomposing and how to use those numbers to find the total.

The most powerful strategy for division facts is to use its relationship to multiplication. To find 28 ÷ 7, think *what do I multiply by 7 to get 28?* (3.OA.4; 3.OA.6). Linking the three numbers within any multiplication or division equation strengthens this relationship and increases the likelihood that students can quickly and accurately identify quotients.

For students to become fluent, they need considerable time to investigate strategies and to practice. Apps and online sites often provide practice in motivating settings. Programs that keep track of facts a student does and does not know are valuable, as they can focus the practice where it is most needed. Competition among peers can also be motivating, but should be monitored carefully to be sure that students are competing with others at a similar level and that there is no humiliation involved, such as reporting low results aloud. Also avoid games where the winner continues to play, while the non-winner must drop out. Such games provide the winner with practice that is not needed and deny the other student access to such practice. Paying attention to particular strengths students have within Gardner's multiple intelligences is also beneficial (Dacey, Lynch, and Salemi 2013). For example, some students may wish to write poems or sing songs to help them remember particular facts.

Other algebraic ideas related to these operations are introduced in grade 2 and are the focus of this domain at grades four and five, including extending division to 100, including quotients with remainders, working with patterns, identifying factors and multiples, and the order of operations. These ideas further students' understanding of these operations as well as provide support for other domains and later study.

Remainders in Division

Unlike any other operation, division does not always result in an answer that is a whole number. In fact, if random numbers were divided, many more would have remainders than not. While common, remainders can be challenging. Introduced in fourth grade, directly modeling situations with remainders does not prove difficult, rather, it is computation and interpretation that are more problematic (Dacey and Collins 2010) (4.OA.3).

MP7
Structure

MP8
Regularity

In terms of computation, it is helpful if students conceptualize the number line or hundreds board in groups, according to a particular divisor. For example, instead of just thinking that $24 \div 8 = 3$ and $32 \div 8 = 4$, students need to realize that if each of the numbers between 24 and 32 were divided by 8, the quotient would be 3 with remainders of 1–7. Such a model will allow students to better recognize the whole number portion of the quotient and to estimate when working with greater numbers. The problem in Figure 5.12 emphasizes remainders while focusing on structure and repeated reasoning. An example of student work is included and demonstrates that some students do not necessarily recognize that whole number quotients have a remainder of zero.

Figure 5.12 Student Work Related to Remainders

Problem: I have between 30 and 50 pennies. When I put them in piles of five, I have 1 penny left over. When I put them in groups of four, I have 1 penny left over. How many pennies do I have?

	31	32	33	34	35	36	37	38	39	40	41	42	43	44	45	46	47	48	49
÷5	6R1	6R2	6R3	6R4	7	7R1	7R2	7R3	7R4	8	8R1	8R2	8R3	8R4	9	9R1	9R2	9R3	9R4
÷4	7R3	8	8R1	8R2	8R3	9	9R1	9R2	9R3	10	10R1	10R2	10R3	11	11R1	11R2	11R3	12	12R1

1, 2, 3, 4, 0, 1, 2, 3, 4, 0, 1, 2, 3, 4, 0, 1, 2,
3, 0, 1, 2, 3, 9, 1, 2, 3, 10, 1, 2, 3, 1, 1, 2, 3,

(Dacey 2012c)

Interpretation of remainders is also problematic as it requires students to decide whether they should report the remainder (as either a whole or rational number), round up to the next whole number, or ignore the remainder. Students need to be involved in explicit conversations about these choices. Have students solve problems such as the following, dramatize similar situations, and pose their own situations for different interpretations of remainders to help make the interpretations explicit and potentially limit answers such as two and a half people in each car.

- There are five cookies that two children want to share equally. How many cookies will each child get?

- If you needed 27 valentines and they were sold in packs of 10, how many packs should you buy?

- The tennis player collected 16 tennis balls to return to their cans. Each can holds 3 balls. How many cans will be filled?

Patterns and Structure

Lynn Stern (1990) famously identified mathematics as the study of patterns, and certainly algebra, with its focus on generalizations and structure, involves patterns. In second grade, students explore the patterns within even and odd numbers (2.OA.3). In third grade, students identify patterns such as those found within the addition and multiplication tables (3.OA.9). In fourth grade, students make generalizations by creating rules for shape or number patterns (4.OA.5). In fifth grade, in preparation for middle school work with ratios, this focus extends to making connections between two patterns and graphing their associated ordered pairs on the coordinate grid (5.OA.3). Multiplication and division are further understood, as students begin to use the terms factors and multiples as well as to identify prime and composite numbers, and precise understanding of these terms is developed. The ability to identify factors and multiples supports work with common denominators.

MP6
Precision

Consider this example: A fourth-grade teacher has displayed the following problem to the class.

Grandma Nell has 24 special necklaces. She has decided to give them all to her granddaughters. She is pleased that they will each get the same number of necklaces. How many granddaughters could Grandma Nell have? How do you know?

The teacher asks each student to independently write down what they know from the problem statement. When she observes that a few students are no longer recording, she asks students to share an idea from their lists. She records their thinking and the following list is created:

- Grandma Nell has 24 necklaces.

- She is going to give them all away.

- She is going to give them to her granddaughters.

- She will give each granddaughter the same number of necklaces.

- Each granddaughter gets a fair share.

- We need to find the number of granddaughters there could be.

- We need to explain our thinking.

Once the students agree on the information, the teacher tells them they may work alone or with a partner to solve the problem. Most of the students chose to work with someone, but a few choose to work independently. The teacher is particularly interested in whether or not they will find all of the factor pairs (4.OA.4).

As students investigate these ideas, their vocabulary associated with multiplication and division expands as summarized in Figure 5.13. There are a variety of ways for students to develop their mathematical vocabulary. They can:

- Play password or dictionary or some other common word game using these terms.

- Interact with a mathematics word wall by creating their own definitions for the terms, organizing them as they see fit, or play a game of 20 questions to identify the correct word.

- Write definitions in their journals or complete a Frayer diagram (Figure 2.4).

- Write a mixed-up story in a small group, where the mathematical terms are used incorrectly. They read the story to the class and the story listeners try to find the errors and correct them.

- Dramatize math words for other students to identify.

Figure 5.13 Vocabulary for Operations and Algebraic Thinking: Multiplication and Division

Grade 3	Grade 4	Grade 5
array	common factor	algorithm
associative property	composite number	divisibility
commutative property	dividend	divisible
distributive property	divisor	
divide	expression	
division	factor pair	
equal groups	identity property	
equal shares	multiple	
factor	number pattern	
multiplication	prime number	
multiply	quotient	
product	remainder	
repeated subtraction		

Recording and Interpreting Equations

Driscoll (1999) has identified building rules to represent functions as an algebraic habit of mind that all students should develop. In third grade, students begin to use a letter for missing values, a significant step along the way to this goal (3.OA.8). As students record equations to represent their solutions to multiple-step problems, their equations become more complex and precision becomes important. They begin to include

MP6
Precision

parentheses and become familiar with the order in which we have agreed to perform operations. They are also able to extend their understanding of operations and the relationships among equations (5.OA.1; 5.OA.2).

True/false questions can highlight how algebraic ideas permeate arithmetic (Carpenter, Franke, and Levi 2003). In this example, one fifth-grade teacher gives the following examples to his students early in the fall. (The basic framework can be used across the grades.) The goal is for them to quickly

MP3
Construct

decide whether they think the expressions are true or false. Then, the items are discussed as students try to convince others of their choices and to understand their peers' arguments. Over the year, the teacher provides similar examples, but includes rational numbers in the equations.

True or False?

$3 \times 234 + 2 \times 234 = 5 \times 234$

$2{,}345 + 179 = 2{,}346 + 178$

$3{,}250 = 3{,}000 + 200 + 5$

$3(65 - 4) = 3 \times 65 - 3 \times 4$

$321 + 432 + 644 = 644 + 321 + 432$

$3{,}276 - 1{,}345 = 1{,}345 - 3{,}276$

$34 \times 9 = 29 \times 9 + 5 \times 9$

$72 \times 5 = 80 \times 5 - 8 \times 5$

Assessment Note

It is essential that students connect meanings of operations, representations, and situations. One way to assess these connections is to have students complete the general template shown in Figure 5.14 and available in Appendix A. You can complete one of the three segments and have students complete the other two or have students choose their own example and complete all three sections. The flexibility of the format allows you to use it several times and to adapt it to meet individual needs.

Figure 5.14 Template for Assessing Understanding of the Meaning of an Operation

Equation:
Drawing or Model:
Word Problem:

It is important that daily mathematical tasks meet expectations for complexity. Standardized assessments are likely to assess fluency through more complex items than 6 x 6 = _____. Instead, students might be asked if the equation 6 x 6 = 4 x 9 is true. Similarly, items might combine domains, so that the relationship between multiplication and division might be assessed within a question about area, connecting to the domain Measurement and Data.

Voice from the Classroom

As a third-grade teacher, I have struggled when students do not know their basic addition facts. They often lose fluency over the summer and end up relying on strategies such as using their fingers to find the solution to simple problems they should know rotely. How was I supposed to get them to learn their multiplication facts, when they weren't yet fluent with simple addition?

This summer, my school system had three days of professional development related to the new standards. I was thrilled to learn the explicit expectations there were for fluency and how they began as early as kindergarten. I know some teachers don't believe these young students should be memorizing facts, but I don't look at it that way. It's only facts to five and it's such a great way to develop these students' visual skills. When I am at a restaurant waiting for food with my daughter, we play a What's Hiding? game with five sugar packets. She loves guessing how many I am covering up.

At the meeting, the K–3 teachers made a pact to meet the basic facts expectations. We decided that three times a year, in October, February, and May, we would assess our students' basic fact knowledge. When we met by grade level, we shared games and activities for learning and practicing facts. Some of the newer teachers used different games than some of us who had been teaching awhile, and it was wonderful to learn new games, especially electronic ones. We also found that teachers from different schools used different strategies. It all felt so useful and I gained such appreciation for my colleagues. I am looking forward to using these ideas in my classroom and think a year from this fall I may meet a group of students much more ready for third-grade work.

—Third-Grade Teacher

Let's Think and Discuss

1. Are the various addition and subtraction situations included in your current curriculum materials? If not, how can you best introduce them?

2. How do you manage your classroom so that you can work with small groups of students needing extra time to review ideas related to the meanings of the operations or basic fact strategies?

3. What are some of your favorite ways to engage students in developing their basic fact fluency?

$\frac{1}{2} + \frac{3}{4}$

132

Chapter 6

Number and Operations in Base Ten

 **Snapshot**

It is early in the year and these fifth-grade students are working on a cryptarithm, which is an arithmetic puzzle. They have solved a cryptarithm earlier this week, and they just reviewed the three rules:

- ✏ The math must be correct.

- ✏ The same letter always represents the same number in a given puzzle.

- ✏ Each different letter in a puzzle represents a unique number.

Today, students are working in small groups on the following puzzle. There are three students in each group, and the triads have assigned each member to one of the following roles: facilitator, recorder, and reporter. **Note:** If this task is not familiar to you, try to find the value of each letter before reading further.

$$\begin{array}{r} \text{P O T S} \\ \times \quad\quad 4 \\ \hline \text{S T O P} \end{array}$$

The teacher wants every group to solve the problem on its own, so that the students all conclude that they are capable mathematicians. She knows some groups will need support, but she wants it to come from other students, not clues she gives them. She does this by asking questions and by having the students initially work together for a few minutes and then stop and share with the larger group. She tries to have the groups share in order of the sophistication of their ideas or approach, with the most accessible ideas presented first. She believes this order increases students' access to more complex ideas and gives everyone different ways to succeed.

After about five minutes, the teacher stops the class for what she calls a *problem update*. She has four of the reporters update the class about their group's thinking. The other reporters will share later in the lesson.

Kevin: We each made up a number to try for POTS. We chose 7325, 6901, and 6126. We made sure all of the digits were different, and then we multiplied and all of the products were way too big. Now, we are trying smaller numbers.

Ming: Our group started like Kevin's group did, but then we noticed how the letters go backward and forward. So now we are thinking about how the same number for S could go in the two different places.

Peyton: The first thing we did was to make a times 4 table. It reminded us that P had to be an even number. We can also use it as a reference when we are wondering what factor will give us the product we need.

Aaliyah: We started by making a list of everything we knew. The idea that has helped us the most so far is that POTS and STOP are both four-digit numbers. We decided that STOP had to be less than 10,000, because that is a five-digit number. Then, we thought about POTS and decided it had to be less than 2,500 because 2,500 x 4 = 10,000.

If you solved this problem earlier *What strategies did you try? What might you do now?*

The teacher chose this problem to reinforce the structure of the standard algorithm for multiplication with a single-digit multiplier, before giving attention to two-digit multipliers. Though the students are successful with multiplication of multi-digit numbers, several do not use the standard algorithm, and she does not think that all those who do have a deep enough understanding of it (NBT.5). She circulates as the students work and hears Michaela tell her group, "Wait, we can get an odd number if there is regrouping. We just need to find a product that ends in eight, so when we add three, it will end in one." She later hears Max make a comment about regrouping. He suggests, "There can't be grouping from the hundreds place because that would mess up the 2 and the 8."

This problem incorporates several of the Mathematical Practice Standards, though in this lesson, the teacher wants to focus most on reasoning quantitatively and on the structure of the standard algorithm for multiplication. To reinforce these practices, the teachers ask students to make a list of what they learned by solving this problem. She records the responses for all to see. Pavel offers, "I learned that there is a lot going on in a multiplication example that I never really thought about before this." (Answer: 2178 x 4 = 8712)

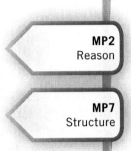

MP2
Reason

MP7
Structure

Big Picture

Number and Operations in Base Ten builds on ideas in the Counting and Cardinality and Operations and Algebraic Thinking domains. It is within Number and Operations in Base Ten that the structure of our number system is established, computation strategies are applied to greater numbers and decimals, and standard algorithms are established. In turn, as computation skills are further developed, students' conceptual understanding of the operations, relationships among them, and their properties deepens. Until grade five, this domain focuses on whole numbers. In fifth grade, place value and the operations are extended to thousandths. Number and Operations in Base Ten connects to ideas within the Number and Operations and Fractions domain through decimals, and is supported by the Geometry (reinforcement of the concepts of composition and decomposition) and the Measurement and Data (opportunities to apply the operations) domains. Each of these domains has a separate focus, but they are all interconnected.

In this domain, particular attention is given to students gaining a deep understanding of our number system. Understanding the base-ten structure allows us to better comprehend numbers in our world and relationships among them. It allows us to understand just how much greater than a million a billion is; a billionaire has a thousand million dollars! It also supports our understanding of our computational strategies. For example, knowing that 10 ones can be composed as 1 ten and that 1 ten can be decomposed to 10 ones, without changing value, provides an essential foundation for adding, subtracting, multiplying, and dividing greater numbers and decimals.

When students first extend use of the operations to numbers other than single-digit numbers, the progression in the domain is often the same, regardless of the grade level. That is, it applies to grade one students first adding two-digit numbers as well as fifth graders first adding decimal numbers. Students will find totals, differences, products, and quotients with multi-digit numbers and decimals through the following three-step progression:

(**Note:** The only time this progression is not explicitly stated as beginning with the use of concrete materials or drawings is in grade four with multiplication and division. Though not included, such models should be used then as well.)

- use of concrete objects or drawings and strategies related to place value, properties, and relationships between inverse operations

- use of strategies related to place value, properties, and relationships between inverse operations (Note the omission of objects and drawings.)

- use of standard algorithms

The phrase *the standard algorithm* is controversial, and many mathematics educators, myself included, would prefer use of the phrase, *a standard algorithm* or *efficient general method*. Historically, various standard algorithms have been highlighted and different algorithms are used today in different curricular materials and in different parts of the world. So just what is *the* standard addition, subtraction, multiplication, or division algorithm, and why must it be used by all students?

In the Progressions Document for Number and Operations in Base Ten, the authors suggest a distinction between special strategies and general methods

(Common Core Standards Writing Team 2012a). For example, if you were multiplying 199 x 4, you could recognize that this would be one less four than 200 x 4, or 796, allowing you to calculate mentally. The authors identify this as a special method, as it would not be applied as easily to, for instance, 56 x 4. General methods are defined as applicable to all numbers. The authors further state that general methods based on place value "...can be viewed as closely connected with the standard algorithms" (3). The document also suggests different recordings for algorithms generally recognized as standard and makes use of diagrams.

So what does this mean for you as a classroom teacher? In *Principles and Standards for School Mathematics*, the development of computational fluency was emphasized and such fluency was considered to include efficiency, accuracy, and flexibility (NCTM 2000). Russell, in her seminal article on computational fluency, stated that, "Being able to calculate in multiple ways means that one has transcended the formality of the algorithm and reached the essence of the numerical operations—the underlying mathematical ideas and principles" (2000, 154). It also means knowing the circumstances in which different strategies work best. Regardless of the operation or the numbers involved, it is most important that instruction be balanced. This domain focuses on place value strategies, an area needing further development, but we don't want to lose recent gains made in whole-number thinking, which often leads to flexible computational strategies.

MP5
Tools

In a balanced approach, students achieve the following:

- Develop a conceptual understanding of the operations.

- Gain special strategies that are particularly beneficial given particular examples (e.g., to find 399 + 501, think 400 + 500).

- Learn to estimate so that they have an intuitive sense of what the answer will be.

- Develop an efficient and accurate general strategy for each operation.

We will keep these ideas in mind as we explore the development of place value, addition, subtraction, multiplication, and division in more depth within the next sections of the chapter.

Understanding Our Base-Ten Number System

Kindergarten students focus on the teen numbers—problematic because they don't follow the usual rules for naming numbers (See Chapter 4) (K.NBT.1). They learn that each teen number is composed of 1 ten and some remaining ones. For many years, students have been bundling craft sticks in groups of ten, though it was not a formal expectation at this level.

It is important that young students begin with concrete models that can be composed or decomposed by the students themselves. Craft sticks and linking cubes both provide such opportunities. Students might count a group of 15 cubes for example, and then link ten of them to make 1 group of ten with 5 other ones. Similarly, they could be given 1 group of bundled sticks and 5 loose sticks and asked to find how many there are. The students can then unbundle and count the 15 ones. Students need many of these concrete experiences, perhaps in connection to stories such as the following that they could dramatize:

There are frogs hopping around all over the place. Then, 10 of the frogs decide to rest on a log. They hop over to it and sit close together in a group. Now there is one group of 10 frogs resting and seven other frogs still hopping around. There are 17 frogs in all.

Blank ten frames are an excellent graphic organizer for tens and ones. Given a pile of 11–19 counters and two such frames, students could count the objects as they place them (one at a time) into an individual empty cell until a ten frame is completely filled. Then, the remaining counters can be placed within the next empty frame. Note that many educators suggest that ten frames be filled in a particular manner, that is, the top row (left to right) first and then the bottom row (left to right). Establishing this routine helps

MP6
Precision

students recognize numbers in relationship to five (the first row) as well as the ten. Figure 6.1 shows the configuration for 14. The use of ten frames can be particularly helpful for students with learning challenges (Losq 2005).

Figure 6.1 Two Ten Frames Used to Organize 14 Ones as 1 Ten and 4 Ones

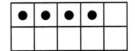

In first grade, the relationships between 1 ten and 10 ones deepens and extends to all two-digit numbers (1.NBT.2; 1.NBT.2a). Once again, students need many opportunities to compose and decompose tens. Initially, they also need to do this grouping and ungrouping themselves, though later they can use materials that are pre-grouped such as base-ten materials or pre-made ten frames (Van de Walle, Karp, and Bay-Williams 2013). These students also are expected to compare two-digit numbers and record the comparisons using the signs for greater than, less than, or equal to. Initially, students might suggest that 18 is less than 24 because they say 18 first when they count. As they continue to explore place value, they develop the understanding that any two-digit number with 2 tens is greater than any number with only 1 ten.

Conceptual Challenge

To nonteaching adults, the relationship between tens and ones may seem both simple and obvious. Experienced primary-level teachers know this is not the case. A first-grader who has just counted 30 objects by ones may be guessing when responding to the question *If you grouped these by tens, how many groups of ten do you think you could make?* Also, after forming the three groups of ten, that same student may separate the groups and recount by ones when asked *How many are there?* It is important to ask students such questions to access their knowledge and to offer them appropriate instructional opportunities.

It takes time for students to be able to move easily between a ones view and a base-ten representation of numbers. With meaningful hands-on activities, conversations, and practice, representations such as those shown in Figure 6.2 become linked. As you work with students, ask questions such as:

MP4
Model

➠ How many groups of ten do you think we can make?

➠ How many ones are there in these groups of ten?

➠ What can you write to show how many there are?

Figure 6.2 Varied Representations for 23

Ones Representation   Base-Ten Representation   Symbolic Representation

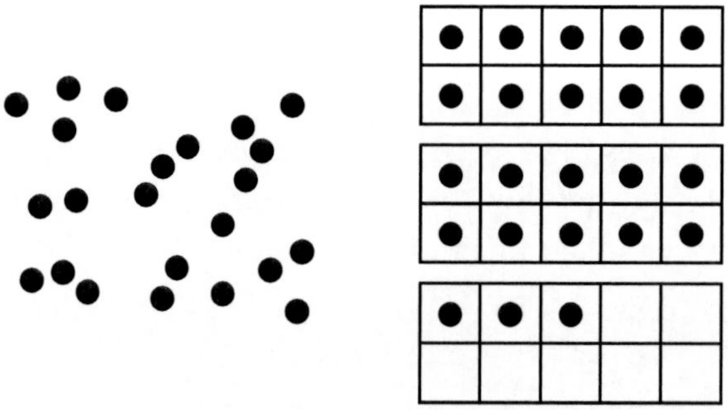

2 tens and 3 ones

20 + 3

23

twenty-three

Numbers to 1,000 are considered in the second grade (2.NBT.1). As with first graders in relation to tens, these students also need to understand that a hundred is the new unit formed from 10 tens and that in numbers such as 100, 200, 300, and so forth, the digit in the hundreds place tells you that there are, for example, three hundreds (2.NBT.1). Students need concrete experiences to note that three-digit numbers indicate two groupings of tens; that is, ones have been grouped to tens, and then those tens also have been put into groups of 10 to form hundreds. A variety of applets can be found on the Internet that allow students to see visual models of regrouping among ones, 10s, and hundreds (Suh and Seshaiyer 2012). Consider this example: in one second-grade classroom a small group of students are counting the number of beans in a bag of kidney beans. Individual students are placing groups of ten beans in individual 5 oz. cups. When there are 10 beans in a cup, they write *10* on the front of it. Groups of 10 filled cups are placed in a shoebox lid. When there are 10 cups in a lid, one of the students writes *100* on the front of it. Mischa comments, "This reminds me of a doll my grandmother gave me. Smaller dolls are put inside larger dolls" (2.NBT.2).

Second-grade students also are expected to read, write, and compare numbers. At this level, expanded form is also an expectation (2.NBT.3; 2.NBT.4). When first asked to write the written numeral for three-digit numbers such as 324, some students may record 30024, or even 300204. Stacked number cards (Figure 6.3), based on Montessori materials, help students understand how numbers in expanded form are represented in a written numeral (Lillard 2005).

Figure 6.3 Stacked Cards to Show Relationship Between Expanded Form and Written Numeral for 324

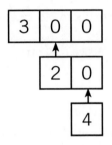

Students do not extend the number of digits in grade three, perhaps as so much focus at this grade level is on multiplication and division, which do not involve large numbers. They do learn about rounding numbers to 10 or 100, which can support their understanding of place value and their abilities to estimate (3.NBT.1).

Grade four students are expected to read, write, compare, and round any multi-digit whole number. It is here that a fuller generalization can be made about *every* place to the right being exactly ten times the value as its digit to the left. This allows students to understand *why* dividing by multiples of ten results in a quotient with one less zero than the dividend. Making a connection to place value language can be helpful for some students with ten just used as a noun. For example, 300 ÷ 30 = 10 can be thought of as 30 tens divided into groups of 3 tens makes 10 groups. Students also discover that in the United States, names for the places continuously follow the ones, tens, and hundreds pattern, for example; one million, ten million, and hundred million (4.NBT.1; 4.NBT.2; 4.NBT.3).

Fifth graders extend all of these same skills to the thousandths place. (In grade four, decimals are introduced, to hundredths, within the Number and Operations and Fractions domain.) Note that students can be distracted by whole-number thinking when comparing decimals with a different number of places such as 0.189 and 0.2 (Suh et al. 2008). Adding zeros to make each decimal have the same number of places is helpful as 0.200 can be more easily recognized as greater than 0.189, as 200 > 189. When writing decimals in expanded form, students also recognize that each digit to the right is $\frac{1}{10}$ of the value of the digit to the left and can use whole-number exponents to represent

MP7
Structure

MP8
Reasoning

powers of ten. Further, students are expected to use their understanding of place value to explain the patterns of where to place the decimal point when multiplying or dividing a decimal by powers of ten (5.NBT.1; 5.NBT.2; 5.NBT.3; 5.NBT.4). Note that students are expected to *explain* the patterns, not just *recognize* them, requiring students to truly understand the impact of the 10 ones to 1 ten and 1 ten to 10 ones relationships in our number system.

Expectations for students' understanding of place value across the grade levels are summarized in Figure 6.4. If you teach grade three, you no doubt noticed that no expansion from grade two is listed in terms of the size of the numbers. Prior to these new standards, many third-grade students extended their knowledge to ten-thousands. This lack of expectation gives more time for the identified critical areas at this grade level. Also, one could argue that it doesn't make sense to introduce ten thousands without also introducing hundred thousands, so that the continuation of the ones, tens, and hundreds structure could be observed.

Figure 6.4 Summary of Place Value Expectations in Grades K–5

Level	Expectations
Kindergarten	Compose and decompose 11–19 into a ten and some ones
Grade 1	• Count to 120 from any number 1–119; read and write the number names for numbers 1–120; and represent such a number of objects with the written numeral • Understand that the digits in a two-digit number represent tens and ones • Compare two-digit numbers
Grade 2	• Understand that the digits in a three-digit number represent hundreds, tens, and ones • Skip count to 1,000 using 5s, 10s, and 100s • Read and write numbers to 1,000 (numerals, number names, and expanded form) • Compare three-digit numbers
Grade 3	• Round numbers to the nearest 10 or 100
Grade 4	• Generalize place value concepts to all whole numbers including recognizing the 10:1 relationship between the value of a digit and the value of a digit to its right • Read and write numbers (numerals, number names, and expanded form) • Compare multi-digit whole numbers • Round numbers to any place
Grade 5	• Recognize the 10:1 relationship between the value of a digit and the value of a digit to its right as well as the 1:10 relationship between the value of a digit and the value of a digit to its left • Explain patterns in the number of zeros in a product when multiplying by a power of 10 and the placement of a decimal point when a decimal is multiplied or divided by a power of ten • Use whole number exponents to represent powers of ten • Read and write decimals to thousandths (numerals, number names, and expanded form) • Compare decimals to thousandths; round decimals to any place

There are a variety of activities or problems that are valuable for all students to explore. Some examples are provided below, many of which can be adapted for different grade levels. Have students:

👉 Make a *My Favorite Number* book or poster. A variety of representations of the number can be included as well as examples of the number in real-world contexts.

👉 Solve number riddles such as *I have 2 tens and 14 ones. What number do I have in all?*

👉 Look at a representation of a number with base-ten materials and predict the number of ones there would be if every hundred and ten were traded for ones.

👉 Estimate where to put number cards on a number line that has been turned face down. Then, turn the line over to check. (The number cards could show written numbers, numbers in expanded form, or number names.)

👉 Create lists of physical or contextual referents for numbers such as the fact that 1,000,000 seconds is about 11.5 days and a billion seconds is about 32 years.

👉 Answer and create animal questions such as:

About how many muscles does an elephant have in its trunk?

752   14,200   1,500   15,000   26,000   18,000

The number is between 1,000 and 20,000.

It is greater than 15 hundreds.

When rounded to the nearest ten thousand, the number rounds to 20,000.

It is not 18 x 1,000.

An elephant has about _____ muscles in its trunk.
(15,000)

↪ Play "Between." Two numbers are given and the first player must name a number between them. Then another player names a number between that new number and one of the original numbers. Players continue taking turns, trying to name between numbers.

Addition and Subtraction

As with Operations and Algebraic Thinking, the K–2 levels in this domain focus on addition and subtraction. Development of the operations is closely tied to place value knowledge and emphasizes base-ten models. Some educators believe that our teaching of place value has been inadequate and thus, unable to support the development of computational concepts and skills. Cawley, Parmar, Lucas-Fusco, Kilian, and Foley (2007) contend that all students, but especially students with mild disabilities, should have extended experiences with place value to understand and develop computational strategies.

Recently, many primary classrooms have found open number lines to be important visual models for addition and subtraction. Number lines are given little or no attention within this domain, where base-ten models dominate. It's possible to think of open number lines as being similar to tape diagrams, which help students to understand a problem they are trying to solve, as well as to reinforce the relationship between addition and subtraction (Figure 6.5). In both cases, the two parts and the total are represented and a question mark can be used to identify the unknown or missing number. Number lines work best when students relate their use to measurement, that is, they focus on the distance between two points (Diezmann, Lowrie, and Sugars 2010). You do not need to avoid using open number lines just because their use is not indicated in this domain; however, you may want to take this opportunity to consider the representations you present.

↪ Which ones are best for understanding problem situations and relationships?

↪ Which ones are best for developing special computational methods?

↪ Which ones are best for developing general computational methods?

Figure 6.5 Open Number Line and Tape Diagram Models of 23 + ? = 47

In first grade, students compose tens to add within one hundred. They begin with drawings and objects from which a written record can be established (1.NBT.4). Some teachers directly model the recording process, while others prefer to let students develop written work that makes the most sense to them. When students use a variety of techniques, gallery walks, where student work is posted or displayed on desks or tabletops, allow classmates to see different recordings and to make sense of the work of others. Such sharing allows students to broaden their thinking and ready themselves for the adoption of new techniques (O'Loughlin 2007). In one classroom, such work included the examples shown in Figure 6.6. The less common recording of the composed 10 just below the addend, as in the second example, is suggested in this domain's Progression Document and allows the original example to remain more visible than when the composed 10 is placed above the addends (Common Core Standards Writing Team 2012a). Also, note that presentation of an expression in a horizontal format may stimulate whole-number thinking, while vertical presentations may suggest place value strategies. While place value strategies are emphasized in this domain, both types of thinking need to be addressed.

MP3
Construct

Figure 6.6 Examples of Student Recordings for 27 + 35

$$
\begin{array}{r}
27 \\
+35 \\
\hline
50 \\
12 \\
\hline
62
\end{array}
\qquad
\begin{array}{r}
27 \\
+35 \\
\hline
1 \\
62
\end{array}
\qquad
\begin{array}{r}
{}^{1}27 \\
+35 \\
\hline
62
\end{array}
$$

$$27+35 \quad \diagdown\!\!\!\diagup \quad 50+12 \quad 62$$

$$
\begin{aligned}
27+35 \\
27+1+4+30 \\
32+30 \\
62
\end{aligned}
$$

146

Place value is further connected to addition and subtraction with the expectation that students can mentally identify 10 more or less than a number, without counting. It can be helpful to represent two-digit numbers within a place value mat adding a new ten or taking away a ten while asking *What number is shown now? How do you know?* (1.NBT.5). Subtraction of two-digit numbers is only extended to multiples of ten, such as 70 – 20. Place value language can be helpful, such as 7 tens minus 2 tens is 5 tens or 50 (1.NBT.6).

In second grade, students extend their addition and subtraction abilities in several ways. They fluently add and subtract within 100, while developing addition and subtraction skills within 1,000. They are also expected to mentally add or subtract 10 or 100 to or from any number 100–900 (2.NBT.5; 2.NBT.6; 2.NBT.7; 2.NBT.8). When three-digit numbers are involved, students have the opportunity to realize that the composition and decomposition of tens continues. It also exposes students to examples where more than one regrouping is necessary. For example in 394 + 106, the ones make a ten, which when added to the 9 tens, makes 10 tens or 1 hundred. Even more challenging to most students is an example such as 401 – 234, requiring one of the hundreds to be decomposed to tens, before a ten can be decomposed to ones.

It is important that students in grade two have ample opportunity to explore various strategies and recording techniques to solidify their conceptual understanding. Too often, students learn these techniques rotely and do not understand why algorithms work. Fortunately, fluency with three-digit numbers is not expected until grade three (3.NBT.2).

Note that while concrete models and drawings are no longer included as strategies at this level, using the relationship between addition and subtraction remains. So a student could find 401 – 234 as shown in Figure 6.7. This missing addend approach can be particularly helpful to some students. A number line could also be used as a written record. Jason, who uses this technique, explains, "I like to find differences by adding up from one number to the next. I add to get to a ten or hundred because that makes the addition easy." Note that the focus on tens and hundreds is an example of using place value strategies.

Figure 6.7 Using Addition to Solve a Subtraction Example

$$234 + ? = 401$$
$$234 + 6 = 240$$
$$240 + 60 = 300$$
$$300 + 101 = 401$$
$$6 + 60 + 101 = 167$$
$$401 - 234 = 167$$

Honoring Individual Differences

It is important for many students to explain their thinking aloud, perhaps verbalizing to themselves, to you, to a partner during a pair-share, or to a larger group as they present their work. Think-alouds allow teachers to better access students' understanding and, for students with learning disabilities, such experiences can serve to limit impulsive approaches. The following example shows the common error of subtracting the smaller number from the larger, rather than decomposing a ten for more ones. When talking aloud, some students will recognize their error and others will do so when prompted with a statement such as, "What is the number you are subtracting from 461?" Witzel, Ferguson, and Mink (2012) suggest that while the verbalization of mathematical ideas is important for all students, it can be particularly helpful to those at risk.

$$\begin{array}{r} 461 \\ -\underline{158} \\ 317 \end{array}$$

Grade three provides an opportunity to focus on the use of place value strategies as the development of addition and subtraction culminates in grade four, when students are expected to fluently add and subtract multi-digit numbers using the standard algorithm (4.NBT.4). As shown in Figure 6.8, recordings may still differ, depending on how the regrouping is viewed. For example, the first recording is based on 7,000 being the same as 699 tens and 10 ones.

Figure 6.8 Different Recordings for 7000 – 1928

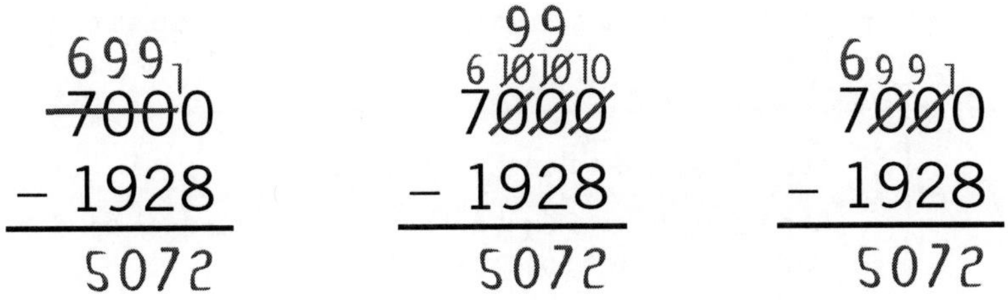

$$
\begin{array}{r}
\overset{699}{\cancel{7000}} \\
-\ 1928 \\
\hline
5072
\end{array}
\qquad
\begin{array}{r}
\overset{99}{6\ \cancel{10}\cancel{10}\cancel{10}} \\
\cancel{7000} \\
-\ 1928 \\
\hline
5072
\end{array}
\qquad
\begin{array}{r}
\overset{699}{\cancel{7000}} \\
-\ 1928 \\
\hline
5072
\end{array}
$$

In grade five, addition and subtraction are applied to numbers with tenths and hundredths as well, though use of the standard algorithm is not required until sixth grade (5.NBT.7). Figure 6.9 provides a summary of the addition and subtraction expectations in grades K–5.

Figure 6.9 Addition and Subtraction Expectations in Grades K–5

Level	Expectations
Kindergarten	No expectations beyond those established in Operations and Algebraic Thinking
Grade 1	• Add a two-digit number and a single-digit number or a two-digit number and a multiple of 10, such as 23 + 20 • Use mental arithmetic to find 10 more or 10 less than a given two-digit number, without counting • Subtract two-digit numbers that are both multiples of 10 such as 80–20
Grade 2	• Add and subtract fluently within 100 • Add up to four two-digit numbers using strategies based on place value of properties of the operations • Add or subtract within 1,000, using objects or drawings and strategies based on place value, properties, or relationships between addition and subtraction and relate the strategy to a written record • Mentally add or subtract 10 or 100 to or from a number 100–900 • Explain why addition and subtraction strategies work using place value or properties
Grade 3	• Fluently add or subtract within 1,000, using strategies based on place value, properties, or relationships between addition and subtraction and relate the strategy to a written record
Grade 4	• Fluently add and subtract multi-digit numbers using the standard algorithm
Grade 5	• Add and subtract decimals to hundredths using objects or drawings and strategies based on place value, properties, or relationships between addition and subtraction, relate the strategy to a written record, and explain reasoning used

Students should have many opportunities to apply these new place value and computational concepts and skills to a variety of word problem situations. Practice can also be embedded in a variety of formats and questions such as those suggested below. Increasing or decreasing the size of the numbers and/or changing the operation allows you to adapt them to a variety of levels. Have students:

- Play Win 100 with base-ten materials and two number cubes. Each player rolls the number cubes and collects that many units. Whenever there are enough units, students trade them for 1 ten. As students play more, encourage them to make predictions. *Will there be enough to make a ten? What number will I have after I get these units and I make a ten, if I can?* For younger students, this activity can be modified to have a smaller target number and use only one number cube. Older students can play Win 1,000 and roll one number cube to identify the number of tens to be collected and the other to identify the ones.

- Use money as a concrete model for work with tenths and hundredths. Money is not a proportional model of base-ten as 10 pennies are not proportional in size to one dime, nor are 10 dimes proportional in size to a one dollar bill. So while not the best model for students just learning about place value, money is appropriate at grade five, as students are quite familiar with composing and decomposing numbers. Most students more easily recognize $0.30 = 0.3$ when they think about 30 pennies having the same value as 3 dimes. Such analogies are important and serve as better conceptual underpinnings than the often-heard comment, *Oh, the zero doesn't matter.*

- Include a number of the day routine into your daily schedule. A number such as 23 is chosen and students create a variety of equations for the number such as $10 + 10 + 3$ or $22 + 1$.

- Present a practice page of subtraction examples with the following directions. *Look at these 10 subtraction examples. Estimate to find how many will have a difference between 25 and 59. Justify your answer.*

- Use the digits 1–6 to write two three-digit numbers. What two numbers would give the greatest sum? The least difference? (642 + 531; 234 − 165)

- Complete the following task. How many different whole numbers could you add to 378 to get a sum that when rounded to the nearest 10, is 450? (10)

- Find the missing digits in this example: (A is 8, B is 2, C is 9)

$$
\begin{array}{r}
9\,A\,0\,3 \\
-\,B\,8\,7\,C \\
\hline
6\,9\,2\,4
\end{array}
$$

- Write three addition examples with a sum of 45. Explain how you could use one example to find others.

- Write a word problem for the example 324 − 125 and solve it.

Multiplication and Division

The strategies and properties of multiplication and division are introduced at the basic fact level within the Operations and Algebraic Thinking domain at grade three. Within that domain, students are introduced to the distributive property of multiplication over addition and the inverse relationship between multiplication and division. Some educators have questioned whether third grade is too early to introduce this property to students. Benson, Wall, and Malm (2013) designed an instructional sequence to connect the property to the geometric model of area and link it to computational strategies. They concluded, "We found that the distributive property is naturally logical to most students if we first allow students to think through problems, view them from multiple perspectives—numerically and geometrically—and then connect other models and more efficient procedures to those original models" (505).

This domain identifies the expectation that third-graders also find products of single-digit numbers and multiples of 10, such as 3 x 50 (3.NBT.3). As with addition and subtraction, place value language can be helpful. To find 3 x 50 students can think 3 x 5 tens is 15 tens or 150.

In fourth grade, students are expected to multiply up to a four-digit number by a single-digit multiplier. Though the standards do not explicitly begin with the use of concrete models or drawings, it is the place to start (4.NBT.5). Students have learned that they can multiply in parts, for example that 7 x 7 = 7(5 + 2) and so the product can be found by thinking 7 x 5 + 7 x 2 = 35 + 14 or 49. This distributive property of multiplication over addition can be applied to greater numbers as well. As students in grade three also learned how to multiply single digit numbers by multiples of 10, they have the tools to find, for example, 3 x 64 by separating the expression into two parts: 3 x 60 + 3 x 4 and then combining these partial products.

Array or area modes are helpful to reinforce the view of multiplication as two-dimensional. Potential recordings include those shown in Figure 6.10. Note that the first and second records explicitly indicate the partial products and could be completed left to right or right to left. The third recording shows the regrouped number written below the line as suggested in the Progressions Document for this domain and the fourth recording is currently common.

Figure **6.10** Four Sample Recordings for 7 x 64

	60	4
7	7×60=420	7×4=28

$$\begin{array}{r} 64 \\ \times\ 7 \\ \hline 28 \\ +420 \\ \hline 448 \end{array}$$

$$\begin{array}{r} 64 \\ \times\ 7 \\ \hline \overset{2}{420} \\ \hline 448 \end{array}$$

$$\begin{array}{r} \overset{2}{64} \\ \times\ 7 \\ \hline 448 \end{array}$$

Multiplying a two-digit number by a two-digit number is more complex as four partial products are involved. One fourth-grade teacher has students make drawings, use stamps of, or use base-ten blocks to show the area model formed when multiplying two-digit numbers (Figure 6.11). Once students recognize the four partial products that are formed, they can adopt one of the recordings shown in Figure 6.12. Note that non-proportional models of these larger numbers are fine; they serve to organize the partial products and make the process transparent.

Figure **6.11** Area Model of Partial Products for 12 x 25

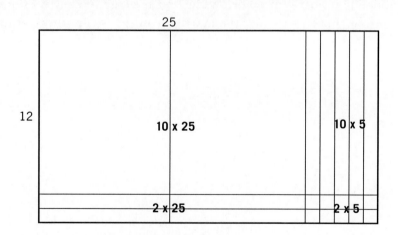

Figure 6.12 Sample Diagram and Potential Recordings for 32 x 46

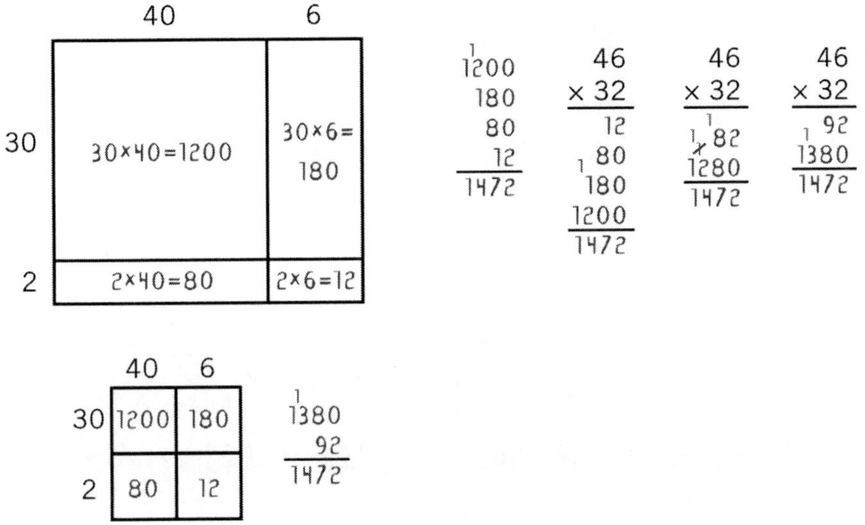

In fifth grade, students are expected to multiply multi-digit numbers using the standard algorithm (5.NBT.5).

Division with greater numbers begins in grade four and again, though not indicated, students should begin with materials and drawings (4.NBT.6).

If conceptual understanding is expected, we must consider alternative strategies. First and foremost, students must establish a written record while initially using models so the multi-step process makes sense (Figure 6.13).

Figure 6.13 Written Record Using Models

65 ÷ 5

Show the 65.

Share the tens fairly among 5 groups.

5 tens are shared.

1 ten and 5 ones remain.

Regroup the 1 ten as 10 ones.

Share the 15 ones.

There are 13 in each group.

Honoring Individual Differences

The language often associated with division is challenging and especially so for English Learners. Consider the expression 258 ÷ 4 to which the phrase *4 doesn't go into 2* is often said at the beginning of the standard algorithm. *Goes into* is not mathematical language and is especially problematic when solving a problem asking about the number in each group. Also, two can be divided by four, as students will learn with decimal division. Further, with the emphasis on place value, we want students to recognize that the 2 represents 200, which is divisible by 4, without decimals. It is important that our language supports, rather than interferes with, mathematical understanding.

Like multiplication, division can be done in parts as illustrated in Figure 6.14. At first, the student was unsure as to how to proceed. He looked at the division example 235 ÷ 5 for some time, and as a result, his teacher was ready to assume that he had forgotten what he learned before the winter break. Then, his eyes got wide and he said, "I know. I can do it in parts."

Figure 6.14 Student Sample of Dividing in Parts

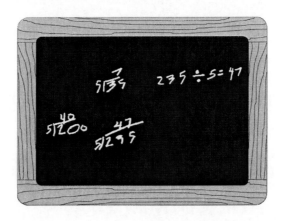

With the place value emphasis in this domain, students should become familiar with dividing by tens, hundreds, and thousands. When thinking of the whole number, instead of about parts of the number such as shown in the first two examples in Figure 6.15, students are far less likely to make common errors such as thinking that $4907 \div 7 = 71$. Note that in these recordings, partial quotients are noted along the way. This way of thinking allows students to work with facts they know, as they gain efficiency. The second example shown includes more steps but does result in the correct quotient. An alternative recording scheme is called an explicit trade method (Van de Walle, Karp, and Bay-Williams 2013). The advantage of this recording is that the decomposing of place value units is clearly identified.

Figure 6.15 Three Sample Recordings for Division

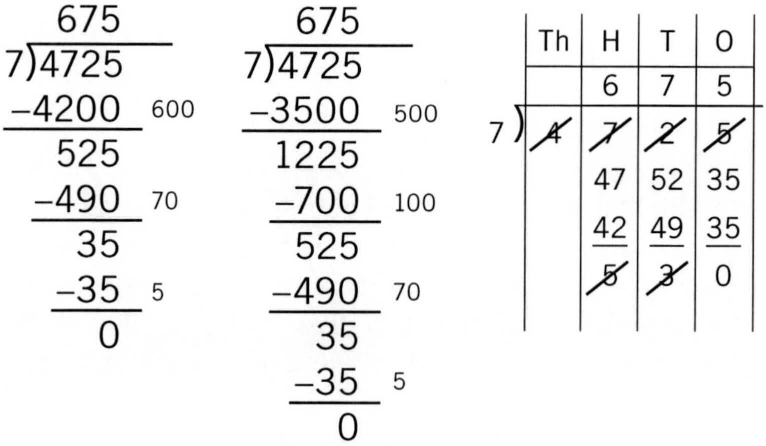

In fifth grade, division is extended to two-digit divisors (5.NBT.6). Note that the standard algorithm for division is not listed as a standard until grade six. Two-digit division is particularly problematic as you can follow prescribed steps of estimate and divide, and still have to erase and start over, as the product is too great when you multiply (Figure 6.16). In this example, the product is too great. Consider having students use strategies illustrated in Figure 6.15, or initially provide students with a times table for the divisor so that they can focus on the process, not the specific arithmetic.

$$70 \div 30$$ is about 2

$$
34 \overline{\smash{)}655} \\
 68
$$

(quotient: 2)

In this domain, fifth graders also multiply and divide with decimals to hundredths (5.NBT.7). While students can follow a rule such as count the total number of decimal places in the factors and place the decimal point so there are that many places in the quotient, we must build understanding as well.

Students should begin with simple decimal examples and when there is understanding, apply a general rule to more complex computations, perhaps making predictions as to how many decimal places there will be, without computing, and then using a calculator to check. Patterns can be generalized from solving a series of related problems such as $200 \div 5$, $200 \div 0.5$, and $200 \div 0.05$. You should also model strategies for estimating and making sense of where to place decimal points when multiplying and dividing before students use a rote rule, including:

MP7
Structure

- **Use rounding:** think of 3.9×4.12 as about 4×4 or about 16

- **Translate to fractions:** recognize 0.4×0.5 as $\frac{4}{10} \times \frac{5}{10}$ or $\frac{20}{100}$

- **Refer to money:** think of $4 \div 0.1$ as finding the number of dimes in four dollars or 40, or think of $6 \div 0.05$ as finding the number of nickels in six dollars, or 120

The last two examples and others similar to them can be particularly useful for students who do not understand how division with two such small numbers could possibly result in such a relatively large quotient.

Expectations for multiplication and division at the 3-5 grade levels are summarized in Figure 6.17.

Figure 6.17 Multiplication and Division Expectations in Grades 3–5

Level	Expectations
Grade 3	• Multiply one-digit numbers by multiples of ten less than 100 such as 3 x 40
Grade 4	• Multiply up to a four-digit number by a one-digit number and two two-digit numbers using strategies based on place value and properties, and illustrate or explain the calculation using equations, arrays, or area models • Divide up to a four-digit number by a one-digit number using strategies based on place value and properties, and illustrate or explain the calculation using equations, arrays, or area models
Grade 5	• Fluently multiply and divide multi-digit whole numbers using the standard algorithm • Divide up to a four-digit number by a two-digit number using strategies based on place value and properties, and illustrate or explain the calculation using equations, arrays, or area models • Multiply and divide decimals to hundredths using objects or drawings and strategies based on place value, properties, or relationships between addition and subtraction, relate the strategy to a written record, and explain reasoning used

Most students need many opportunities to discover and rediscover all of the relationships within the compact multiplication and division algorithms. Students need many opportunities to make connections among visual models, explanations, and written work, with specific attention given to place value. They also need to estimate products and quotients so they strengthen their number sense. Ideas include:

☞ Use the multiplication example on the left to find the other products.

$$
\begin{array}{r}
387 \\
\times\ 42 \\
\hline
774 \\
+\ 1548 \\
\hline
2{,}322
\end{array}
$$

What is 42 x 397?

What is 200 x 42?

What is 40 x 387?

What is (42 x 287) – (2 x 387)?

☞ Use estimation to match multiplication or division expressions with five products or quotients and justify their choices.

☞ Prepare a teaching poster that addresses such questions as *Why does the standard algorithm for multiplication involve addition? Why does the standard division algorithm involve subtraction? How do you estimate a product to check your work? How can you predict the number of digits there will be in the quotient?* Share the posters at a classroom math fair.

☞ Identify whether statements such as 36 x 5 = 30 x 5 + 6 x 5 are true or false.

☞ Solve a problem such as *Use the digits, 3, 4, 5, and 6 to create a division expression with a quotient of 89.*

- Play *Jeopardy!* with the categories word problems, single-digit divisors, two-digit multipliers, and remainders. If, for instance, a team chose two-digit multipliers for $500, they might get the answer 1,392 and have to ask a question such as *What is 58 x 24?*

- Place decimal points so that equations such as 32 x 46 = 1.472 become accurate.

Assessment Note

Given limited time, teachers may find themselves examining written work only to determine whether answers are correct or not. If you don't have time to look at all work carefully, choose the work of five students a day and consider it from the following perspectives:

- Can I follow the written record?

- If an error is made, what might be the source?

- Does the task appear to be at about the right level, that is, is there enough challenge without being too frustrating?

Some teachers copy and save examples of work in folders they keep for each student. Such artifacts provide comparisons for later work as well as documentation that can be reviewed when writing report cards or preparing for parent conferences. It can be helpful to record your observations of the work before it is filed. A template for such recordings is provided in Figure 6.18 and in the Appendix.

Figure 6.18 Form for Organizing Comments About Students' Work

Examining Written Work

Name: _____ Date: _____

1. Is the work accurate?

2. If errors are made do they appear to be
   Careless?   Basic fact related?
   Due to a faulty procedure?   From an unknown source?

3. Can I follow the written record? If not, what would make it clearer?

4. How does this work show progress the student is making?

5. What should this student work on next?

Standardized test items are likely to include items that require several steps for their solution. The need to provide complex tasks and to teach content through the lens of the mathematical practices cannot be over-emphasized. An example of such a task is provided in Figure 6.19.

Figure 6.19 Example of a Multi-Step Assessment Task

The tennis coach wants to buy tennis balls while they are on sale. She wants to buy 560 tennis balls and does not want to buy any extra ones.

1. What should she buy?

2. What will be the total cost?

Tennis Balls On Sale!		
Size	Number	Cost
Can	3	$5
Bucket	24	$40
Case	144	$240

 Voice from the Classroom

About 10 years ago my school system adopted new curriculum materials that emphasized use of a variety of strategies for addition, subtraction, multiplication, and division. At first, I was really resistant. Why did I want to teach four different ways to subtract, some of which seemed quite inefficient to me? That first year didn't go so well as I didn't really understand exactly what I was supposed to do. As I think back on it, I was teaching in the same way as I always had, just teaching more algorithms. Some of the students really got confused about all the different techniques. We had some professional development that summer and the leader modeled a different way to teach. She had us share our ideas and we used lots of chart paper to record our thinking. My own understanding of these operations solidified and I was excited to try this way of teaching in the fall. After a couple of years, I began to really appreciate the power of students understanding what they were doing. We were having these great conversations and I was really enjoying teaching math. Some of my students were amazing, with all the connections they were making.

I did notice that a few students were struggling in different ways. They couldn't follow so many different ideas and sometimes they would combine strategies in incorrect ways. I began to provide a bit more modeling and to work with small groups to make sure everyone had one or two techniques they could really understand. But I always had a nagging feeling that some students were being left behind, and I worried about what would happen when they got to middle school.

In thinking about these new standards, I first had that same feeling I had when we adopted the new curriculum. Things seemed to be going fairly well, so why did we have to change again? Place value seems so dominant. I mean, that makes sense and I think it could really help my students in later years, but I also want to keep up some of my practices from before these standards were adopted. I'm hoping that with the greater focus on computation that I can more fully develop place-value skills while still developing young mathematicians who think about an example such as 399 + 8, and realize that they can find the sum mentally, without using a standard pencil and paper algorithm.

—Fourth-Grade Teacher

Let's Think and Discuss

1. What are some common misunderstandings that your students have about our number system? How might new standards give you the opportunity to rethink how you address those ideas?

2. How are the computation-related standards in this domain similar and different from your current expectations for students?

3. What are some ways you have found for helping students create written records of their work?

$\frac{1}{2} + \frac{3}{4}$

Chapter 7

Number and Operations— Fractions

Snapshot

A fourth-grade class is comparing fractions. The teacher displays $\frac{5}{12}$ and $\frac{3}{4}$. He tells students to quickly write down which amount of the same-sized container of lemonade they would like to have if they really liked lemonade. He counts aloud to five as they decide and record one of the fractions. He glances around the room as he counts and is pleased to see that, based on his quick observation, all of the students have written a number. He has used this routine of counting to five often as he likes to capture students' intuition. In the beginning of the year, many of the students seemed afraid to write an answer unless they were certain it was correct. Now they understand that they can record their ideas and later change their minds. Many students even enjoy finding out more about what the student, Erica, calls *my hidden thinking that even I don't know about.*

The teacher asks, "Who wants to tell us which number you chose and why you did so?" As students report, the teacher records their thinking on chart paper. The following statements are among those shared. Finley says, "I chose five-twelfths right away because three and four are such small numbers and I do love lemonade." Eloise says, "I chose three-fourths because it only takes one more fourth to make a whole container and five-twelfths has lots missing." As Eloise shares, the teacher concludes that Eloise has good intuition but could over-generalize from this example. He records $\frac{6}{10}$ and $\frac{2}{5}$ as a comparison he wants students to investigate later, to make sure Eloise and other students with similar thinking are focusing on the distance from 1, rather than just thinking about the numerators of the fractions that remain. After a couple more students report, he directs them to turn to a neighbor and take some time to make a final decision about which fraction represents the greater amount of a container. He distributes blank paper so they can record their thinking.

After an allotted time, students present their recordings and discuss which ones make the most sense. Lei says, "I really like Gino's picture. With five-twelfths and three-fourths on the same tall rectangle, I can see that three-fourths is more and the rectangle looks like a container." Saul says he likes Gino's picture, too, but also likes Rosa's idea about comparing each fraction to one-half. He comments, "I mean, I could recognize five-twelfths as less than six-twelfths, and three-fourths as greater than two-fourths, in my head, before you even got to five!"

MP2
Reason

MP3
Construct

The teacher chose this task as it allows students to think about fractions both concretely and abstractly and requires them to communicate their thinking. He set the comparison in a context (same-sized container), rather than just having them compare two fractions, to reinforce the idea that to compare fractions you need the same whole. He also chose a situation that involved a continuous model (liquid), as so often students think about discrete, countable parts. He closes the lesson by asking students to each decide individually if they would rather have two-thirds or three-eighths of same-sized containers of chocolate milk if they loved chocolate milk. He told them to explain their thinking as well as write the answer. He will use the students' responses to decide how to group students tomorrow.

 ## Big Picture

Many students find fractions and solving word problems involving fractions quite challenging (Lamon 2012, Alajmi and Reys 2010). Over the years, research has identified several student misconceptions or partial understandings, such as the whole number thinking that Finley demonstrated in comparing five-twelfths and three-fourths. Students appear to lack a conceptual understanding of fractions and even when able to apply procedural knowledge correctly, are unable to justify their thinking (Siemon, Izard, Breed, and Virgona 2006). As the Common Core demands both conceptual and procedural knowledge, our instructional focus and methods need to change.

Number and Operations—Fractions is a separate domain at grades 1–2 though fractions are integrated within the Measurement and Data and the Geometry domains in grades 1–5. For instance, in second grade within the Geometry domain, students partition shapes into equal shares and describe those shares as halves, thirds, or fourths. It is important to note such connections when thinking about the organization of your curriculum. A focus on fractions is a critical area at each of these grade levels.

Within this domain, the number line or linear model of fractions is given significant attention, rather than near sole reliance on the traditional visual mode of shaded parts of a shape. Unit fractions, fractions with a numerator of one, and equivalent fractions are also significant and provide the foundation for operations with fractions. Bringing this focus to our curriculum supports middle school investigation of unit factors and equivalent ratios in the Ratios and Proportional Relationships domain. Figure 7.1 details the six clusters found in this domain.

Figure 7.1 Cluster Names at Each Grade Level 3–5

Grade Level	Clusters	Denominators
Grade 3	• Develop understanding of fractions as numbers	2, 3, 4, 6, 8
Grade 4	• Extend understanding of fraction equivalence and ordering • Build fractions from unit fractions • Understand decimal notation from fractions, and compare decimal fractions	2, 3, 4, 5, 6, 8, 10, 12, 100
Grade 5	• Use equivalent fractions as a strategy to add and subtract fractions • Apply and extend previous understandings of multiplication and division	unlimited

Fractions as numbers

The familiar language of *five out of six*, accompanied by a fraction pie that shows five of six parts shaded, strongly suggests that fractions are two numbers, not one number. In grade three, all of the fraction standards are within the cluster titled *Develop understanding of fractions as numbers.* Partitioning and copying (iterating) become the vehicles through which fractions are understood (3.NF.1). One-fourth is understood as the quantity identified by one part when a whole is divided into four equal parts (partitioning). It can also be viewed as the part that when copied four times, makes the whole (iterating).

Unit fractions are the building blocks of fractions, just as ones are when it comes to whole numbers (Common Core Standards Writing Team 2013). A number such as $\frac{5}{6}$ is understood through a two-step process that involves finding the unit fraction $\frac{1}{6}$ and then copying it five times as shown in Figure 7.2.

Figure 7.2 Model with Unit Fractions

Step 1:

A whole is *partitioned* into six equal parts, identifying $\frac{1}{6}$.

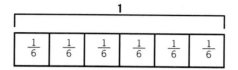

Step 2:

Five of the one-sixths are put together to identify $\frac{5}{6}$.

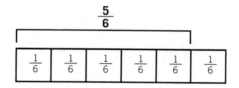

number Line Models

Part of understanding fractions as numbers is to be able to locate them on a number line. This ability requires the student to apply the basic partitioning and copying processes and to recognize that the distance from 0 to 1 defines the whole. It also requires students to understand that there are numbers other than whole numbers. Mills expresses this challenge in her statement, "For many students who have spent their early mathematics lessons focusing on counting (whole) numbers, recognising that there are many numbers between those whole numbers called fractional numbers is quite revolutionary" (2011, 7–22) (3.NF.2; 3.NF.2a; 3.NF.2b). Knowing where a fraction is on a number line, such as whether it is closer to 0 or 1, supports number sense and estimation skills. For example, if students can place $\frac{11}{12}$ on a number line, they should eventually be able to recognize that $\frac{11}{12} + \frac{11}{12}$ is close to 2. Being able to place a fraction on a number line is also one of the ways that students can compare fractions. As with whole numbers, fractions to the right are greater, and those to the left are less.

Shaughnessy (2011) warns us to recognize the complexity of placing or identifying a fraction on an open number line. She encourages teachers to present tasks in a variety of ways so as to unmask possible misconceptions. Pfotenhauer, Kleine, Sitabkhan, and Earnest (2013) suggest the importance of assessing students' abilities to place fractions on a number line without tick marks or units identified. Consider the variations in Figure 7.3. What do you think might be discovered about student understanding through one of these formats that would not be discovered in another?

Figure 7.3 Various Forms of Number Line Tasks

Write $\frac{2}{3}$ where it belongs on the line.

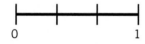

Write the number.

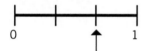

Write $\frac{2}{3}$ where it belongs on the line.

Write $1\frac{2}{3}$ where it belongs on the line.

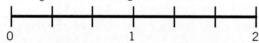

Write $\frac{2}{3}$ where it belongs on the line.

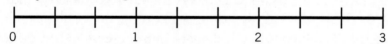

Write the number.

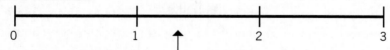

Write $\frac{2}{3}$ where it belongs on the line.

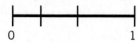

172

Equivalent Fractions

Students learn about equivalent fractions in third grade. Through drawings, fractions strips, and number lines, students recognize that there can be several labels for the same fraction, for example, three-fourths and six-eighths. The initial focus is exploratory, in preparation for more formal and generalizable approaches in grade four. Note that work with equivalent fractions is not restricted to number lines; in fact, it is important that students develop a variety of visual models (3.NF.3a).

Consider the following classroom example:

> Nick's mother put two small pizzas on the table.
>
> Nick cut one of the small pizzas into halves and ate one of the pieces.
>
> His sister Brianna cut the other pizza into fourths. She ate two of the pieces.
>
> Draw to show the amount of pizza each one ate.
>
> Write the fractions to show how much pizza each one ate.
>
> Did they each eat the same amount of pizza or did one of them have more? Explain.

Fadi and Johanna are working together. Johanna reads the whole problem aloud. Then, she reads again as Fadi represents the two pizzas. They agree that the fractions are $\frac{1}{2}$ and $\frac{2}{4}$, which Johanna records. They decide the amount of pizza looks the same. Fadi asks, "Does this mean that one-half is the same as two-fourths?" Johanna replies that they are the same amount, but they are different, too. She adds, "I'd always rather eat two pieces."

In another third-grade class, students are folding strips of paper to make fractions. One group reports that it did a lot of double folding. They folded a strip in half and wrote $\frac{1}{2}$ in each part. They folded the next strip in half and then folded it in half again. When they opened the paper, they counted to make sure there were four parts. Then, they wrote $\frac{1}{4}$ in each part. They repeated this process, this time folding a strip in half three times to form eighths and marked them appropriately. They glued their strips on a piece of paper, lined up carefully one below the other. As a class, they talked about different names for the same fractions and how they knew they were the same (NF.3b). The teacher writes $\frac{1}{2}$ = $\frac{2}{4}$ and asks students to write three other equations with equivalent fractions.

Students should see different fraction names on number lines as well. Students can write numbers below and above the lines to show equivalences (Figure 7.4). The understanding of the numerator as the number of copies and the denominator as indicating the size or denomination that is being copied can also help students understand that every whole number can be written as a fraction (e.g., $\frac{3}{1}$ can be thought of as three ones, just as $\frac{3}{4}$ can be understood as three one-fourths) (3.NF.3c).

Figure 7.4 Equivalence on a Number Line

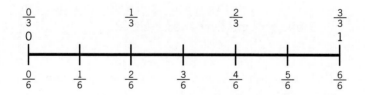

In fourth grade, students formalize their understanding of how to recognize and generate fractions. Area models and number line models can be used. Both models are shown in Figure 7.5. Note that when the whole is further partitioned, so are the parts, but the fractions are the same size. With repeated experiences, students can conclude that multiplying the numerator and the denominator by the same number results in an equivalent fraction. This same reasoning could be used to simplify fractions, that is, by dividing the numerator and denominator by the same number, but this skill does not receive attention in these standards (4.NF.1).

Figure 7.5 Area and Number Line Models Showing Equivalent Fractions

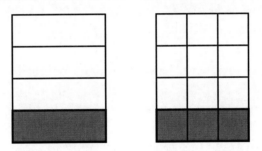

$$\frac{1}{4} = \frac{3 \times 1}{3 \times 4} = \frac{3}{12}$$

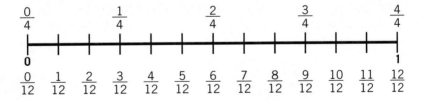

Comparing Fractions

To compare fractions, many adults cross multiply, without knowing why that method works, or they use their calculators to translate the fractions to decimals and compare the decimals. Neither of these techniques builds understanding of fractions. Conversely, Common Core comparisons are based on students' ability to reason about the size of fractions or on the use of common denominators (3.NF.3d; 4.NF.2). Students also must recognize that comparisons require that the fractions refer to the same whole.

Pictures of different units, such as shown in Figure 7.6, illustrate this importance. Sharing the following scenario draws students' attention to this idea.

Enrico ate one-third of the slice of pumpkin bread.

Jonas ate half of the slice of banana bread.

Did they each have the same amount of bread?

MP3
Construct

One teacher assigns the students to two groups: those who will present an argument that Enrico ate more bread, and those who will argue that Jonas ate more bread.

Figure 7.6 Representations Showing that $\frac{1}{3}$ of a Larger Whole Can Be More than $\frac{1}{2}$ of a Smaller Whole

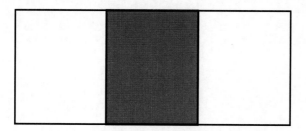

Figure 7.7 gives examples of abstract reasoning students could use to compare fractions. Note that the use of benchmarks in grade four does not require all of the strategies described. Rather it is the use of benchmarks that is expected. Similar reasoning could be used to explain why one fraction is less than another.

MP2
Reason

Figure 7.7 Using Conceptual Reasoning to Compare Fractions

Grade 3	• $\frac{1}{3} > \frac{1}{5}$ because it only takes three of the thirds to make a whole and it takes five of the fifths. The thirds must be bigger. • $\frac{2}{3} > \frac{2}{5}$ because there are two of each and thirds are greater than fifths. • $\frac{5}{8} > \frac{3}{8}$ because 5 one-eighths is more than 3 one-eighths.
Grade 4	• $\frac{3}{4} > \frac{1}{3}$ because $\frac{1}{3}$ is less than $\frac{1}{2}$ and $\frac{3}{4}$ is more than $\frac{1}{2}$. • $\frac{7}{8} > \frac{1}{10}$ because $\frac{7}{8}$ is close to 1 and $\frac{1}{10}$ is close to zero. • $\frac{5}{6} > \frac{3}{4}$ because $\frac{5}{6}$ is $\frac{1}{6}$ away from 1 and $\frac{3}{4}$ is $\frac{1}{4}$ away from 1. Since $\frac{1}{4}$ is greater than $\frac{1}{6}$, $\frac{3}{4}$ is to the left of $\frac{5}{6}$ on the number line. • $\frac{4}{6} > \frac{5}{8}$ because $\frac{4}{6}$ is $\frac{1}{6}$ more than $\frac{1}{2}$ and $\frac{5}{8}$ is $\frac{1}{8}$ more than $\frac{1}{2}$. Since $\frac{1}{6} > \frac{1}{8}$, $\frac{4}{6}$ is to the right of $\frac{5}{8}$ on the number line. • $\frac{7}{12} > \frac{2}{4}$ because $\frac{2}{4}$ is the same amount as $\frac{6}{12}$ and $\frac{7}{12}$ is greater than $\frac{6}{12}$.

Conceptual Challenge

Some of the reasoning suggested in Figure 7.7 can be quite challenging, even for adults who have not been previously exposed to such thinking. A number line model can be particularly helpful. Have students show, for example, $\frac{5}{6}$ and $\frac{3}{4}$ on the same number line. Their placement will clearly indicate their relative size, but draw students' attention to the unit fractions that represent the distance of these fractions from 1. Ask questions such as *Which fraction is farther from 1, $\frac{5}{6}$ or $\frac{3}{4}$? Which unit fraction is greater, $\frac{1}{6}$ or $\frac{1}{4}$? If we placed $\frac{9}{10}$ on the number line, what fraction would represent the distance from this number to 1? How can the distance that remains help us figure out whether it is greater or less than the other two fractions?*

A variety of whole number games can be played as fraction games to provide practice with understanding fractions, recognizing equivalent fractions, and comparing fractions. You just need to replace a regular deck of cards with a fraction deck. You can download examples of fraction decks from the web. Some games include:

- A game based on *Go Fish*, where the questions become *Do you have any three-fourths?* Matches of four cards could be based on matching multiple visual representations of a fraction, on equivalent written fractions, or on combinations of both.

- A *Concentration* game that matches two visual representations of the same fraction, a visual representation to a written fraction, or two equivalent written fractions, depending on the practice the students need.

- ☞ A *War* game where each player turns over a fraction card and the player with the greater number claims the two cards. When the fractions are equivalent, there is a war. Each player places three cards down and turns up a new fraction. Whichever player has the greater of these two numbers collects all of the cards from this war.

- ☞ *Closest to 1/1 is* a game that can be played with a regular deck of cards, without the face cards or only keeping numbers appropriate for your grade level. Each player is dealt three cards and chooses two of them to form a fraction. The player with a fraction closest to 1 gets a point; a total score of 10 points wins the game.

- ☞ There are also many games online that require students to match fractions with their visual representations. Other games ask students to compare fractions with and without visual models. Most sites allow you to choose among different levels of challenge, allowing you better individualized practice.

Addition and Subtraction of Fractions

As mentioned earlier, fractions are built on unit fractions. In fourth grade, the notion of copying a unit fraction to form fractions with numerators other than 1 is represented with addition. Thus, $\frac{3}{8}$ can be understood as $\frac{1}{8} + \frac{1}{8} + \frac{1}{8}$. Within this model, $\frac{5}{4}$ is understood as $\frac{1}{4} + \frac{1}{4} + \frac{1}{4} + \frac{1}{4} + \frac{1}{4}$ (3.NF.1; 4.NF.3). Note that the "out of" model and language does not support an understanding of such fractions. Five one-fourths makes sense; five out of four does not (Siebert and Gaskin 2006). This understanding allows a variety of fractions to be understood, without notions of *improper* fractions, a term that sounds derogatory.

Consider the following task investigated by fourth graders (Figure 7.8).

Figure 7.8 Fourth Grade Fraction Task Involving Partitioning and Iterating

If [rectangle] represents 2/3, draw a rectangle to show 1 1/4.

MP5
Precision

Kellian suggests they make a line down the middle so they can see each of the thirds. His partner, Gemma, says they should fold it in half so the middle will be more exact. Once they identify the unit fraction they extend the figure that amount and agree they now have the whole. Kellian writes $\frac{1}{3} + \frac{1}{3} + \frac{1}{3} = 1$ on their paper. They appear stalled for a bit, which is not an uncommon reaction when students complete a significant portion of a multi-step task. They make some sketches trying out some of their ideas. Then, Gemma says, "Now we have to find fourths, right?" Kellian agrees and this time he suggests they trace and cut out a copy of the whole. Once cut, they fold the length of the strip in half twice and cut out one of the fourths to add to the length of their whole. This time Gemma records $\frac{1}{4} + \frac{1}{4} + \frac{1}{4} + \frac{1}{4} = \frac{4}{4} + \frac{1}{4} = 1\frac{1}{4}$ (4.NF.3b).

MP1
Make Sense

Honoring Individual Differences

As difficult as it can be to change language we have used for years, we need to change our habits when it comes to how we describe fractions. Though all students will potentially develop a less complete understanding of fractions when they are defined as *the number of parts out of the number of parts in all*, such language is particularly harmful to auditory learners who rely on oral input for understanding. Another example of inappropriate language related to fractions is the phrase *reduce it*. Reduce suggests that something is lessening, which suggests two representations are no longer equal. Vocabulary with everyday meanings that differ from their mathematical uses is particularly challenging to English Language Learners (Rubenstein and Thompson 2002). Practice the language of *dividing into equal shares* and the *joining of unit fractions* and develop an internal censor that eventually will keep you from use of common but inappropriate language.

Students' previous experience with the composition and decomposition of whole numbers provides the basis for adding and subtracting mixed numbers with like denominators. With fractions, the focus is on composing wholes rather than tens and decomposing to unit fractions rather than ones (4.NF.3c). To find $2\frac{3}{4} + \frac{3}{4}$, students can think of $2\frac{3}{4}$ as $\frac{4}{4} + \frac{4}{4} + \frac{3}{4}$ or $\frac{11}{4}$. Then they find that $\frac{11}{4} + \frac{3}{4} = \frac{14}{4}$. This number is then used to compose wholes or thought of as $\frac{4}{4} + \frac{4}{4} + \frac{4}{4} + \frac{2}{4}$ or $3\frac{2}{4}$. With repeated experiences, students can learn to recognize they can divide to find the number of wholes and remaining parts. Once understanding is established, applying the properties of arithmetic can simplify the process. For example, the example above can be thought of as $2 + (\frac{3}{4} + \frac{3}{4})$. After understanding is established through several experiences, prod students' thinking by asking *Is there another way to do this?* If such a process is not shared, model it yourself and encourage students to consider a variety of choices.

MP5
Tools

MP7
Structure

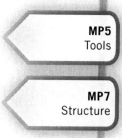

181

Note that students' understanding of fractions based on copies of unit fractions transitions well to addition and subtraction with like denominators. It makes sense that when taking three one-sixths from four one-sixths that you would be left with one-sixth. Sixths can be thought of as a noun in the same way as the number of trucks or dolls could be added or subtracted with whole numbers. Further, previous language use would translate $\frac{3}{4} + \frac{3}{4}$ to three out of four plus three out of four, suggesting six out of eight, or $\frac{6}{8}$, an incorrect answer.

Particular attention is given to decimal fractions in fourth grade. (Investigation of decimals continues in fifth grade within the Numbers and operations in Base Ten domain.) Here the focus is on tenths and hundredths. Students are expected to translate between tenths and hundredths and use these translations to allow them to add tenths and hundredths by rewriting one of the numbers so that there are like denominators. So $\frac{3}{10} + \frac{27}{100}$ becomes $\frac{30}{100} + \frac{27}{100}$ (4.NF.5). Decimal grids as shown in Figure 7.9 help students make the connection between tenths and hundredths.

Figure 7.9 Decimal Grid Models Showing the Equivalency of $\frac{2}{10}$ and $\frac{20}{100}$

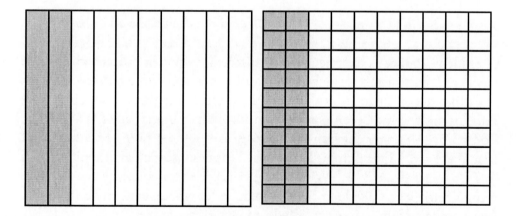

The decimal grids can also help students recognize that 0.10 is less than 0.9, a comparison that can be challenging to students used to whole numbers, where they have learned that 10 is greater than 9 (Roche 2005; Glasglow et al. 2000) (4.NF.7). Students are also expected to write fractions with denominators of tenths or hundredths in decimal form, connect decimal notation to meters, and locate a decimal on a number line diagram (NF.6). As we would not expect students to divide a whole into 100 equal shares, related tasks should be limited to such tasks as identifying the correct number within choices for a decimal in the hundredths, placing hundredths within an identified tenth (Figure 7.10), estimating placement, or indicating whether such a decimal would be to the left or right of an identified number.

Figure 7.10 Sample Number Line Task

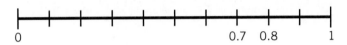

Show where 0.72 would be on the number line.

In fifth grade, addition and subtraction expands to unlike denominators of all kinds, including those involving mixed numbers (5.NF.1). One could argue that if students know how to generate equivalent fractions, recognize the need for a common denominator, and know how to add or subtract with like denominators, students only need to combine these abilities to meet this standard. Yet teachers have known for years that many students struggle with this multi-step process, especially when one denominator is not a factor of the other, such as $\frac{1}{6} + \frac{1}{4}$, requiring both fractions to be rewritten. There are two changes within the Common Core that may prove helpful; only time will tell. Delaying this expectation until fifth grade may increase the likelihood that students can keep track of multi-step procedures. Further, the standards give no attention to the use of least common denominators, which removes an additional criterion.

Both fourth and fifth-grade students are expected to solve word problems involving fractions. It is important that the problems we give students indicate that the fractions being added or subtracted refer to the same unit. Consider the following problem:

Wilma drank $\frac{1}{2}$ of her glass of juice.

Deidre drank $\frac{1}{4}$ of her glass of juice.

In total, how much juice did the two girls drink?

If the amount of juice the girls drank was given in cups or pints or if the problem referred to the amount of juice poured from the same container, this problem can be answered. As written, however, there is no way to know that the two girls are drinking from the same size glasses.

At grade four, students solve problems with like denominators (4.NF.3d). In fifth grade, word problems extend to fractions with unlike denominators. These students are also expected to use their number sense of fractions to estimate the reasonableness of their answers (5.NF.2). Students at both grade levels can use visual models and equations to represent problem situations.

We should remember to vary the situations in the problems we offer students, just as expected with whole numbers. Further, the type of problem we present can influence the type of visual models students use. Consider the following two problems. The first is more suggestive of a number line model, while the second is more likely to be represented by an area model. It is important that we provide both types of examples.

Brooke and Isabella are riding dirt bikes on a trail. Brooke has ridden $\frac{5}{12}$ of the trail and Isabella has ridden $\frac{7}{12}$ of the trail. How much further has Isabella ridden than Brooke?

Jamal used $\frac{4}{6}$ of the poster board for a social studies project. Then, he used some more of the poster board to make a sign for his bedroom door. He had $\frac{1}{6}$ of the poster board left and gave it to his younger brother. How much of the poster board did Jamal use for the sign?

Sometimes students who are successful solving word problems with whole numbers become uncertain as to how to solve a problem with fractions. Simplifying the numbers can help students better recognize the structure of the problem. Consider the following example.

> *Dionne had several yards of orange cloth. She used $2\frac{3}{4}$ yards to make a costume and $\frac{3}{4}$ of a yard to cover a pillow. Now, $1\frac{1}{2}$ yards of orange cloth remain. How many yards of cloth were there before Dionne made the costume and the cover for the pillow?*

Ask students how they might simplify the numbers in the problem. In this case, rounding each number up to the nearest whole number works well. Have students identify the steps they would use to solve the problem with these numbers and then apply their thinking to the original example.

Multiplication and Division of Fractions

Multiplication of fractions is introduced in the fourth grade. Students are expected to understand that a fraction with a numerator other than 1 can be represented by a multiplication equation. So, for example, $\frac{5}{6}$ can be represented as $5 \times \frac{1}{6}$ and $\frac{7}{4}$ as $7 \times \frac{1}{4}$ (4.NF.4a). This idea is then generalized to the multiplication of any fraction by a whole number and the solution of word problems involving such multiplication. This thinking is built on the idea of "copying" and thus, relies on the repeated addition model of multiplication (4.NF.4b; 4.NF.4c).

Consider Parker and Maya solving the following problem.

Li wants to make 4 loaves of corn bread. Her recipe lists $1\frac{1}{3}$ cups of cornmeal for each loaf. She had 5 cups of cornmeal. Does Li have enough cornmeal to make 4 loaves with this recipe?

Their teacher has asked them to do their own thinking first and then talk to each other about their ideas. After the allotted time, Parker tells Maya that he thought of $1\frac{1}{3}$ as $\frac{3}{3} + \frac{1}{3}$ or $\frac{4}{3}$. Then he multiplied by 4 because of the four loaves and got $\frac{16}{3}$ or $5\frac{1}{3}$, which is not enough. Maya agrees, but adds, "I got the same answer, but I multiplied the 1 and the $\frac{1}{3}$ separately. I know that four times one is four and so I just found four of the one-thirds. Three-thirds would be another cup, for five cups, and then there is the one-third that is still needed." The teacher is pleased by the conceptual understanding these two students have. She decides to have both of them present their thinking to the class as a whole. She wants students to practice following the thinking of others and to compare these two approaches to their own.

MP7
Structure

MP8
Reasoning

In fifth grade, students learn to multiply a whole number or a fraction by a fraction. To find $\frac{1}{4} \times 6$, often associated with the language *one-fourth of six,* the six is divided into four equal shares or parts and one of them is identified. When the numerator is not one, multiple copies are combined. For example, to find $\frac{2}{3} \times 6$, the six is divided into three parts and two of those parts are combined. Visual models of these examples are provided in Figure 7.11 (5.NF.4).

Figure 7.11 Models of Multiplication of a Whole Number by a Fraction

 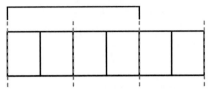

A unit of 6 divided into 4 equal shares.

One share is $1\frac{1}{2}$.

$\frac{1}{4} \times 6 = 1\frac{1}{2}$

A unit of 6 divided into 3 equal shares.

One share is two. Two shares is 4.

$\frac{2}{3} \times 6 = 4$

Conceptual Challenge

For many years, students have lacked a conceptual understanding of operations with fractions. After learning how to multiply fractions, students might rely on the same type of algorithm for addition or subtraction, incorrectly believing that $\frac{3}{4} + \frac{1}{8} = \frac{4}{12}$. Note that such an error is also supported by whole number thinking in that the whole numbers are being added across. Conversely, a student distracted by addition with like denominators may incorrectly find $\frac{2}{3} \times \frac{2}{3} = \frac{4}{3}$. Such errors are less likely when algorithmic rules are only introduced after conceptual understanding is firm. It is also worthwhile to have students return to visual models on occasion to reinforce understanding. Requiring students to create word problems for given expressions also underlines the meaning of multiplication with fractions.

Multiplication with two fractions is best represented with an area model of multiplication that has been established with whole-number multiplication in grade three (Figure 7.12). Applying the same models across numbers helps students to recognize that the concept of multiplication remains the same, regardless of the type of numbers.

Consider this problem.

Marti had $\frac{3}{4}$ yd. of yellow felt.

She used $\frac{2}{3}$ of the felt to make a puppet.

What fraction of a yard of this felt did she use to make the puppet?

To solve this problem, the student needs to recognize that the $\frac{2}{3}$ represents the part of the $\frac{3}{4}$ yd. that was used (not $\frac{2}{3}$ of a yard). The task is then to find $\frac{2}{3}$ of $\frac{3}{4}$.

Figure 7.12 Representation of $\frac{2}{3}$ x $\frac{3}{4}$ = $\frac{6}{12}$

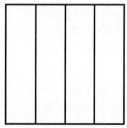
Divide into fourths.

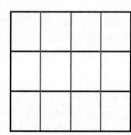
Divide into thirds.

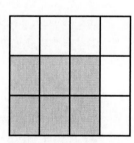
Identify the area.

With repeated exposure, students can recognize the general rule for multiplying fractions as multiplying the numerators and denominators (5NF.4a; 5.NF.4b).

The emphasis on understanding is also demonstrated by the expectation that students can explain why multiplying by a fraction greater than one results in a product greater than the other factor, while multiplying by a fraction less than one results in a smaller product. This can be a surprise to students who have over-generalized their experiences with whole numbers and incorrectly concluded that a product is always greater than either of its factors. Focusing on this idea allows students to better estimate products, and this notion of scaling (changing the size of) helps to prepare students for the sixth and seventh grade domain, Ratios and Proportional Relationships (5.NF.5; 5.NF.5a; 5.NF.5.b).

 Another strategy for supporting student understanding of multiplication and division of fractions is to assign different problems to the students according to their readiness levels. Consider this example from a fifth-grade class: Inez is solving one of five problems students in her class are exploring. Each problem is similar, but the specific numbers are different, based on student readiness. Inez is completing the following task.

The three children in the Stenson family are sharing four ears of corn. Each child will get the same amount of corn. Write a fraction to tell how much corn each child will get.

Inez draws four rectangles to represent the ears of corn. She divides each rectangle into three parts, counts the parts to find that there are 12, and records $\frac{12}{3}$. Inez knows her multiplication facts, but it is not unusual for a learner to revert to earlier techniques such as counting when exploring an unfamiliar situation. She then divides and decides each child will get $\frac{4}{3}$ ears of corn.

When appropriate, the teacher calls the students back together. As students report, the teacher records the number of people, the number of ears of corn, and the number of ears of corn each person gets. As the teacher is recording the third example, Joshua exclaims, "The numbers are all the same." Through this activity, students are exploring the idea that a fraction can be interpreted as division; that is, $\frac{5}{3} = 5 \div 3$ (5.NF.3).

In fifth grade, students also investigate division with unit fractions as either the quotient or the divisor. Pattern blocks are a great way to explore initial unit fraction ideas. (Other representations of fractions could easily be used.) Here is an example from a fifth-grade teacher. After investigating with the pattern blocks, the teacher knows that students are surprised when they find, for example, that $9 \div \frac{1}{2} = 18$ and thinks that the kinesthetic component of working with the blocks helps. He distributes the blocks and asks students to build the hexagon as many different ways as they can, using multiple copies of only one shape. It doesn't take long for the students to recognize that the triangles, large rhombuses, and trapezoids can each be used. He then asks, "If we assign the hexagon a value of 1, what would be the value of each of these three blocks?" Once the students agree, he draws and labels each piece on chart paper, similar to that shown in Figure 7.13.

Figure 7.13 Pattern Blocks Fractions

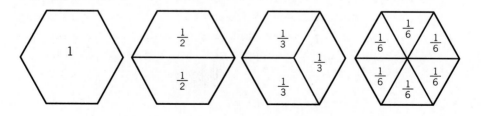

The teacher then displays the following problem and asks students to use their blocks to find the answer.

Mr. Chen has 3 cookies to give to his grandchildren. He gives each of his grandchildren $\frac{1}{2}$ a cookie. How many grandchildren does Mr. Chen have?

The students use three hexagons to represent the cookies. Some students place trapezoids on top of the hexagons to show the halves and some use one trapezoid and move it on top of the hexagons as they count. The teacher writes $3 \div \frac{1}{2} = 6$ on the chart paper along with a sketch of the blocks. Jessie asks, "How come we divided and got a bigger number?" The teacher does not respond but rather looks at the students with expectations for them to explain. Chris says, "It's like how many halves are there in three." Jessie nods, but the teacher senses some uncertainty remains. He gives a few more examples and Jessie begins to enjoy how quickly he can find the answers.

As an exit card, the teacher asks students to make a drawing to show how to find $4 \div \frac{1}{6}$. Over time, students will explore examples such as $\frac{1}{2} \div \frac{1}{6}$ using the pattern blocks and drawings. They connect their division equations to the related multiplication equations (5.NF.7).

- ✏ Apply and extend previous understandings of division to divide unit fractions by whole numbers and whole numbers by unit fractions (5.NF.7a).

- ✏ Interpret division of a unit fraction by a non-zero whole number, and compute such quotients. *For example, create a story context for $\left(\frac{1}{3}\right) \div 4$, and use a visual fraction model to show the quotient. Use the relationship between multiplication and division to explain that $\left(\frac{1}{3}\right) \div 4 = \frac{1}{12}$ because $\left(\frac{1}{12}\right) \times 4 = \frac{1}{3}$* (5.NF.7b).

- ✏ Interpret division of a whole number by a unit fraction, and compute such quotients. *For example, create a story context for $4 \div \left(\frac{1}{5}\right)$, and use a visual fraction model to show the quotient. Use the relationship between multiplication and division to explain that $4 \div \left(\frac{1}{5}\right) = 20$ because $20 \times \left(\frac{1}{5}\right) = 4$.*

Honoring Individual Differences

Pattern blocks are part of many classrooms, and by fifth grade, most students have used them in previous grades. Some students may feel that such blocks are only for younger students and be hesitant to use them. Using a concrete material for a day or two lets all students know that you think they are appropriate for older students as well. You can then leave them in an accessible location, available for use by students as they wish. If there are students distracted by the sound of the blocks, have students use them on top of small rug samples. Some students find the hexagon shape challenging to draw as well as to show it divided into thirds. You can make stamps or shape templates available for use.

Fifth graders are also expected to solve and create story problems involving these limited fractions. It should be noted that research has previously documented that teachers find the creation of such problems challenging, most likely due to the lack of attention given to conceptual understanding in their own educations and the fact that teachers tend to replicate the way they were taught (Green, Piel, and Flowers 2008). The fact that fifth graders will now be expected to accomplish this task highlights the rigor of the standards and the power of learning with understanding (5.NF.7c). Remember that both uses of division should be included, that is, to find the number in each group and the number of groups (Figure 7.14).

Figure 7.14 Two Types of Division Problems

How Much in Each Group?	How Many Groups?
Four students were given $\frac{1}{2}$ a bag of balloons to share. What portion of the bag of balloons will each student get?	Four yards of shoelace material will be used to make shoelaces, each $\frac{1}{2}$ yard long. How many shoelaces may be made?
$\frac{1}{2} \div 4 =$	$4 \div \frac{1}{2} =$
This problem lends itself well to using the sharing interpretation of division.	This problem lends itself well to using the measurement interpretation of division.
This visual model shows $\frac{1}{2}$ of the whole, divided into 4 equal shares with each student receiving $\frac{1}{8}$ of the bag of balloons.	This visual model shows measuring out how many $\frac{1}{2}$'s there are in 4.
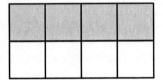	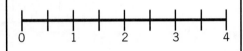

Assessment note

Formative assessment data can be gathered in many ways. One example is through a game format. To do this, several versions of a tic-tac-toe game should be created. One version is shown in Figure 7.15. Other versions focus on finding sums, and different numbers are used in both the addition and subtraction formats to meet a variety of readiness levels. The game rules are as follows:

1. Players take turns.

2. On each turn choose a number in Box B to subtract from Box A.

3. Find the difference and put your initials on that number in the Game Board. The other player may not place his or her initials in this same location.

4. The first player whose initials are on three numbers in a row, column, or diagonal wins.

Figure 7.15 Sample Fraction Game with Addition and Subtraction of Fractions

Box A

1	$1\frac{1}{2}$
$\frac{7}{12}$	2

Game Board

$\frac{1}{2}$	$1\frac{2}{3}$	$\frac{1}{6}$	$\frac{3}{4}$
1	$1\frac{1}{12}$	$\frac{1}{12}$	$1\frac{1}{12}$
$1\frac{1}{4}$	$\frac{2}{3}$	$1\frac{1}{6}$	$1\frac{7}{12}$
$\frac{1}{4}$	$\frac{7}{12}$	$1\frac{3}{4}$	$\frac{1}{3}$

Box B

$\frac{5}{12}$	$\frac{1}{3}$
$\frac{1}{4}$	$\frac{1}{2}$

As the teacher circulates the classroom, he or she can carry a clipboard and a form to summarize the observations (Figure 7.16 and in Appendix A). As students demonstrate one of these skills, the teacher writes their names in the appropriate box. On another day, the teacher might use the same form, but only observe one student, looking for evidence of each of the conceptual and procedural understandings listed.

Figure 7.16 Sample Game Observation Summary

Activity:	Date:
Uses number lines to find the sum or difference	Uses drawings to find the sum or difference
Uses abstract reasoning or arithmetic to compute	Computes mentally
Finds accurate sum or difference	Uses estimation and/or number sense to choose numbers that will yield a strategically located sum or difference

195

Standardized tests are likely to include fractions on a number line as this is such a major focus within the standards. They may also connect such representations with problem solving. An example would be as follows:

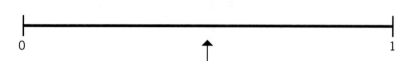

Figure 7.17 Fractions on a Number Line

Jason and Sorel both started walking at the beginning of the nature trail. The arrow points to Jason's location on the trail now.

1. Which number best represents Jason's location on the trail: $\frac{1}{4}$, $\frac{3}{8}$, $\frac{2}{3}$, or $\frac{1}{2}$?

2. Sorel started walking before Jason. Sorel is $\frac{3}{8}$ farther along the trail than Jason right now.

3. Draw an arrow on the number line to represent Sorel's location on the trail.

   a. Explain why you think the arrow goes there.

   b. What number matches this location on the number line?

Voice from the Classroom

I participated in a professional development institute this fall about fractions. I couldn't believe what I didn't really understand. To start, the leader wrote $2\frac{1}{3} \div \frac{2}{3}$ and asked us to write a story problem that we could solve by finding this quotient. We all just looked at each other. We were encouraged to work in groups, but there we didn't have much to say. My group made a few attempts, but none were successful.

Then, the leader asked us to make a drawing to find the quotient. Even this was challenging. Next, we were asked how to find the quotient. Finally, something I knew, invert and multiply! But what good did that do me if I couldn't create a story problem for this expression?

By the end of the two-day institute I had learned to understand fractions in a whole new way. I feel so much better prepared to teach fractions!

—Fifth-Grade Teacher

 # Let's Think and Discuss

1. What representations do you like students to use to model fractions? Why?

2. What concepts related to fractions do you think you understand best? What do you think contributed most to this level of understanding?

3. The Common Core emphasizes real-world problems. When do you use fractions and decimals outside of the classroom?

Chapter

Measurement and Data

 **Snapshot**

The second-grade teacher gathers the students at the rug area to listen to the story *Inch by Inch* (Lionni 1995). The students are easily engaged with the smart inchworm who measures to keep from being eaten. The teacher reads the book again, asking volunteers to find the inchworm on each page among the illustrations. Then, she says, "Use your fingers to show how long you think the inchworm is." As she glances at their responses, she notes that though there is variation, the students appear to recognize that an inch is a relatively small unit. She gives each student an inch-long paperclip. She asks the students to hold it between their pointer finger and thumb to feel the length of an inch. Then, in pairs, without holding the paperclip, students take turns trying to place their pointer finger and thumb an inch apart and then have their partner place a paperclip there to check.

Next, the teacher places a large piece of paper on the rug with a bold line drawn on it that is 14 inches long. She asks students to bring up their paperclips, one at a time, until the line of paperclips has matched that of the drawn line. She has a couple of students check if the clips are placed end-to-end, without gaps or overlaps. Once they are satisfied, she asks all the students to join her as she counts the paperclips. She then announces that the line is 14 paperclips or 14 inches long. She asks, "Is this the same way that the inchworm measured the birds?" Benjamin suggests it is the same because they used inches, too. Martin says, "I agree with Benjamin, but it is also different."

The teacher asks the students to close their eyes and imagine the inchworm measuring their line. When the students open their eyes, the teacher asks them what they saw in their mind's eye. Responses include "a green inchworm," "an inchworm crawling," "an inchworm moving slowly along the line," and "an inchworm counting."

The teacher asks the students to tell why they think that the inchworm was counting. When Rosalie says, "He had to keep track. There was only one of him," the teacher places another paperclip on the other side of the room and asks the students to think about how they could use just one paperclip to measure the length of the line. It is decided that the paperclip could be moved along the line. "Can I move it anywhere?" the teacher asks. Some of the students look perplexed by this question, but a few clearly state that it should be moved right next to where it was. The teacher then demonstrates marking the end of the clip and moving it to this new marked position. This time she writes the numbers 1–14 just below the corresponding lines. Once students agree that the measure is still 14 inches, the teacher gives them a piece of paper with a 6-inch line on it and asks them to work in pairs to find the length of the line, using their paperclip.

This teacher realizes that some of the students are familiar with this award-winning book, but she thinks reading is an excellent way to draw their attention to measuring length by using one unit multiple times. This iterative process is very different from lining up multiple copies of the same unit, the way in which these students measured in first grade. She knows students are challenged by this transition and that many such experiences will be necessary.

Big Picture

One of the greatest changes to the organization of the K–5 curriculum within the Common Core State Standards for Mathematics is the coupling of measurement and data within one domain. Measurement is identified as a critical area in grades 1, 2, 3, and 5; data is not identified as critical at any level within this grade span. The lessening of attention to data and probability at the elementary level is in line with the curricula of Hong Kong, Korea, and Singapore, all with students who perform well in mathematics on standardized tests (Ginsburg, Leinwand and Decker 2009).

Geometric measurement concepts related to length, area, and volume are given considerable attention within these standards. The term geometry measurement is introduced as a subheading in grades 3–5, but length is included in some way, at each of the K–5 levels. At the middle school level, measurement is no longer a separate domain but rather considered within the geometry domain. Prior to the Common Core, area and volume were introduced much earlier in the curriculum, with some programs exploring volume as early as grade two. In these standards, area is introduced at grade three and volume is delayed until grade five. According to Smith and Gonulates (2011), the focused attention at these grade levels accomplishes more than was done previously across the wider grade span.

The domain does include attention to other measures such as time, money, liquid volume, temperature, and weight or mass, though none of these are identified as a critical area. Few elementary classrooms have the necessary tools for students to measure temperature or to measure weight/mass, or liquid volumes with standard units. Such measures are often considered within the science curriculum. Hopefully, new STEM initiatives will give students greater access to a wide variety of measurement tools. A summary of the measurement clusters is provided in Figure 8.1.

Figure 8.1 Summary Clusters

Grade	Summary Clusters
K	• Describe and compare measurement attributes
1	• Measure lengths indirectly and by iterating length units • Tell time and write time
2	• Measure and estimate lengths in standard units • Relate addition and subtraction to length • Work with time and money
3	• Solve problems involving measurement and estimation • Understand concepts of area and related area to multiplication and addition • Recognize perimeter
4	• Solve problems involving measurement and conversion of measurements • Understand concepts of angles and measure angles
5	• Understand like measurement units within a given measurement system • Understand concepts of volume

The data standards involve categorical data (grades K–5), that is data that results from sorting objects. The focus is first on classifying objects and then on representing and interpreting such data in picture graphs or bar graphs. Measurement data is the other focus, which results from taking measures. Line plots are used to organize this type of data.

There are a variety of ways in which the standards in this domain connect to the three number-focused domains (Operations and Algebraic Thinking, Number and Operations in Base Ten, and Number and Operations—Fractions). Figure 8.2 provides examples of such connections across the grade levels.

Figure 8.2 Connections Between the Measurement and Data Domain and the Number-Related Domains

Grade	Measurement and Data Concepts	Connections to Number Domains
K	• Classify objects and sort them by their count	• Counting and comparing numbers
1	• Organize data and count the number in each category; determine how many more or less compared to another category	• Addition and subtraction situations
2	• Create bar graphs and use information in the graphs to solve put-together, take-apart, and compare problems • Show whole-number measures in a line plot	• Addition and subtraction situations • Number line
3	• Create scaled picture and bar graphs and solve related two-step how many more and how many less problems • Make a line plot to show measures to the nearest one-fourth of an inch • Use multiplication to find areas	• Multiply and divide (to create and interpret graphs) • Addition and subtraction situations • Show fractions on a number line • Commutative and distributive properties of multiplication
4	• Make a line plot to show measures to the nearest one-eighth of an inch and use data to solve problems involving addition and subtraction • Find relationships among metric units	• Show fractions on a number line • Add and subtract fractions • Solve addition and subtraction problems involving fractions • Base-ten system
5	• Make a line plot to show measures to the nearest one-eighth of an inch and use data to solve problems • Multiply to find volume	• Add and subtract fractions • Multiply and divide fractions • Solve problems involving fractions • Associative property of multiplication

There are also connections between measurement and data. These connections will be highlighted in the discussions of these two components of this domain. Finally, geometric measurement, of course, connects to the geometry domain.

Measurement

When we measure, we identify the physical attribute to be measured and choose an appropriate unit with that attribute. We then determine the number of units necessary to match, fill, or cover that attribute of the object, for example, the number of square feet needed to cover a rug (Van de Walle, Karp, and Bay-Williams 2013). Measurement has sometimes been taught as a series of explorations of different units, without attention to central ideas that permeate the measuring process. When we draw students' attention to these ideas, we help them to recognize the repeated reasoning and structure that hold across the measurement of different attributes, rather than to view measurement as a series of isolated experiences. Such common ideas include the following:

MP7
Structure

MP8
Reasoning

- use of identical units

- iteration of units without holes or gaps

- understanding of the inverse relationship between the number of units needed and the size of the units

- use of tools

- understanding that measures are additive

Research suggests that students do not understand measurement (Lehrer and Lesh 2003). International test results indicate that students perform less well on measurement-related questions than on any other mathematical topic (Thompson and Preston 2004). Establishing new standards gives us the opportunity to rethink how measurement is taught and to decide how to best develop students' conceptual understanding of measurement as well as their procedural skills for taking measures. Thinking about common challenges or misconceptions can help us. As you read about the different aspects of measurement, think about your students and where they struggle.

Early Beginnings

Initial exploration of measurement focuses on attributes. Young learners need to recognize the various aspects of an object that can be measured. Within this context, kindergarten students might explore length, area, volume, and weight/mass (K.MD.1).

Students often make informal comparisons of measures in their daily interactions claiming, for example, that they are taller or that the building they built is bigger. Such comparisons are not based on specific measures, but rather on perceptions or direct comparisons. Perceptual comparisons are conclusions drawn on how objects look or feel to viewers. In direct comparisons, one object is lined up and matched to another. Young students do this naturally when they stand back to back to compare their heights. Though it is not uncommon to find a child increasing his or her height by standing on tip toes, this is recognized as "cheating." In this instance, students recognize that their feet need to be firmly on the ground. This concept does not transfer to the comparison of two sticks, for example, where the start point might be more ambiguous or even ignored by some learners. You can make an analogy to comparing heights to help students recognize the importance of the starting or zero point (K.MD.2).

Consider the following conversation at the block area in a kindergarten classroom:

Marcus: My building is bigger.

Patty: Well, mine is bigger this way.

Teacher: Tell me more about how your building is bigger.

Marcus: Look at this. (Said as he points to indicate the height of his building.)

Teacher: Oh, I see. Your building is taller. Do you agree, Patty?

Patty: Yes, but look. (Said as she spreads arms to longest length of her building.)

Teacher: So you think your building is longer at the bottom. Do you agree, Marcus?

Marcus: I think we each have bigger in different ways.

Such comparisons occur often and provide opportunities to emphasize the different attributes of objects and the language associated with those attributes. Note how the teacher encouraged the students to be more specific about the ambiguous term *bigger*.

Length

In kindergarten, students explore length as part of their general exploration of attributes. They compare lengths of two objects directly. Length is a critical area at both grades one and two. In first grade, students are expected to order three objects by length directly and compare two objects indirectly. Note that the use of rulers is not a standard at this level (1.MD.1). To compare the lengths of three objects, students must make sure there is a common start or end point.

When lengths cannot be placed side-by-side, direct comparison is impossible and use of an indirect or intermediary length is required. Families do this when they mark their children's height each year on a wall. This allows them to compare the heights from year-to-year, something that cannot be done directly. In school, students might use a piece of string to compare the length of a poster on one side of the room to that on another side. First, one poster would be measured and the length marked on the string, perhaps by holding that point with fingers or by tying a knot there. The string would then be brought to the other poster, allowing for the length marked on the string to be compared directly to the length of this poster.

The measurement of length begins in first grade, when units to measure are introduced. Here students use multiple copies of the same-sized unit. Linking cubes, paperclips, or craft sticks are length units that students can manage easily. Over time, students need to learn to place such length units end-to-end, with no gaps or overlaps (Figure 8.3), until the entire length is matched. The idea of placing units without gaps or overlaps needs to be modeled, both correctly and incorrectly, for students to understand the difference. Observe students carefully as they measure. One teacher uses the phrase *I spy* as in *I spy a gap* or *I spy an overlap* as a way to remind students how to place their units. Then, just as students need to recognize that the last number they say when they count tells the number in all, they need to learn that the count of units is the measure. At this grade level, the standards limit the process to a whole number of units. This limitation can be met easily with lines prepared by you, but is unlikely when measuring real objects. Do not keep students from exploring the lengths of real objects, rather, let them informally identify such lengths as five sticks and a little more (or less) (1.MD.2).

Figure 8.3 Examples of Gaps and Overlaps

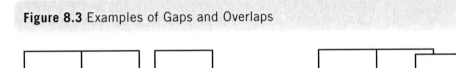

Honoring Individual Differences

We expect to support young children as they develop the language of measurement, but may not realize how challenging this vocabulary is for many learners, especially those learning English, regardless of their age. The variety and overlap within our comparative language can make the task of developing precise vocabulary particularly perplexing. In comparing lengths, we might identify one object as being wider, shorter, taller, longer, deeper, or higher than another. Also, a term such as *longer* is not just associated with lengths or distances; we also might use it to compare time.

MP6
Precision

When we do so, we are comparing the lengths of duration, but that concept is one with which many learners at this level are unfamiliar. When measuring units are introduced, students focus on the number of units and may confuse the language of arithmetic with the language of measurement through such statements as *mine has more* or *four is more than three*. Note that the number alone is not enough to draw conclusions, as 2 yards is longer than 14 inches. Measures must consider the number of units and the unit used. Revoice such statements with comments such as *You think yours is longer because it is 4 inches long and the other is 3 inches long.*

Students in second grade are expected to make several qualitative leaps in terms of their understanding of length. Tools are introduced for the first time; and students are expected to choose among such tools as rulers, yardsticks, meter sticks, and measuring tapes to measure particular lengths. Using these tools is not simple. First, as it is unlikely that students will have access to multiple copies of these tools, they must be iterated, that is, they must be picked up and moved. As indicated at the beginning of this chapter, placing any unit from one position to the next is complex. Doing so with a ruler is even more complex as there are usually spaces before and after the zero mark and final inch or centimeter mark, which need to be taken into consideration. While standardized tests will have students only measure lengths less than what can be shown on a page or screen, in real life, they may only have a ruler to measure a longer length (2.MD.1).

Conceptual Challenge

Use of rulers is also complex in the same way that number lines are. Even fifth graders can lack a conceptual understanding of a ruler as being composed of inch-long segments (McCool and Holland 2012). Twelve separate one-inch segments represent a discrete quantity, that is, discrete objects that can be counted. Once composed as a ruler, they form a continuous quantity, without separations. When counting them, students could place their fingers on any part of the inch, but to measure, it is the endpoint of each inch that is important. Each number marks a location. In grades 3–5, use of rulers is further complicated by the inclusion of fractions. Note that measuring to the nearest half-inch was often an expectation at grade 2, but is now delayed until grade 3, where fractions on a number line are developed.

With use of tools comes the expectation of using standard units to measure lengths. Students are also expected to estimate lengths in inches, feet, centimeters, and meters. To do so, they must have a sense of how long each unit is as well as everyday referents. For example, the height of a doorknob is nearly a meter. Focusing on these four units makes sense, as they are common measures that students can visualize (2.MD.3; 2.MD.4).

Another conceptual idea of measurement that is introduced at grade two is the inverse relationship between the number of units needed and the size of those units (2.MD.2). For example, as feet are longer than inches, it will take more inches than feet to measure the same length. Students should use a variety of standard and nonstandard units to measure same lengths until they can make this generalization about their findings. You can also ask questions such as the following:

✏ *We just measured this length in feet and now we are going to measure it in inches. Will we need more or fewer inches? Why do you think so?*

MP2
Reason

➥ *Do you think you will need more craft sticks or paperclips to measure the length of your arm? Why do you think so?*

➥ *What could you say to someone who thought it took more centimeters than meters to measure your height?*

While students at this level are quite familiar with adding and subtracting numbers, they need to realize that lengths can also be added and subtracted and to solve word problems involving lengths. Further, there is an explicit expectation that they use number lines, among other models, to represent such problems. These standards reinforce those within the number domains and students should be exposed to the variety of addition and subtraction problem situations. (2.MD.5; 2.MD.6).

What's most important is that students have many opportunities to compare and measure length. Some ideas include:

➥ Create a "length bag" by placing several objects in an opaque bag such as a paperclip, a crayon, a craft stick, and a new pencil. Students close their eyes and, based on their readiness, pull out two to four items. By touch, with their eyes still closed, students organize the items from shortest to longest.

➥ Have students measure the width of the room in baby steps, walking steps, and giant steps and talk about the differences among the measures.

➥ Have students make their own rulers to use as measuring tools, by gluing 12 one-inch segments together on cardstock and writing the correct numeral at the end of each segment. Close supervision of this process completed in small groups would be helpful. It's a great opportunity to involve a parent volunteer, if available.

➥ Give each student a strip of heavy stock paper that is 1 in. or 1 ft. long. Have students search the classroom for four shorter and four longer items.

✏️ Create concentration-type games where students match items pictured above rulers with their measures. Include items that are not lined up to the zero point of the ruler.

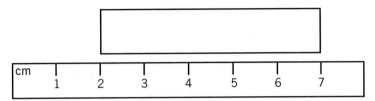

Establish a daily length routine. You could have a length drawing contest where measures are given, such as 7 inches, and students draw a line they think is that long. Similarly, you could draw a line or name a distance, such as from the classroom door to the window, and have students estimate its length in inches, feet, centimeters, or meters, before finding the actual measures.

Perimeter

In third grade, students continue to explore length through their introduction to perimeter (3.MD.8). Perimeter, with its corners (or any path with corners), presents new challenges. For example, Battista (1999) indicated that some students would count squares at corners, rather than the two line segments, when figures are shown on grids (Figure 8.4). Also, fractional parts are likely to occur when students measure the perimeter of a face of a real object. When measuring continuously, rather than finding the length of each side and then adding, students may choose to use string and then measure the string. If using a nonstandard unit or a ruler, however, students need to note where the measure ended on one side so that this can become the start point for the next side. Finding the perimeter of a rectangle relying on a formula is a standard at fourth grade.

Figure 8.4 Incorrect Iteration of Length Units at Corners

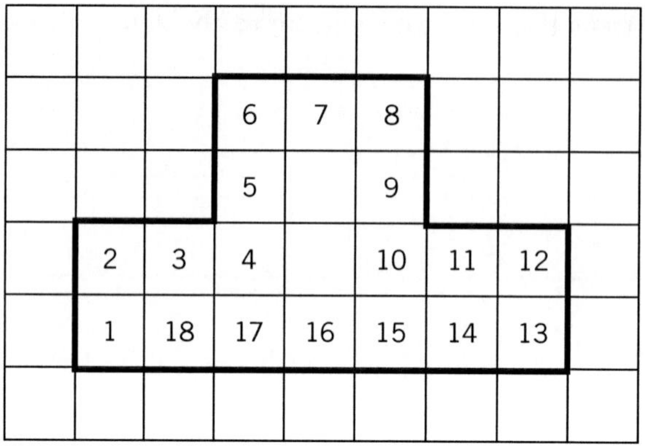

Standards in grades four and five include a greater variety of length units, and students are expected to convert from one to another within a single measurement system. (Note that such expectations hold for measures of other attributes as well.) In grade four, the conversions are from a larger unit to a smaller one, as this coincides with standards for multiplication at this level (4.MD.1). Fifth-grade students use their division and decimal skills to convert from a smaller to a larger unit, and there are no restrictions on the types of units involved. For example, students might be solving a problem related to estimating the cost of buying ribbon to place along the border of a bulletin board. The perimeter of the bulletin board is likely to be measured in inches, but ribbon is often sold in yards. Thus, the total number of inches would then need to be converted to yards, by dividing by 36 (or by dividing by 12 to find feet, and then by 3 to find yards) to estimate the cost (5.MD.1).

Area

Ideas related to area might be explored as early as kindergarten within the investigation of attributes of objects. Partitioning rectangles into same-sized squares within the geometry domain is also central, but explicit attention to area begins in grade three. The significant emphasis on area corresponds to the focus on multiplication at this grade level.

Students first need to understand that area is the amount of two-dimensional space within a region (Common Core Standards Writing Team 2012b). Like many other aspects of measurement, NAEP data suggest that students do not have a complete conceptual understanding of area (Blume, Galindo, and Walcott 2007) (3.MD.5). Though not indicated explicitly in the standards, students need repeated experiences measuring and comparing areas to reinforce the notion of covering a two-dimensional figure.

The standards focus on the use of square units, and initially, students could use multiple copies of one-inch squares to cover a figure without gaps or overlaps. These experiences could include irregular shapes for which students estimate, for example, two empty spaces that could be filled by decomposing a whole unit (3.MD.5a; 3.MD.5b; 3.MD.6). The counting of these square units or those shown on a grid then leads to connecting this process first to addition, by counting a row and then adding or skip-counting based on the number of rows, and then to multiplication (3.MD.7). Learners should tile rectangles with square units until they can explain clearly why multiplying the lengths of the sides of a rectangle results in the same outcome as counting (3.MD.7a).

Once students gain conceptual understanding of a rectangular array structured into squares, students can work with given length dimensions to find areas (3.MD.7b). As with other measures, area may be added and subtracted. The composition and decomposition of figures to find area should be prominent in tasks in general and can be used to reinforce the distributive property of multiplication (Figure 8.5) (3.MD.7c; 3.MD.7d).

Figure 8.5 Model of How to Connect Finding Area to the Distributive Property

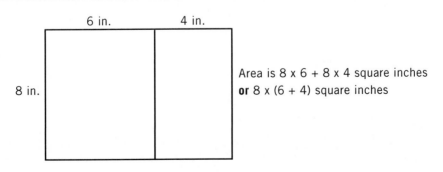

Area is 8 x 6 + 8 x 4 square inches
or 8 x (6 + 4) square inches

In fourth grade, students apply the area formulas for rectangles and find the missing lengths of a rectangle by recognizing it as a missing factor problem. They can solve real-world problems related to area, including the variety of multiplication and division situations. Too often area and perimeter are studied briefly with an emphasis on formulas. The result is that students often confuse the two measures, applying the incorrect formula to solve problems. They also do not always attend to whether the measure should be given in units or square units. The progression within these standards encourages conceptual understanding from which formulas emerge and should lessen students' confusion when solving, for example, problems about gardens (Figure 8.6) (4.MD.3).

MP6
Precision

Figure 8.6 Examples of Area and Perimeter Problems

1. You are going to make a vegetable garden and enclose it in a fence. What measurements will you want to take. Why?

2. Arlo made a small herb garden. It is 4 ft. wide and has an area of 52 square feet. What is the perimeter of this garden? What other perimeters could a garden with this area have?

3. Corrine made this drawing to solve two problems about a garden. She found the correct answers to be 20 square feet and 34 feet. For each answer, write a problem Corrine might have solved.

8 ft.	2 ft.	3 ft.	
tomatoes	herbs	carrots	4 ft.

Angles

The concepts and language associated with angles are not part of most students' everyday experiences. Coaches might refer to angles, but rarely to specific measures. There are few, if any, opportunities for students to use or to see adults use protractors outside of school. So while young students are able to count the number of angles in shapes and perhaps be aware of their "pointiness," everyday experiences with angles and their measure are limited. In school, students' exposure to angles is usually restricted to static angles, that is, angles drawn on a page or viewed on a face of an object. Given this inadequate exposure, it is no wonder that students rarely understand basic concepts of angles.

An angle is formed when two rays extend from a common point *P*. The point is the vertex of the angle. How far the rays are spread apart determines the size of the angle (Figure 8.7). Dynamic models of angles are available online, which allow users to move one of the rays to form narrower or wider angles. Using such visual models can help learners recognize angles as turns or rotations of one of the two rays. Students can also use two strips of heavy stock paper connected with a brad to form a variety of angles (4.MD.5).

Figure 8.7 Angles as Rotations

Angle CPD is larger than Angle APB; it has a wider rotation.

Students learn about angles and particular types of angles as they explore attributes of shapes. In the fourth-grade geometry domain, students draw angles and classify shapes according to whether or not they have certain types of angles. Angles are also part of the measurement domain at this level. As you know, there are 360 degrees in a circle. If you stood in one spot and turned completely around, you would have turned that many degrees. Angles are measured in degrees, with each degree being $\frac{1}{360}$ of a circle. As those units are so small, it would be extremely difficult to cut up a circle into 360 pieces so that students could use multiple copies of one-degree wedges to measure angles. Thus, tools are needed to measure angles and protractors are used to both measure and to create angles of given sizes. As with rulers, students need specific instruction on how to use a protractor, made more challenging by its small numbers and need for proper alignment and interpretation (4.MD.5a; 4.MD.5b; 4.MD.6). As with other measures, students are expected to recognize that angle measures are additive and to solve problems related to such measures (4.MD.7). It is important that students have many opportunities to compare angles before measuring and to develop a sense of how angles of 30, 45, 60, and 90 degrees look. Such referents will help students to check their angle measures when using their protractors and, over time, develop understanding that lessens common misconceptions.

Conceptual Challenge

The Common Core Standards Writing Team (2012b) identifies the following misconceptions related to angle measures:

☞ A right angle is an angle that points to the right.

☞ Two right angles in different positions do not have the same measures.

☞ All angles formed by slanted rays measure 45 degrees.

- ✏ Protractors are placed with their base parallel to the edge of the paper, regardless of the position of the angle.

- ✏ Angles with longer rays are greater than those with shorter ones.

It is important to include such examples (e.g., left-facing right angles) within tasks and representations.

Volume

As with area and perimeter, volume is often confused with surface area. It can be beneficial to introduce closely related, often confused concepts at different times. The Common Core does this by making volume a critical area of study in grade five and introducing surface area in grade six. The related standards are similar to that of all attributes in that they begin with understanding what volume is and then establish cubic units as the way to measure it. The notion of items holding more or less is common to even young students, but measuring volume is not (5.MD.3; 5.MD.3a; 5.MD.3b; 5.MD.4).

Students can begin to measure using multiple cubic units such as one-inch or one-centimeter cubes. As with area, it is the counting process that helps students to connect finding volume to multiplication and addition, and eventually, to use of formulas. At this level, the goal is to use formulas to find the volume of right rectangular prisms with whole-number lengths. As the multiplication of the three dimensions can be done in any order, the associative property of multiplication is reinforced. Students should recognize and be able to explain that they can count the cubic units in one layer and then multiply by the number of layers to find the area, which leads to the formula $V = b \times h$. Alternatively, they can multiply to find the number of cubic units in one layer and then multiply by the height, leading to the formula $V = l \times w \times h$. It is key that students have a visual model of the relationships among two of the length measures, the area associated with those dimensions, and the volume when several rows of that layer are combined (Figure 8.8). Finally, students recognize volume as additive and use this property to find areas of shapes composed of two right rectangular prisms (5.MD.5; 5.MD.5a; 5.MD.5b; 5.MD.5c).

Figure 8.8 Visual Model of Formula for the Volume of a Right Rectangular Prism

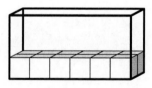

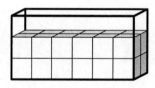

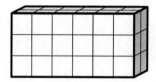

The width and length tell us the area of the base.

The area tells us the number of cubic units in the first layer.

The height tells us how many layers there are.

Liquid Volume and Weight/Mass

Given the many standards associated with geometric measures of length, area, volume, and angle, it may surprise you to learn that there is only one standard specific to liquid volume and mass and it is limited to the metric units of grams, kilograms, and liters (3.MD.2). Liquid volume can confuse students as the common image is one of watching liquid being poured into a container, with the height of the liquid in that container rising. The focus on height can suggest a one-dimensional measure. Emphasize that the liquid is filling the whole container and thus has three dimensions.

It is unlikely that elementary classrooms would have scales accurate to the nearest gram, but students can learn common referents such as the mass of a nickel is 5 grams and product labels can be brought to class or explored within store flyers. Students can also explore these measures in relation to areas of interest by finding, for example, the mass of different balls used in sports or how much water is needed for an aquarium.

This third-grade standard is later supported in grade four and grade five standards related to solving problems and conversions (4.MD.2). Those standards also include ounces and pounds, and conversions among liquid volumes suggest cups, pints, quarts, and gallons, though these units are never mentioned explicitly. Such problems can include fractional or decimal numbers. Scale problems such as the one shown in Figure 8.9 provide an excellent model for equality as well as highlight the need to persevere in solving problems.

MP1
Make Sense

Figure 8.9 Sample Balance Scale Problem

Blocks with the same size and shape have the same mass.

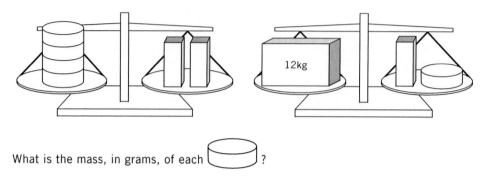

What is the mass, in grams, of each ⬭ ?

"Fit the Unit" problems can also provide an interesting format for this standard as well as estimation expectations in third grade and the notion of relative size suggested in grade four (4.MD.1). These problems also can be written with an emphasis on real-world data. An example of such a problem is provided in Figure 8.10.

Figure 8.10 Sample Fit the Unit Problem

years	millimeters	kilograms	meters	centimeters	minutes

Sydney likes to read about leatherback sea turtles, the largest of the sea turtles. These turtles are usually about 2 _____ long and weigh about 590 _____. When they hatch, they are only about 65 _____ long or between 6 and 7 _____ long. Sea turtles can stay underwater for up to 35 _____ and live for about 45 _____.

(Used with permission from *50 Leveled Math Problems, Level 4, Shell Education* 2012)

Time and Money

Time and money are not identified as critical areas within the Common Core, yet they are clearly important areas of mathematical literacy. So while not essential to further mathematical study, these topics are important to students' lives and can reinforce learning in other domains.

Time

Time is unique to the measures considered at the K–2 levels as the units cannot be represented with physical objects. Also, both adults and children experience durations of time differently under various circumstances. For example, when you are very hungry and waiting for a server to take your order, the wait may feel much longer than that same period of time spent eating your food once it arrives. Though not mentioned in the standards until grade four, first- and second-grade students should also gain a sense of the relative sizes of the time units they are using. You can have students do the following:

- Close their eyes until they think a minute has passed. Repeat so that students have the opportunity to refine their estimates.

- Experiment to find how many times they can write their first name, do a jumping jack, or take baby steps in one minute.

- Respond to questions such as *Do you think it will take you 3 minutes or 3 hours to brush your teeth? What might take 2 hours?*

Within the standards, time is limited to reading clocks and determining intervals of time. Time related to calendars is not included. According to the National Research Council (2009), "…using the calendar does not emphasize foundational mathematics." Teachers of younger students, who have long included calendar activities in their morning meetings, might continue to do so, but this ritual should not be thought of as significant mathematics instruction, which should encourage grouping by tens at these grade levels, not sevens. Units such as days, weeks, months, and years could be included in standards that emphasize solving problems, learning the multiplication table for seven, or converting units.

Telling time is introduced in first grade with measurement to the hour and half-hour, using both analog (face) and digital clocks (1.MD.3). Telling and writing time are relatively simple tasks with a digital clock; students learn to read or write what they see. The only issue would be the writing of the colon. Some students initially write only one dot, perhaps because they are more familiar with periods. Analog clocks have become less and less prevalent and are more challenging to read. Yet it is use of an analog clock that helps students to relate times to one another. Visually, on an analog clock, students can recognize that 9:57 is very close to 10:00 without knowing how to tell time to the minute or that there are 60 minutes in an hour.

In second grade time is measured to the nearest five-minute interval and includes use of a.m. and p.m. Skip-counting by fives is important here and provides support for multiplication in grade 3.

You can make connections to literature to reinforce a.m. or p.m. by asking questions such as *Do you think this part of the story is happening during the a.m. or p.m.?* It is important not to simplify these labels to day and night. While day and night might make sense when comparing 9:00 a.m. to 9:00 p.m., this over-simplification makes differentiating noon and midnight even more challenging as we experience noon as day (though it is p.m.) and midnight as night (though it is a.m.). One teacher sets an alarm to ring for one week at noon. Each day she announces, "It's now p.m." (2.MD.7).

In grade three, students are expected to tell time to the nearest minute and to measure intervals of time or elapsed time (3.MD.1). With an analog clock, students can better visualize time intervals and count them. It may help students to recognize that an analog clock can be thought of as a number line in a circular formation. Most problematic are intervals that include noon or midnight, which require particular attention, as the number sequence begins again at one. Empty number lines, suggested in the standard, are also useful. Students tend to include a time within the 12:00 hour on such a line, making such time intervals less problematic (Dixon 2008). As with all open number lines (lines without numbers), students can choose the "jumps" or intervals to mark in ways that make the most sense. Consider the following task and representations shown in Figure 8.11. Such models can also be used to find beginning (when given interval and end time) and ending times (when given beginning time and interval).

Figure 8.11 Use of Open Number Lines to Determine Time Intervals

Today, the third-grade class has P.E. at 9:20 and a school-wide meeting at 2:17. How much time after gym begins is the meeting supposed to start?

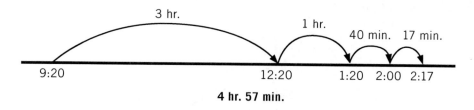

4 hr. 57 min.

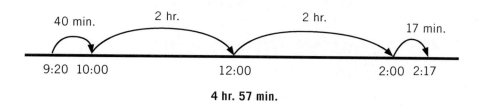

4 hr. 57 min.

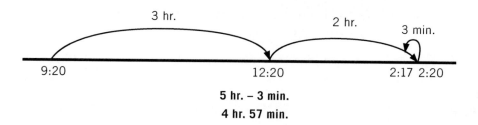

5 hr. – 3 min.
4 hr. 57 min.

Money

There is only one measurement standard specific to money, most likely because, although it involves standard units, we don't apply the measurement process to money; we count it, convert among units, and solve problems with it. These skills are the focus of the grade two standard (2.MD.8). Students often find problems related to money motivating, and money is a clear connection to the usefulness of mathematics in the real world. As such, it makes sense to include money-related problems within number-focused standards when appropriate. Problems related to this standard will require students to find the total value of collections of coins. Examples include:

✏ I have

I spend 19 cents. How much money do I have left?

✏ I have four coins of the same value. How much could these coins be worth?

✏ Janis has 2 dimes and 6 nickels. Can she use these coins to buy something for 59¢?

✏ I have 6 coins in my piggy bank. I have 80 cents in my piggy bank. What coins do I have?

Data

Data provide real-world contexts for mathematical analyses. Though there are only a total of eight standards focused on data within the K–5 levels, once students are familiar with data displays, they can be included in problems throughout the curriculum and support the idea that mathematics is useful. The standards focus on two types of data: categorical data that results from organizing information in categories and measurement data generated from actual measures.

Categorical Data

Standards related to categorical data most often connect to standards within the Operations and Algebraic Thinking domain. In kindergarten, students classify objects into given categories such as *living* and *nonliving; lives on land* and *lives in the water;* or *rolls* or *doesn't roll.* Once items are classified, students can count the number in each category as well as compare those numbers (K.MD.3). In first grade, this expectation is extended to up to three categories, and students respond to questions about the number in each category and how many more (or less) there are in one category compared to another (1.MD.4). Students also organize and represent such data, though no clear expectations are given for the format such a representation should take. This openness allows students to develop representations that are meaningful to them. This student has taken a handful of shapes from a bucket, sorted them, and recorded the number of each shape (Figure 8.12).

Figure 8.12 Student Example of Sorting

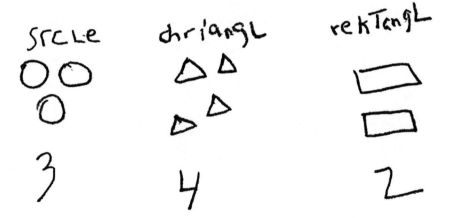

In second grade, students generate data sets with up to four categories and represent the data in picture graphs and bar graphs. They then solve one-step put-together, take-apart, and compare problems related to the data. Be sure to emphasize how organizing the data makes it easier to compare the number in each category. Bar graphs can be horizontal or vertical and the categories can be given in any order, though many graphs list categories alphabetically. Draw students' attention to the two axes; one names the categories and the other is a number line segment that indicates the count. Some students may find it difficult to read back (or down) from the top (or end) of the bar to the scale. Making bar graphs on grid paper can help students identify the correct number aligned to each bar. Note that generating data is not the same as taking a survey.

While surveys are one way of generating data, they are not given any explicit attention in the standards. Students also can be given data to categorize and graph and solve word problems that require use of data presented in a picture graph or bar graph. As students' knowledge of shapes progresses, they can be asked questions about data that require them to apply that knowledge. Figure 8.13 shows an example of a task for this level (2.MD.10).

Figure 8.13 Sample Grade Two Categorical Data Task

Show the number of each shape on the graph.

circles	
hexagons	
quadrilaterals	
triangles	

How many shapes are not quadrilaterals? _____

In third grade, students represent data in several categories and solve one- and two-step addition and subtraction problems related to the data. At this level, data is represented in scaled picture graphs or bar graphs, connecting to students' developing multiplication skills. Figure 8.14 provides a sample task. Generating the data is not part of the standard, but that does not mean that these students should not also have the opportunity to collect such data. Doing so often increases their engagement (3.MD.3).

Figure 8.14 Sample Grade Three Categorical Data Task

Third Graders Like to Read!	
Type	**Chosen**
Biography	📖 📖 📖 📖
Fiction	📖 📖 📖 📖 📖 📖 📖 📖 📖 📖
Graphic Novels	📖 📖 📖 📖 📖
Joke	📖 📖
Sports	📖 📖 📖 📖 📖 📖 📖

Each 📖 stands for 4 books

All of the third graders at the Blaine Elementary School were asked the type of book they liked best. The graph shows how many students chose each type. How many more students chose fiction than joke books?

Show two ways to find your answer.

Measurement Data

Standards involving measurement data include opportunities for students to measure and reinforce concepts related to number lines. In grade two students generate measurement data related to length, measured to the nearest whole unit (2.MD.9). They represent the measures on a line plot. A line plot shows numbers spaced appropriately to show their relative size.

One way for students to practice measurement is by using measurement centers. One center may include six one-inch-wide cardboard strips of different lengths for students to measure. Students measure each strip and show the data on a line plot, which might look like the one shown in Figure 8.15. If the X's on a line plot are of varying heights, visual comparisons may be inaccurate. Using lined paper makes it more likely that X's will be placed in a way that enables accurate comparisons.

Figure 8.15 Sample of Line Plot for Measures of Cardboard Strips

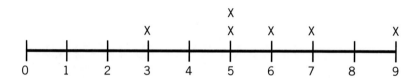

In grade three, expectations extend to measuring to the nearest half and quarter-inch, which supports identifying fractions on a number line (3.MD.4). Students often find measuring to a fractional part of an inch quite challenging. It is important to develop this skill as students learn about fractions. Just as younger students benefit from making rulers showing inches, these students should have the opportunity to construct a ruler showing half and quarter-inches. This process will help them gain a deeper understanding about both fractions and how to use a ruler.

Once some understanding of fractional parts of a ruler exists, students can measure to generate data for line plots.

Consider this classroom scenario as an example. In one classroom, third-grade students are measuring the distance around their wrists to the nearest quarter-inch. Rulers, string, and measuring tapes are available so that students will reflect on the tools they use. As a class, the students talk about the way they measured and why they did so. Then the teacher asks for six volunteers to share their measures. Responses are recorded in a list on the white board as the measures are given. The teacher draws an open number line and says, "We are going to show these lengths on a graph, a line plot. What numbers should we put on the line?"

MP5
Tools

A few comments are made about needing fractions and then Lanie says, "All of the measures are between 4 inches and 6 inches, so let's use those numbers and then add the numbers between." Her suggestion is supported by others and so the teacher writes these three numbers, evenly spaced, with room for more numbers to be included. The teacher then models placing one of the measures, $5\frac{1}{2}$ inches, on the line by saying, "I know this measure is between 5 and 6 inches. I am going to mark the point right in the middle to show the two parts needed to make the one whole between five and six. Now, I write $5\frac{1}{2}$ below the line, and an X above the line to show this one measure." Following this process, the teacher asks students to make their own line plot showing these six measures.

Standards in grade four and grade five do not require students to generate data, but rather, to make line plots of given data and solve problems related to the information. Students at both grades measure to the nearest one-eighth of an inch and solve problems about the measures. In fourth grade, such problems are limited to addition and subtraction, while in fifth grade, multiplication and division examples, aligned with expectations with the Number and Operations—Fractions, are included (4.MD.4; 5.MD.2). The fifth-grade standard also includes a new idea, that of redistributing data shown on a line plot so that all show an equal amount. So, for example, if three measures of liquid were shown, $2\frac{1}{2}$ cups, 3 cups, and $3\frac{1}{2}$ cups, pouring $\frac{1}{2}$ cup of liquid from the cup holding the most to the cup holding the least results in each container holding 3 cups. The notion of redistributing data this way is one way to find the mean average, considered in the sixth grade. In fifth grade, students only consider the leveling process, without attaching it to the concept of mean.

Honoring Individual Differences

Connecting to students' interests is an important way to differentiate instruction and provide motivation (Tomlinson and Imbeau 2010). Students come to school with all kinds of preferences about what they like. Many students also develop keen interests in school in relation to particular subject areas. You can differentiate data instruction by encouraging students to find data sets that match their interests or by providing such data yourself. You can set up data learning centers focused on such topics as sports, music, particular topics in social studies such as the civil rights movement, or books by a particular author such as Eric Carle or J. K. Rowling. Have students complete an interest survey at the beginning of the year and also ask parents about their children's interests. As interests change over time, you may wish to repeat the survey midyear or return the original responses for students to update.

Assessment

Formative assessment is always important, but may have a particular value in relation to measurement. Students are likely to have very different levels of measurement experience outside of school, of which you are not likely aware. "Do Now" tasks at the beginning of a lesson can provide quick formative assessment information that can inform your instruction. Examples of such questions/statements include:

- Draw an object for each word: tall, short, heavy, light.
- Each box weighs the same. What might be in each box on the scale?
- What are three length measures you would use a tape measure to find? Why would you choose this tool?
- What is something in our classroom that measures about 8 cubic feet? Why do you think so?
- What different things could you measure about a cup of cocoa? What unit would you use for each measure?
- How many times bigger is a square foot than a square inch?
- How tall do you think our classroom door is? Why do you think so?

Length, area, and volume all progress in a similar manner. A general checklist can be used for organizing data about students' understanding. Consider the form in Figure 8.16 and in Appendix A as a model focusing on those items that match the level of your students.

Figure 8.16 Measurement Assessment Checklist

Student Name: _____Attribute: _____

Measurement Assessment Checklist

The student can:

❏ identify this attribute of an object

❏ identify the standard unit to measure this attribute (unit, square unit, or cubic unit)

❏ use multiple copies of same-sized units to measure this attribute

❏ use one copy of a unit to measure this attribute

❏ identify appropriate tools to use to measure this attribute

❏ identify appropriate units to use when measuring this attribute of various sized objects

❏ use tools to measure this object

❏ use formulas to measure this attribute (if appropriate)

❏ recognize the relative sizes of units

❏ estimate the measure of a particular item

❏ solve problems involving this attribute

❏ convert from larger to smaller standard units of this attribute within the same system

❏ convert from smaller to larger standard units of this attribute within the same system

Standardized tests will emphasize the critical area of measurement at grades 3–5, but because this domain connects with so many other domains, do not assume for example, that grade five measurement items will only focus on volume. Though volume will certainly be included, other measurement concepts may be as well. For example, the task below incorporates the expectation for finding the area of a rectangle with that of multiplying fractions.

Consider this example:

Janetta and Wayne are making scenery for the school play. Janetta cut a piece of heavy cardboard that was $\frac{1}{2}$ yd. long and $\frac{2}{3}$ yard wide. Wayne cut a piece of heavy cardboard that was $\frac{1}{3}$ yard long and $\frac{3}{4}$ foot wide. Whose piece of cardboard had the greater area? Explain how you know.

Voice from the Classroom

There are so many skills related to measurement that I learned easily because they were part of my everyday life. It was not unusual for one of my parents to send me to the corner store to pick up something they needed and they expected me to make sure I got the correct change. My father had a woodworking shop and often made things for our house or toys for me and my sister. As we got older, we helped him make things for our younger nieces and nephews. My mother always had some sort of craft or baking project going and she usually involved us in some way. Measurement was a daily activity in our house.

I know that's not the way my children are growing up. There are some special times of year, near holidays, when some baking and other projects occur, but certainly not on a regular basis. The same seems to be true of my students. As a result, measurement seems very unfamiliar to them. I teach second grade and I see students make all kinds of errors when they use a ruler. For example, some of them measure from the twelve, rather than the zero and still think it's okay to just read the number where the object ends. I'm so glad we no longer require these young students to measure to the nearest half-inch.

Last year we made a class book report quilt. Everyone made a square with something from their favorite book or character. I gave each student an eight-inch square and told them that they could decorate it with other pieces of fabric, but that first they had to make a plan and that plan had to include measures. The students were much more interested in measuring correctly when it came to their fabric. They knew they wouldn't get a second chance, if they cut a piece incorrectly. This year I think we'll make books about time and have them measure the large paper and where to fold it. I know it is these real-world measurement opportunities that have the greatest impact on their conceptual understanding.

—Second-Grade Teacher

Let's Think and Discuss

1. What measurement misconceptions have you found to be common among your students?

2. What projects in other subject areas could include specific measurement directions? What other ways might you link standards in this domain with other subjects?

3. Do you think the teacher who modeled creating a line plot with fractions modeled too little, too much, or just right? Why?

Chapter 9

Geometry

Snapshot

A third-grade teacher is leading her students in a game of "What's My Shape Rule?" The students are sitting in a circle on the rug; there is a collection of shapes in front of the teacher. She takes two of the shapes and places them in one group and then two different shapes that she places in another group. She tells students, "I am asking myself a question each time I place a shape. I am saying *Is this an example of my shape rule, yes or no?* Talk with your neighbor about what you think my shape rule might be."

Cathleen and John suggest that the shape rule is triangle. The teacher records this idea on a piece of chart paper and asks them to point to the shapes that fit this rule. They point to the shapes in the group on the right and the teacher asks the other students to put their thumbs up if they agree that triangles is the shape rule and thumbs down if they disagree.

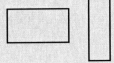 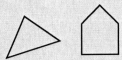

More students put their thumbs down than up, but there are some of both. Luther puts his thumb sideways, explaining that he is unsure. Pedro, who held his thumb down, says, "The last one on the right is not a triangle. That can't be the rule." To make sure the other students understand what Pedro is saying, the teacher points to that shape and says, "So you do not think this shape is a triangle." Pedro nods and then John explains that the top of it is a triangle. The teacher invites John to come up to the shape to show what he means and after he does so, the class decides to change the shape rule to *is a triangle or has a triangle part*. The teacher changes the recording of the rule on the chart.

When asked if there were any other ideas, Mia and Chang offer the shape rule *rectangles,* while pointing to the group on the left. The teacher records this new idea and finds that nearly all of the students support it. She then adds another shape to each group. Several students look perplexed and incredulously ask, "What?" The teacher asks them to talk with a neighbor about why they are surprised and what the shape rule might be.

At this point, the students agree that the rule cannot be "rectangles"; some think that "is or has a triangle part" is still a possibility and some do not. The teacher adds another four shapes, one at a time.

There is a conversational buzz as each shape is added. The teacher smiles as she hears, "I got it, oh, wait," more than once. Juno announces that she doesn't think there is a rule since the shapes are all so different and several others agree with her. Finally, Jazz says, "I've finally got it." The teacher holds her finger to her lips to keep Jazz from stating the rule. Instead, she shows Jazz a shape and asks where to place it. The teacher then shows a new shape and asks, "Can someone else tell me where this shape should be placed?" This continues until many of the students are smiling as they think they know the rule. She then gives Jazz the opportunity to tell the shape rule *has four sides*. Marley adds, "Oh they're all quadrilaterals." The teacher recognizes that many of her students have forgotten this term. She writes it on the chart paper and has the students practice saying it several times.

The teacher knows that the name for quadrilaterals is introduced in second grade, but knowing that four-sided geometric shapes have this name and recognizing that these shapes that look so different yet share a characteristic is quite different. She knows that if she had shown them several shapes, the students might have sorted them according to number of sides. In fact, this is a common way students sort shapes, but that's different than struggling a bit to notice a common feature. She thinks the students' success with that challenge will help them to remember that four-sided geometric shapes are called quadrilaterals and to recognize that a shape can be a quadrilateral and also, for example, a rectangle.

Big Picture

Geology, geography, geometry, and geode all begin with *geo,* which means earth. Since shapes and space are all around us, geometry clearly connects the mathematics curriculum with the real world. Geometry allows us to visualize other mathematical topics, for example, an area model of multiplication, fractions as parts of wholes, and the measurement of length, area, and volume. It also connects with other subjects such as architecture and engineering. Based on its presence in our lives, it would make sense to predict that students would do particularly well on tests of their geometric knowledge. Unfortunately, students in the United States have performed lower in geometry on international standardized mathematics tests than in any other area according to the Trends in Mathematics and Science Study (TIMSS) (Mullis, Martin, and Foy 2008).

How might Common Core standards, along with the opportunity to reflect on our teaching, develop greater geometric proficiency in our students? The Common Core has identified geometry as a critical area at each of the K–4 levels. It embraces a clear model for the development of geometric thinking and it does not have a traditional narrow view of geometry.

Pierre van Hiele and Dina van Hiele-Geldof developed a model for the development of geometric thinking that influences geometry curriculum worldwide (Van de Walle, Karp, and Bay-Williams 2013). Research is generally in support of the theory (Battista 2007). The van Hiele model identifies levels of geometric thinking. No ages are attached to the levels, and according to Pierre van Hiele (1999), development is more dependent on instructional activities than age. He describes three levels of thinking (visual, descriptive, and informal deductive) necessary before the formal deductive reasoning required in traditional geometry courses at the high school level:

☞ At the **visual** level, learners rely on nonverbal thinking. A circle is a circle because it looks like one and students may include some oval shapes within the categories.

☞ At the **descriptive** level, learners can identify shapes according to their properties. Language is used to describe shapes, and their properties are used to form classes of shapes. As a result, a square is a square because it has four right angles and four sides of equal length.

☞ At the **informal deductive** level, students understand relationships between classes of shapes. Students at this level can explain why all squares are rectangles and make conclusions such as *if it is a rectangle, then it is a quadrilateral.*

As you read this chapter, note the focus the standards give to students attending to the attributes and properties of shapes and to reasoning about them.

In the United States, geometry at the K–5 levels has often focused on the learning of vocabulary (Van de Walle, Karp, and Bay-Williams 2013). Attention must be given to the full range of geometric content goals. Yet there are many terms associated with geometry, and the explicit teaching of vocabulary is essential for comprehensible input. When possible, however, vocabulary should be introduced and reviewed in a manner similar to that within the opening vignette of this chapter; that is, it should be grounded in conceptual development. Figure 9.1 summarizes new terms stated within the standards at each level. Note that this list is not inclusive; in fact, one would expect parallelograms to be included in our curriculum, regardless of whether or not it is explicitly specified in this domain.

Honoring Individual Differences

A common suggestion for making content more accessible to all learners and especially English Language Learners, struggling readers, and students with language-related learning disabilities is to preview new vocabulary. Yet, Bay-Williams, Livers, and Livers (2009) warn that at times "...previewing the content can inadvertently lower the level of cognitive demand by showing students what they would otherwise be figuring out during the lesson" (240). Though new terms must be taught and terms previously introduced must be reviewed, we need to think carefully about when and how we do so. Thinking about the following questions can help you to decide when in a lesson terms should be previewed or reviewed.

- Is this a term related to the context of the problem that students need to know to understand the problem and discuss the mathematical situation? (preview)

- Is this term related to the mathematics of the problem that students need to know to access the new mathematical content of the lesson? (preview)

- Will previewing or reviewing the vocabulary *tell* the mathematics of the lesson, rather than *allow* it to be conceptually developed? (review after the concept is explored)

Figure 9.1 Geometry Vocabulary Specified at Grades K–5

Grade	Terms
K	above, below, behind, beside, in front of, next to flat shape, solid shape corners, sides rectangle, triangle
Grade 1	closed square, trapezoid, cube, half-circle, quarter-circle cube, right-rectangular prism, right circular cone, right circular cylinders (These names of three-dimensional shapes are listed, but with a footnote that indicates students do not need to learn formal names.)
Grade 2	quadrilateral, pentagon, cubes faces, angles rows, columns
Grade 3	rhombus
Grade 4	right triangle line, line segment, point, ray acute angle, obtuse angle, right angle parallel lines, perpendicular lines line of symmetry
Grade 5	origin, x-coordinate, y-coordinate, x-axis, y-axis

In the progressions document on geometry, the Common Core State Standards Writing Team (2012c) organizes the key ideas of elementary geometry into three categories:

1. Shapes, components, properties, and categorization

2. Composing and decomposing shapes

3. Spatial structuring and spatial relations

The discussion of the standards will be organized by these categories in the next section of the chapter.

Attributes and Properties of Shapes

The standards related to this category focus on students' growing understanding of how shapes are identified and categorized. At each grade level, a new layer of understanding is added, allowing students to recognize classes of shapes and develop more precise language to describe shapes and their properties. Young learners, relying on visual thinking, often have limited exposure to geometric shapes in different forms and positions and, as a result, may misidentify shapes. For example, students may name shapes as triangles that are not quite closed or whose sides are not quite straight. Similarly, triangles in less familiar positions or with uncommon angles may not be seen as triangles or may be identified as *sort of triangles* or *upside down triangles* (Dacey and Eston 2002). Examples of misidentified figures are shown in Figure 9.2. Note that even equilateral and isosceles triangles may not be recognized when in a nontraditional orientation. With explicit instruction and exposure to a variety of examples of shapes, young students can learn to recognize various examples of shapes (Sarama and Clements 2009).

MP6 Precision

MP7 Structure

Figure 9.2 Potential Errors of Visual Identification of Triangles

Examples that might be falsely identified as triangles

Examples that might not be recognized as triangles

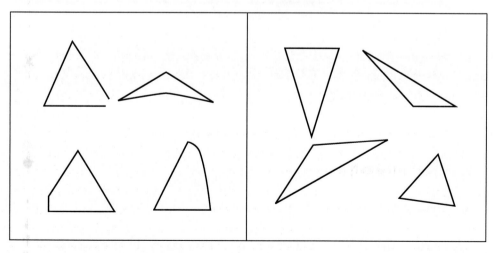

Kindergartners are expected to identify and describe shapes, which complements the standards within the measurement and data domain, where students learn to categorize objects by their attributes. Notably, the standards explicitly state the expectations that students identify shapes regardless of their position (K.G.2; K.G.4). Kindergarten students also model shapes and draw them. Over time, as students use sticks and clay balls, for example, to build rectangles, they learn that they need three clay balls and three sticks to make a triangle (K.G.5). Attention is given to both two-dimensional and three-dimensional shapes with informal language such as flat and solid (K.G.3). Sorting activities focus students' attention to similarities and differences but should be accompanied by explicit discussions and teacher modeling, as appropriate.

Honoring Individual Differences

Consider cultural relevancy when thinking about having students make connections to real-world examples of shapes. Too often traditional examples might show a silo as an example of a cylinder. To students unfamiliar with farms, this example does not provide a real-world connection with a mathematical model. You might wish to highlight picture books in your classroom library, or take out picture books from a library that highlight various parts of the United States or the world. Students are more likely to attend to pictures of architecture, pottery, fabric, and so forth, from a meaningful geographical location.

In first grade, students focus more closely on the attributes of geometric shapes, distinguishing between those that define a class of shapes, such as number of sides, from those that do not, such as size (1.G.1). In second grade, identification of shapes is extended to the ability to draw shapes having a specified number of angles or faces, and the term *quadrilateral* is introduced (2.G.1). Roberts (2007) describes an activity she uses to focus students' attention on the defining properties of shapes. She asks them to describe a square so she can draw it. When given the description *It has four sides,* she draws a nonclosed shape. This process continues until a complete set of necessary conditions are provided.

Sarama and Clements (2003) argue for a wide variety of teaching strategies, such as students using their bodies, manipulatives, and drawings. They are also strong proponents of the inclusion of computer technology. Many apps, websites, and dynamic software programs allow students to manipulate shapes and should be included in lessons. Some other activities at the primary level include the following:

✏ Provide a wide selection of two-dimensional and three-dimensional shapes and name a characteristic such as *has eight corners.* Have students sort the shapes based on those that do and do not have that characteristic.

✏ Organize a shape hunt with students looking for specified shapes. Students can find examples of the shapes in classroom objects as well as in picture books. You might also have magazines available so that students could find shapes in pictures of fabrics, tiles, and so forth.

MP6
Precision

✏ Have students complete shape sheets, which help students to distinguish shapes as well as develop more precise descriptions of them:

Figure 9.3 Shape Sheets

Name:	My Shape:
Drawings of my shape:	Drawings of shapes that are not my shape:
Where I see the shape in the world:	Words to tell how my shape looks:

244

- Have students sit on opposite sides of a divider with the same set of shape cards or three-dimensional shapes available to each of them. One student describes one of the shapes and the other student tries to identify it.

- Provide mini-marshmallows and toothpicks for students to use to build two- and three-dimensional shapes.

In grades 3–5, students explore relationships among classes of shapes and thus move to the informal deductive level of geometric thinking. In third grade, students build on the understanding of quadrilaterals, recognizing that this class of shapes represents a larger category than that of, for example, rectangles. They are also able to draw examples of quadrilaterals that are not rhombuses, rectangles, or squares (3.G.1). The classification of shapes continues in fourth grade with the introduction of angles, perpendicular and parallel lines, and symmetry. These characteristics allow for additional distinctions among shapes and the identification, for example, of subcategories of triangles according to whether they have a right angle, an obtuse angle, or if all of their angles are acute. There is also the opportunity to compare the sides of shapes such as parallelograms, trapezoids, rectangles, squares, and regular hexagons in relation to parallel and perpendicular sides (4.G.1; 4.G.2; 4.G.3). As students make and test conjectures about the properties of shapes, they are making sense of geometric problems and creating justifications for their thinking.

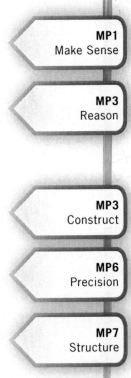

MP1
Make Sense

MP3
Reason

MP3
Construct

MP6
Precision

MP7
Structure

In fifth grade, the hierarchical relationships among shapes are established and students are expected to classify shapes within such a system (5.G.3; 5.G.4). A trapezoid has two definitions in the United States. They can be defined as having *exactly one set* of parallel sides or *at least* one set of parallel sides. The latter is more inclusive and allows for all parallelograms to be considered trapezoids, similar to the idea that all squares are rectangles. This definition is becoming more universally accepted. So, for example, students can recognize that all squares are rectangles and rhombuses, which are all rectangles, which are all parallelograms, which are all trapezoids, which are all quadrilaterals. Whew! Students can complete sentence starters such as *If a shape is a square then it is also a….* and justify their choices.

A variety of models can be used to represent these relationships. Note that the diagram in Figure 9.4 could allow you to start with a shape and ask questions about it as you worked your way through the figure. Or you could start at a lower level and recognize that the shape is also a member of all the classes above it.

Figure 9.4 Hierarchical Representation of Quadrilaterals

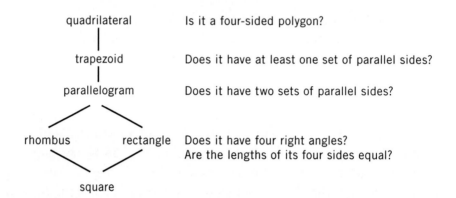

quadrilateral   Is it a four-sided polygon?

trapezoid   Does it have at least one set of parallel sides?

parallelogram   Does it have two sets of parallel sides?

rhombus   rectangle   Does it have four right angles?
                            Are the lengths of its four sides equal?

square

Conceptual Challenge

Though the hierarchical model develops over time, the idea that one could deduce that a shape is a member of one class *because* it is a member of another class is challenging. This type of thinking involves the transitive law of logic that states that if A has a relationship to B and B has that relationship to C, then A also has that relationship to C. If the relationship were *is taller than,* one can usually visualize three people, each one shorter than the person before, and the transitive law makes sense. Equality is another example of such a relationship. If 3 + 7 = 10 and 10 = 6 + 4, then 3 + 7 = 6 + 4. To understand, for example, that all rectangles are parallelograms and all parallelograms are trapezoids, so all rectangles are trapezoids, requires significant familiarity with the properties of each class of shapes. Do not underestimate the need for students to return, over time, to the conclusions one can draw from this schemata. Also, be sure to ask questions about shapes in the reverse, incorrect order, such as *Is every rectangle a square?*

Previously identified activities can be adapted to include new expectations and sorting activities are always appropriate. The National Council of Teachers of Mathematics (NCTM) "Illuminations Shape Sorter" activity provides a computer-based Guess My Rule game presented within a Venn diagram format. Use of such a diagram emphasizes the commonalities and differences among shapes. Students can also:

- Solve and create Shape Riddles such as *I am a parallelogram with right angles. What shape am I?*

✏️ Answer Detective Questions such as *If I am a rectangle, what other shape names do I have? If I have two lines of symmetry, am I a rectangle?*

✏️ Write a letter to a shape factory beginning with the sentence *Hello, I am a (name shape) and I'd like to tell you about myself and explain why I would be a valued employee.*

✏️ Make shapes on geoboards to explore such questions as *Can a triangle have two obtuse angles?*

✏️ Identify a picture of a geometric shape taped or pinned to their back. Each student asks his or her classmates questions about the properties of his or her shape until they think they know what his or her shape looks like. Questions such as *Am I a (name of shape)?* are not allowed. When students think they know their shapes, they draw the shape for a peer to confirm or contradict. Though size and position do not need to be exact, a drawing of a right triangle does not match a picture of an obtuse triangle.

✏️ Write directions for a robot to follow to "walk a shape" such as *Walk forward five steps, turn right 90 degrees, walk forward three steps, turn right 90 degrees, walk forward five steps, turn right 90 degrees, walk forward three steps.*

Composition and Decomposition of Shapes

As with numbers, shapes can be put together (composed) and taken apart (decomposed). When students combine and take apart shapes, they have the opportunity to learn more about the properties of his or her shapes. In kindergarten, students combine shapes (K.G.6). For example, two right isosceles triangles with sides of equal lengths, can be composed to make a larger triangle or a square (Figure 9.5). Students can sketch or trace such shapes once formed.

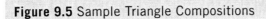

Figure 9.5 Sample Triangle Compositions

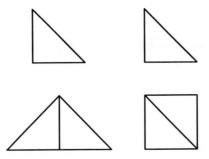

Building blocks at both kindergarten and first grade provide opportunities for students to compose with three-dimensional shapes. The moment when students have used all of the right triangular prisms and want one more to complete a building is often when they discover that two right triangular prisms can be put together to make a right rectangular prism (Figure 9.6).

Figure 9.6 Sample Prism Compositions

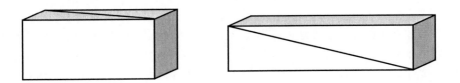

Pattern blocks intrigue most students, and both kindergarten and first grade students can explore different ways to make the hexagon, trapezoid, and larger rhombus using other blocks. They can also fill outlines with several pattern block shapes (Figure 9.7). Tangram puzzles provide similar experiences. You may wish to read aloud *Grandfather Tang's Story* to students, which includes beautiful illustrations as well as tangram-based representations of the different animals in the story (Tompert 1990). In small groups, where students can see the arrangements of the seven tangram pieces clearly, students can model the rearrangement with their own tangram sets.

Figure 9.7 Pattern Block Filling Examples

Write the number to tell you how many of each shape you need.
Draw lines to show the images.

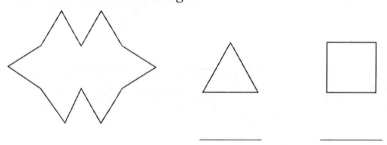

(Used with permission from 50 Leveled Problems, Level 1, Shell Education 2012)

In first grade, students also use a variety of two- and three-dimensional shapes to make new shapes. Most notable is the inclusion of half-circles and quarter-circles. Students use these shapes to compose new shapes, providing early work with the concept of iterating fractional parts to make wholes. Students also decompose or partition circles and rectangles into two and four equal parts, naming those parts halves, fourths, and quarters. Further, they are expected to understand that decomposing a shape into more shares means that those shares will be smaller, an idea essential to the later comparison of fractions with the same numerators (1.G.2; 1.G.3). In second grade, students also decompose shapes to form thirds, recognize that equal shares do not need to have the same shape, and recognize wholes as two halves, three thirds, or four fourths (2.G.3). The partitioning of wholes into equal shares is defined as equal areas in third grade and introduces the concept of a unit fraction (fraction with a numerator of one). Examples of these ideas are shown in Figure 9.8 (3.G.2).

Figure 9.8 Composition and Decomposition of Parts and Wholes

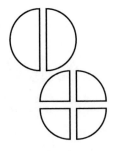  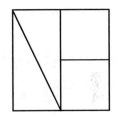

Students use multiple copies of half-circles and quarter- circles to make new shapes—circles.

Students could solve a problem such as: You want to cut the sandwich in half. How could you cut it? Is there another way?

Students can describe the whole as four-fourths and recognize that equal shares can have different shapes. The whole is four-fourths and the area of each part is one-fourth the area of the whole.

At second grade, students also partition rectangles into rows and columns of same-size squares, preparing them for the study of area in grade three (2.G.2). Partially completed diagrams can scaffold this thinking (Figure 9.9), but do not guarantee success. How the students count the total depends on their spatial structuring (see next section). In fifth grade, students partition right rectangular prisms within the measurement domain as they learn about volume.

Figure 9.9 Examples of Rectangles with Partially Completed Partitions

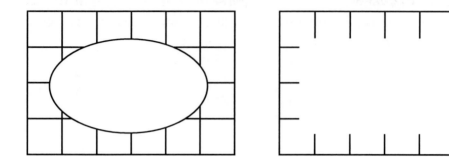

Spatial Structuring and Spatial Relations

Casey et al. (2008) state that "Spatial skills involve the ability to think and reason through the comparison, manipulation, and transformation of mental pictures" (270). Those mental pictures relate to the way in which we have structured space. Space structuring may be a new term to you. Battista (1999) wrote that, "Spatial structuring is the mental operation of constructing an organization or form for an object or set of objects" (171). Such structuring is interwoven with attributes and properties of shapes as well as the composition and decomposition of shapes. For example, when filling in puzzles, younger students might rely on trial and error. Later, they begin to mentally rotate a shape, or compare lengths or angles to determine if a shape is likely to fit. Similarly, a fourth-grade student might imagine a figure being folded onto itself to mentally test for a line of symmetry. To decompose a rectangle into square units, there must be a structure that can recognize rows and columns (Common Core Standards Writing Team 2012c). It is also related to location. Such structuring connects to non-geometric domains as well. Examples are given in Figure 9.10.

MP7
Structure

Figure 9.10 Examples of Connections Between Spatial Structuring and Other Domains

Domain	Connection
Counting and Cardinality	• Recognition of the number of objects, without counting, when they are arranged in a common form such as shown on number cubes or dominoes (subitizing).
Operations and Algebraic Thinking	• Use of visual models of properties of arithmetic • Area models of multiplication
Number and Operations in Base Ten	• Composition of 10 ones as 1 ten within base-ten models • Use of number lines
Number and Operations— Fractions	• Iteration of fractional parts to form wholes • Partition of wholes to form fractional parts
Measurement and Data	• Organization of rows and columns within an array • Organization of layers of cubic units within a right rectangular prism • Forming and iterating composite units • "Chunking" to estimate measures

Location Language

Some standards in the geometry domain focus on location, an aspect of spatial structuring and spatial relations. In kindergarten, the standards identify *above, below, beside, in front of, behind,* and *next to* as examples of words these students should use to describe relative positions. Other such terms include *on, in, top, middle, bottom, under, over, inside, outside, between, before, after, near,* and *far.*

Here is an example of a creative way to incorporate locational language in a purposeful way for students.

A kindergarten teacher was at a garage sale over the weekend where she was excited to find 25 pairs of number cubes for $5. She decided that she would buy them, give one pair to each student, and send home directions for games and activities they could explore at home. As the class was about to begin a mini-unit on spatial language, she decided to organize a scavenger hunt for her students that emphasized positional language. At morning meeting, she announces that there is a special message left for them. She says she is going to read it to them, but that everyone is to stay at the rug area. After confirming their understanding of this expectation, she unfolds a small piece of paper and reads *Look under the circle on the table.* The teacher then leads the students walking quietly and slowly around the tables in the room until they see that the table in the math area has a large circle on it. The teacher says, "I don't see a clue," and many students call out, "Look under it." The second clue is found and the hunt continues for three more rounds until the number cubes are discovered. The teacher decides to wait until the end of the day to tell students they will each get a pair. Now they will recap the hunt, going over the clues. As she reads them again, she represents them visually, for example, she draws a circle, with an arrow pointing under it. The next day they will play "Twenty Questions" with shape cards arranged in the pocket chart. To identify the shape, students will ask questions such as *Is it above the red circle?*

The scavenger hunt taps into one of the ways students develop spatial skills, that is, to think about the relationships among locations of objects and develop language to describe relative positions (K.G.1).

Coordinate System

In fifth grade, students learn about the coordinate system as a way to structure two-dimensional space. As integers are introduced in grade six, the grid is limited to the first quadrant. Students must view the grid as formed by intersecting lines, rather than square units. Students also become familiar with the terms *coordinate, origin, x-axis,* and *y-axis* and understand a coordinate as providing the distance from the origin on the *x*-axis, followed by the distance from the origin on the *y*-axis. Identification of coordinates can be the first focus. Games such as *Battleship*™ and *Connect Four*® (four in a row, column, or diagonal) can be played with coordinates used to identify locations. Students can create pictures relying on coordinates and make a set of directions for peers to follow [e.g., *Start at (5, 2) and draw a line to (4, 1)*]. Students can also solve problems such as shown in Figure 9.11 (5.G.1).

Figure 9.11 Sample Problem Involving the Location of Coordinates

Kaylee and Justin worked together to draw a parallelogram. How might they have completed the figure if they were given the two vertices (5, 8) and (10, 8)? Use a graph to show how they might prove their figure is a parallelogram.

Answer: (3, 4) and (8, 4) or (7, 4) and (12, 4)

(Used with permission from 50 Leveled Math Problems, Level 5 Shell Education 2012)

Conceptual Challenge

It seems as if there are some students who just can't seem to ever remember that the first number of the coordinate indicates the distance from the origin on the x-axis, and the second, the distance on the y-axis. Other students just seem to disregard this convention. Teachers sometimes react to this challenge by posting examples on word walls, writing reminders on problem sheets, or verbally reminding students of this information just before they begin to work independently on a related task. While well-meaning as these behaviors may be, they inadvertently let the students know that they do not need to remember this information; they will always be reminded. Instead, challenge students to create their own way to remember the order within the coordinate. For example, they might suggest that they think about the letters in the alphabet. They are quite familiar with the order and know that x comes before y. It is important that students take responsibility for their learning.

MP4
Model

MP5
Tools

Once students understand the location of coordinates, they can also use the first quadrant of the coordinate plane to solve problems. Use of the grid in this manner prepares students for middle school and can informally introduce students to a constant rate of change. In the process, students learn about a new mathematical tool for solving problems and model a real-world situation.

Two examples of problems are shown in Figure 9.12. In the example to the left, a graph is given to the students, while students must construct the graph in the second example (5.G.2).

Figure 9.12 Examples of Problems That Involve the Coordinate Grid for Their Solution

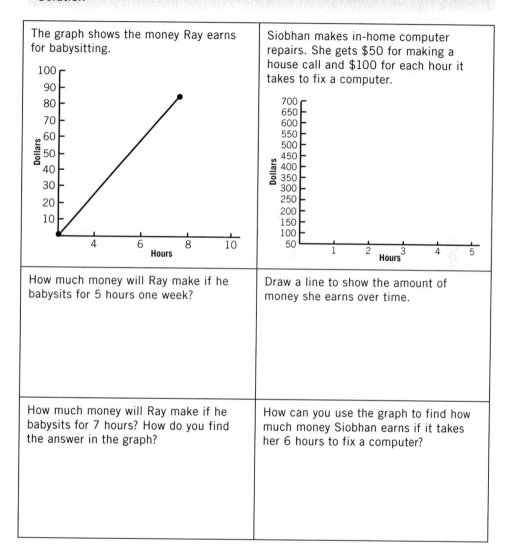

The graph shows the money Ray earns for babysitting.	Siobhan makes in-home computer repairs. She gets $50 for making a house call and $100 for each hour it takes to fix a computer.
How much money will Ray make if he babysits for 5 hours one week?	Draw a line to show the amount of money she earns over time.
How much money will Ray make if he babysits for 7 hours? How do you find the answer in the graph?	How can you use the graph to find how much money Siobhan earns if it takes her 6 hours to fix a computer?

Assessment note

One way to focus your formative assessment in this domain is to think about the van Hiele model of the development of geometric thought. The first three stages are relevant at this level. As you observe your students, you can note anecdotal evidence of their thinking. Figure 9.13 provides a possible recording sheet. It is also available in Appendix A.

Figure 9.13 Observation Form for Levels of Geometric Thinking

Name: _____ Date:_____

Note evidence of the different levels of thinking. Include information about the specific shapes the student was considering as you observed as well as whether or not shapes were in traditional or nontraditional positions.

1. The student identifies shapes visually.

2. The student describes attributes and properties of shapes and uses properties to identify shapes.

3. The student identifies categories of shapes, and relationships among them, based on the properties of shapes.

A task such as that shown in Figure 9.14 can be adapted for all grade levels. For younger students or others who would benefit, cut out shapes that students can feel and manipulate.

Figure 9.14 Sample Task that Focuses on Similarities and Differences Among Shapes

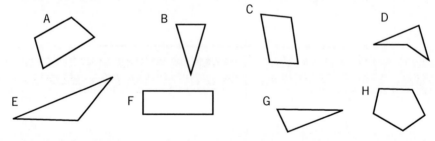

Make a shape rule.

Use the rule to put the shapes in groups.

Write your rule.

Use the letters to tell the shapes in each group.

Voice from the Classroom

When I was a student, I liked solving algebraic word problems, even the ones about when trains would meet. I thought of myself as a student who was good at math. Rather, I thought of myself that way until I took high school geometry. There were so many new terms to learn as well as axioms and postulates that had nothing to do with the properties of arithmetic that I knew so well. Suddenly, math wasn't math and I didn't feel smart anymore.

I remember some activities in elementary school that were fun. I loved tangram puzzles and creating tessellations, but I already had good spatial relations. It wasn't until I was in graduate school and learned about the van Hiele model of geometric thinking that I understood what had happened. I didn't have a sense of the hierarchical structure of shapes or the vocabulary associated with them. And without any experiences in informal deductive thinking, I was ill-prepared for the formal reasoning that was expected of me.

Over my years of teaching, I have filled in many of the holes in my geometric knowledge, but I only learned recently that I should call the diamonds in the pattern block set rhombuses. I know my school will focus on the number domains first, but I hope we will be given time to focus on geometry as well. I don't want my students to experience what I did.

—First-Grade Teacher

Let's Think and Discuss

1. What variety is there among the shape manipulatives in the classroom? What about the shapes depicted in diagrams and pictures or in books in the classroom library?

2. Think of some of your favorite geometry lessons. Which of the three key geometric ideas (shapes, components, properties, and categorization; composing and decomposing shapes; and spatial relationships) are highlighted in those lessons?

3. Think about the students who are stronger in geometric thinking than algebraic thinking. How could you tap into their visual strengths in non-geometric lessons?

Chapter 10

Engaging Parents and Supporting Your Own Work

 **Snapshot**

> Some teachers are meeting to discuss plans for the upcoming Back to School Curriculum Night for parents and guardians. This planning group would like to present a consistent message regarding their current work with the standards in the classroom. One of the teachers suggests that they do a short activity with the parents, perhaps highlighting the focus on conceptual understanding of math and how that differs from rote learning. Another teacher shares his thinking that a broader focus would be appropriate, providing an overarching list of the curriculum changes at their grade levels. One of the veteran teachers brings up the point that it might be difficult to make too detailed a presentation, given the fact that they only have a relatively short period of time that evening in which to make their points. One of the teachers found a presentation online, on their state's department of education website, which provides a good, short summary of the shifts in the standards. The group decides to use that presentation, tweaking it a little to make it more specific to their grade levels, and then to do a very short activity to provide a classroom example.

One of the teachers thinks that the *Guess My Number* game would be fun to play in order to give parents an idea of what the standards could look like in the classroom and would not take too long. While several of the teachers do know the game, two of the newer teachers have not played it before, so she asks the group to play the game together to see if they agree that it would be appropriate for the evening event. As leader of the game, she tells the group that she is thinking of a three-digit number that they must guess. She writes on chart paper, shown below, and asks the teachers to make a guess as to what the number could be, in this case, without repeating any of the digits. One teacher guesses *three-four-five*. The game leader says, "Let's use the base-ten number name *three hundred forty-five*," and then writes into the chart how many of those digits are correct and how many digits are in the right place. Another teacher guesses 352 and explains that she thinks the 3 and the 5 are correct, with the 3 in the right place, and the 5 should remain, but be moved to the tens place. The game leader writes the responses to this guess on the second line in the chart and asks for another guess. Someone pipes up and suggests 524, providing an explanation to the group as to why, and the game leader again writes the responses in the chart. She then asks everyone to stop and talk with a neighbor about what they know and how they know it. Several partnerships are considering all the different arrangements of these three digits and checking them against the previous guesses and responses. Another guess is made and the teacher tells the group that they have found the number.

The group agrees that it is an enjoyable game that is engaging and would not take a long time to play. They also know that it can be played with fewer or more digits or even decimals. Moving on, they discuss how best to present why this game is appropriate for students and how it incorporates the standards. The group decides that the necessity to correctly name the numbers and refer to digits by their place value names is related to early grade standards on our base-ten number system.

Guess	Digits	Place
345	2	1
352	2	1
524	3	1
542	3	3

The teachers note that the logic and problem-solving aspect of the game incorporates what they think the standards for mathematical practice are about, with a focus on making sense of problems and discussing viable arguments. At the end of the meeting, the teachers feel satisfied they have found an appropriate presentation to offer the parents that will engage them in some initial thinking about how these standards are different than what and how their children have learned mathematics in the past. They decide to create directions to the game in English, Portuguese, and Spanish for parents who want them.

This example of how teachers collaborate to present the Common Core State Standards to a group of parents and guardians raises many questions. Is there one way that is better than another to communicate about these standards to parents? Should it be done at a curriculum night or through a special presentation on another evening? While it may not be ideal to make the presentation on such a busy evening with lots of other things to talk about, it is also a good opportunity to take advantage of the captive audience. Teachers are faced with these kinds of dilemmas on a regular basis, as they consider how best to get an important message to parents regarding expectations for their children.

Many parents have heard of the Common Core, but they may not be well informed about how the standards will impact their children's education. These parents often want to know the information, but they need presentations that are clear, concise, and in laypersons' language. Finding ways to work with parents and guardians as a team is essential to your students' success, and so it is one of many things you must attend to in relationship to these standards. This chapter is intended to provide you with a variety of ways you can engage parents in these curricular changes as well as ideas for supporting your work overall during this time of change.

Engaging Parents

We all recognize the important role of parents in their child's education. A school, parent/guardian, and community partnership is a significant factor in student achievement (Epstein et al. 2009). We should recognize parents and caregivers as experts on their children and view them as our partners in their children's learning (Aubach 2011). To form respectful relationships with parents, we must be culturally sensitive to expectations for roles and interactions (Delpit 2006; McKenna and Millen 2013). No doubt your school has specific routines, protocols, scheduled meetings, and other events to promote parent engagement. Here, the focus is on establishing school, family, and community partnerships to increase students' success with the Common Core State Standards.

What Do They Know and Hear?

What do parents know about the Core? In a summary of the 45th Annual Phi Delta Kappan Gallup Poll in 2013, Bushaw and Lopez state that, "Almost two of three Americans have never heard of the Common Core State Standards, arguably one of the most important education initiatives in decades, and most of those who say they know about the Common Core neither understand it nor embrace it" (9). We do not always make sure that parents understand and are able to engage in educational initiatives. Your school and state had learning standards before the Common Core was adopted. How much attention did you and your school administrators give to those standards as you communicated with parents? Yet, this situation is different. Because of its national impact and political polarization, some parents and members of the community may have particularly strong views and, at the same time, have access to incorrect information.

So informing parents about what the standards are or are not is an important place to begin. Parent/teacher organization websites are also helpful in providing information about the standards. It is most important to establish that it is still teachers who determine how to facilitate students' learning of these standards. Also, it is advantageous to avoid lengthy explanations, as they may initially make information about the standards difficult to understand.

Parents need to know that:

- your state has always had standards,

- these standards are intended to cover fewer ideas at each grade level more deeply,

- there are critical areas of focus for each grade level, and

- they are critically important in helping their children succeed and to be college- and career-ready.

How Can Parents Help?

As President of the National Council of Teachers of Mathematics, Linda Gojak (2013), encouraged teachers to view planning how best to engage parents in the learning process as important as planning instruction in the classroom. There are specific ways that parents can best support the likelihood that their children will meet Common Core State Standards. Parents and caregivers should:

1. **Set clear expectations for their children to work hard at their mathematics homework and to convey the message to their children that they believe that mathematics is important to learn.** In today's busy world of extracurricular activities for many students, it is often challenging for them to juggle all of their responsibilities. Urge parents to support their children by finding the space, time, and needed materials to complete their home assignments. Encourage parents to provide adequate time for their children to engage in the math they are learning in a meaningful way, rather than just trying to get their homework done quickly. Suggest to parents that they contact you if their children are struggling at home with the required work.

2. **Connect mathematical ideas to everyday tasks and interactions.** One of the key shifts in the mathematics standards is the emphasis on applying mathematical ideas to real-life problems, and exposure to such thinking is important at home, as well. Suggest that parents engage their children in such tasks as reading a bus schedule and deciding which bus to take to get to an event or appointment on time; estimating the cost of items when grocery shopping; cooking and planning nutritious meals; and setting and planning budgets.

3. **Support fluency expectations and engage with their children in the playing of mathematical games.** Such games could be introduced at a school-sponsored Family Math Night and families could leave with directions and materials necessary to play the games at home. Provide parents with opportunities to learn thinking strategies for basic facts, such as composing and decomposing tens, to support their children using them at home. Help parents understand the higher-level thinking involved in such strategies and why they are more successful than constant one-minute fact tests. Tell parents that it is not possible to solely learn and practice mathematics facts in school, that practicing the basic facts at home is as important as practicing the piano or how to hit a baseball.

4. **Ask their children to explain their thinking about a math problem that comes up naturally in their household or in connection to a homework problem.** Tell parents that this will give them access to how their children are being taught to solve problems as well as provide students practice with justifying their thinking. Explain that such explanations will be included in new standardized tests.

5. **Model for their children how to engage in the learning process.** Help parents understand that if their child is uncertain as to how to do a particular problem or is struggling with a concept, parents should encourage their children to persevere and to seek out a variety of strategies for problem solutions. Remind parents that their children will be more successful if they learn to be self-reliant and take responsibility for their own learning.

Supporting Your Work

Perhaps there has been a time during your teaching career when you have switched grade levels, changed school systems, or been told to use a new textbook purchased by your school. You may have found such changes exciting, worrisome, stimulating, or exhausting. You may have experienced all of those reactions to the same change at different points in the process. Regardless of which response was prominent, it is likely that the change required an additional time commitment, at least in the beginning.

As a teacher, your attention is pulled in many directions, and it's challenging to know how to prioritize your tasks. You know that you need to use your time wisely. More commonly now, professional development opportunities are spent analyzing test results of these standards, rather than on defining best teaching practices. Although you may have teacher meetings intended to learn more about the standards, you will likely agree that these meetings don't give you nearly enough time to learn all there is to know. So what can you do to continue to support the important work of finding the best ways to help every one of your diverse students meet these standards? What could you do to keep your energy strong and support a positive attitude?

Get a Standards Buddy at Your Grade Level

Have you ever heard friends or colleagues talk about finding a new walking partner? Suddenly their exercise program has been reinvigorated. They are excited to get up in the morning to exercise. They claim that the time flies by. The same kind of benefit can be achieved from finding a *standards buddy*. Here are some ways you might want to work together:

- Read an article about the mathematical practices and meet to discuss it. You could even talk about what the practices mean to you while you go for a walk!

- Meet before you begin the next unit and review the related standards and critical areas. Decide what preparation you most need to make the unit successful and divvy up the work.

- If you have a "free" or a preparation period, use it once in a while to visit each other's classroom while your buddy is teaching a new lesson. Talk about what you learned and enjoyed. Once a level of comfort is established, talk about another visit where you focus on one aspect of your teaching you would like to improve.

- Watch a classroom video together and then talk about the evidence you saw of engagement and learning.

- If you are asked to teach a new mathematical topic you don't completely understand, work with your buddy to learn the new math content by doing some research together and practicing the idea prior to teaching it.

✏ Take advantage of local workshops by attending them together so that you can talk about what you both learned.

Connect Across Grade Levels

With the immediate demands of preparing and assessing your students, it can be challenging to think about the mathematics at other grade levels, but working across grade levels is a way to help you and your students. Consider forming a study group, including teachers who are interested in meeting together just once to look at how one of the domains develops or how one of the mathematical practices might look different across grade levels. If it is helpful, you can always decide to meet again. Perhaps teachers from each grade level could bring a few samples of student work and, as a group, you could look at the samples to consider the following questions:

✏ What similarities and differences are there among the mathematical tasks we brought?

✏ What progression of learning do the work samples suggest?

✏ What do we notice about the ways in which students represent their mathematical thinking at different grade levels?

✏ What common errors or misconceptions do we notice, and how can we help students avoid them?

✏ What evidence is there that students are developing the expectations of the mathematical practices?

Take Advantage of Online Resources

There are a variety of tools online to support implementation of these standards. For the first time, national websites and those from other states are helpful and relevant to the standards of your state. Due to the plethora of choices available, it helps to rely on sites that have connections to well-known, highly respected organizations and individuals. Here are some ideas you might want to pursue for learning more about the standards:

↪ Read the progressions documents for yourself. They are available at http://ime.math.arizona.edu/progressions/. You can also participate in discussion forums hosted by Common Core State Standards writer Bill McCallum at http://commoncoretools.me/forums/forum/public/

↪ Join the National Council of Teachers of Mathematics (NCTM). An e-membership is more affordable and gives you access to a variety of online resources, current and back issues of *Teaching Children Mathematics* and discounts for NCTM meetings and resources.

↪ Receive a daily update from a professional organization. You can sign up for the ASCD SmartBrief or the NCTM SmartBrief at http://www2.smartbrief.com/.

↪ Listen to a TED talk. As educators, we can become so focused on educational resources that we miss ideas in other disciplines. TED is a non-profit organization that began in 1984 with the mission of spreading good ideas. The best talks are available online at http://www.ted.com/.

↪ Watch videos of classrooms. The Teaching Channel has dedicated a good number of its videos to demonstration lessons that support the work of the standards at all grade levels. Their videos can be found at http://www.teachingchannel.org.

↪ Look at your state's website. Most state departments of elementary and secondary education are posting quality resources for teachers on state websites as they become available. Do some research on available Common Core materials as provided by these leading state education agencies.

Resources are also needed to supplement or replace outdated materials. Most classrooms are filled with texts published before the Common Core. Though there will be useful sections of those books, it is unlikely that they will provide the deep focus needed, and a good number of books include topics that are now taught at different grade levels. Even those published shortly after the CommonCore may not be as robust as necessary. The following sites have specific curricular suggestions:

↪ Illustrative Mathematics offers tasks, videos, plans, and curriculum modules at http://www.illustrativemathematics.org/. The work is funded by the Bill & Melinda Gates Foundation.

- The NCTM resource for teachers, *Illuminations* at http:// illuminations.nctm.org/, was started before adoption of the Common Core, but its resources have been vetted by experienced mathematics educators.

- The website for the National Council of Supervisors of Mathematics (NCSM) has a link to Common Core resources on their main web page: http://www.mathedleadership.org, including a sample of "great tasks."

- Consider materials made available to you from www.achievethecore.org. Student Achievement Partners, founded by several of the lead authors of the Core Standards, has created a website resource that includes tasks and assessments, lessons, ready-to-use modules, and year-long planning materials. This website also has bilingual materials available for teacher and parent use.

- PARCC items and test prototypes can be found at http://www. parcconline.org/ and Smarter Balanced practice tests are available at http://www.smarterbalanced.org. Both consortiums are likely to continue to release items that can be used in your classroom.

Finally, with an emphasis on fluency, students need practice. Online games can often motivate some students in ways that nothing else seems to do as well. It's important to remember however, that *drill and kill* can happen through technology as easily as paper and pencil. Such practice can support automaticity, only *after* a conceptual framework is established and *before* recall has been established. Consider online activities that encourage students to learn their facts in interesting ways rather than just becoming online flash cards. We must also remember to include games that support higher-order thinking.

Look for Opportunities to Use Project-Based Learning

Our greatest challenges may be to find appropriate tasks as well as the time for students to pursue them. In light of the Common Core's expectation that students apply their mathematical knowledge to real-world problems, many educators have suggested that we give more attention to Project-Based Learning (PBL). PBL offers students authentic questions and problems to pursue. As they are authentic, they are also complex and require a variety of concepts and skills. Usually explored with others, authentic projects give students opportunities to learn how to work collaboratively as they research and synthesize information. John Larnier, Director of Product Development at the Buck Institute for Education (2011), suggests that PBL is appropriate for students of all ages, for ELL students, and for students with learning disabilities. Despite the fact that these kinds of projects do take more time to complete, they are most often very engaging for students and they tend to learn a good number of skills and concepts while doing them. The work of such projects could be started in class by collaborating with others and then continued at home, or you could choose to fully dedicate in-class time for such work.

Mathematics and science are often connected. If your students were studying birds, projects could focus on their migration, their sizes, or counting and categorizing the number of birds that approach a bird feeder over time. Older students might investigate soil quality and other questions related to establishing a school vegetable garden. Another approach would be to ask how mathematical understanding informs a book being read in literacy learning, or a topic in the social studies curriculum. Projects such as *How could mathematical information help us better understand the Revolutionary War?* can engage students in interesting interdisciplinary learning endeavors.

School-wide projects can support school unity and provide opportunities for multi-age interactions. A project such as creating a school garden can connect to various components of the K-5 mathematics curriculum as shown in Figure 10.1.

Figure 10.1 Sample Across Grade Explorations Related to a School Vegetable Garden

Grades K-1	Grades 2-3	Grades 4-5
Categorize and represent data: • What vegetables should we plant? • How many seeds have germinated/not germinated? **Count, solve related addition and subtraction word problems:** • How many of each type of vegetable did we plant? **Measure using informal unit:** • How far apart did we plant the seeds? **Describe shapes:** • What shapes do we see in our garden?	**Length measure with rulers:** • How deep/far apart should the seeds be planted? **Liquid volume measures:** • How much water do the plants need? • How can we measure the water they get from rainfall? **Area measurement:** • How much space do we need for the garden? **Line plots, addition with greater numbers:** • Where can we harvest the plants? **Length and mass measures, bar graphs:** • How big are the vegetables? **Counting, graphing:** • How many vegetables did we harvest?	**Computation with decimals:** • How much will the garden cost? **Volume measures:** • How much compost do we need? **Fractions, area measures:** • What portion of the garden should each type of plant get? **Fractions and measures in recipes:** • How will we use the vegetables? **Computation with greater whole numbers:** • How many of....(one type of vegetable) would we need in order to serve our whole school for one lunch period? • What was our yield in, for example, tomatoes, for each package of seeds that we planted?

Write Your Own Professional Goals

Goal setting is common in education and with good reason. Intentionality gives focus to our work. Many teachers are required to set goals every year, and some do so based on an evaluation calendar. When changes such as adoption of the Common Core State Standards occur, we all need to reflect on our practice and establish clear, meaningful goals that seem doable to us. Such goals might begin with one of the following sentence stems:

- ✏ By using strategies found within resources listed on the website of the National Council of Supervisors of Mathematics website, I will incorporate...

- ✏ By examining PARCC exemplars [or Smarter Balanced practice tests] I will create ...

You may wish to begin with the practice standards. You could start by completing the following worksheet (Figure 10.2).

Figure 10.2 Practice Goal Worksheet

Name: _____ Date:_____

Mathematical Practice:

Two goals I have in relation to this practice are:

Evidence that I have met my goal would include:

A specific action I will take is to:

Resources I will use include:

In six months, I will have:

Being a teacher can bring great sources of satisfaction as well as great challenges. When you are inspired and passionate about your teaching, chances are your students feel energized and excited about learning, too. So it is important that you find ways to support this work. Always remember, standards are only as valuable as the teacher implementing them.

 ## Voice from the Classroom

I had dinner last night with an old school friend. We have both been teaching for 10 years. I love talking with her about teaching as it reminds me how different it can be depending on where you teach. Last night we spent some time talking about our students' parents.

My biggest concern about parents in my school is that I wish they were more engaged. So many of them work more than one job and rarely have time to participate in school activities. My friend describes parents who seem to be constantly available to do their children's homework. It's good to remember that every teacher would probably like to improve something about his or her relationships with both parents and the greater community.

We talked most about how valuable parents' roles are in supporting their children and how we can help them understand ways to do it. My friend told me about a game library she set up for her students with games they could bring home. I thought that sounded like a great idea and am going to try to create one during the spring break. If students learn the game in class, they can teach it to someone at home. It will be a great way for them to practice the basic facts.

My friend told me that her biggest concern was that her students weren't learning to do things themselves, as caregivers or parents were always there with an answer or ready to look something up for them. I told her about the homework website (with paper copies available) I created precisely because I know my students are more likely to be working on their own.

It provides a copy of the assignment, allows them to review basic content, and offers probing questions such as, have you tried making a table? My friend is going to try this idea as she thinks her students might go to such a site before immediately asking their parents for help.

I have tried to attend more community events for the past few years. There is a street festival every fall that my family enjoys and some of my students who attend introduce me to their parents. I've noticed that those parents then seem more comfortable when we meet at the school. I've also done a couple of workshops for the volunteer tutors at the local Boys and Girls Club. Many of my students do their homework there and I want the tutors to understand current expectations of students. One of my students told me that his tutor said, "Now I can do the math just like you can." I could tell that he was pleased that his tutor and I knew each other. I take time to connect well with those in my students' lives, because I know I can't be successful without their support. If only there were more time to do things like this and less time needed for paperwork!

—Fourth-Grade Teacher

Let's Think and Discuss

1. How will parents in your district best engage with the goals of the Common Core Standards?

2. What sources of support have you found during past educational initiatives? How might they help you with this one?

3. What are two "I can..." statements that you can make about yourself in relationship to teaching and learning with the Common Core's mathematics content and practice standards? What are two you could make about your partnership with the community and parents?

The Standards for Mathematical Practice

Standards for Mathematical Practice (National Governors Association Center for Best Practices [NGA] and the Council of Chief State School Officers [CCSSO] 2010)

MP1 Make sense of problems and persevere in solving them.

Mathematically proficient students start by explaining to themselves the meaning of a problem and looking for entry points to its solution. They analyze givens, constraints, relationships, and goals. They make conjectures about the form and meaning of the solution and plan a solution pathway rather than simply jumping into a solution attempt. They consider analogous problems, and try special cases and simpler forms of the original problem in order to gain insight into its solution. They monitor and evaluate their progress and change course if necessary. Older students might, depending on the context of the problem, transform algebraic expressions or change the viewing window on their graphing calculator to get the information they need. Mathematically proficient students can explain correspondences between equations, verbal descriptions, tables, and graphs or draw diagrams of important features and relationships, graph data, and search for regularity or trends. Younger students might rely on using concrete objects or pictures to help conceptualize and solve a problem. Mathematically proficient students check their answers to problems using a different method, and they continually ask themselves, "Does this make sense?" They can understand the approaches of others to solving complex problems and identify correspondences between different approaches.

MP2 Reason abstractly and quantitatively.

Mathematically proficient students make sense of quantities and their relationships in problem situations. They bring two complementary abilities to bear on problems involving quantitative relationships: the ability to *decontextualize*—to abstract a given situation and represent it symbolically and manipulate the representing symbols as if they have a life of their own, without necessarily attending to their referents—and the ability to *contextualize*, to pause as needed during the manipulation process in order to probe into the referents for the symbols involved. Quantitative reasoning entails habits of creating a coherent representation of the problem at hand; considering the units involved; attending to the meaning of quantities, not just how to compute them; and knowing and flexibly using different properties of operations and objects.

MP3 Construct viable arguments and critique the reasoning of others.

Mathematically proficient students understand and use stated assumptions, definitions, and previously established results in constructing arguments. They make conjectures and build a logical progression of statements to explore the truth of their conjectures. They are able to analyze situations by breaking them into cases, and can recognize and use counterexamples. They justify their conclusions, communicate them to others, and respond to the arguments of others. They reason inductively about data, making plausible arguments that take into account the context from which the data arose. Mathematically proficient students are also able to compare the effectiveness of two plausible arguments, distinguish correct logic or reasoning from that which is flawed, and—if there is a flaw in an argument—explain what it is. Elementary students can construct arguments using concrete referents such as objects, drawings, diagrams, and actions. Such arguments can make sense and be correct, even though they are not generalized or made formal until later grades. Later, students learn to determine domain to which an argument applies. Students at all grades can listen or read the arguments of others, decide whether they make sense, and ask useful questions to clarify or improve the arguments.

MP4 Model with mathematics.

Mathematically proficient students can apply the mathematics they know to solve problems arising in everyday life, society, and the workplace. In early grades, this might be as simple as writing an addition equation to describe a situation. In middle grades, a student might apply proportional reasoning to plan a school event or analyze a problem in the community. By high school, a student might use geometry to solve a design problem or use a function to describe how one quantity of interest depends on another. Mathematically proficient students who can apply what they know are comfortable making assumptions and approximations to simplify a complicated situation, realizing that these may need revision later. They are able to identify important quantities in a practical situation and map their relationships using such tools as diagrams, two-way tables, graphs, flowcharts and formulas. They can analyze those relationships mathematically to draw conclusions. They routinely interpret their mathematical results in the context of the situation and reflect on whether the results make sense, possibly improving the model if it has not served its purpose.

MP5 Use appropriate tools strategically.

Mathematically proficient students consider the available tools when solving a mathematical problem. These tools might include pencil and paper, concrete models, a ruler, a protractor, a calculator, a spreadsheet, a computer algebra system, a statistical package, or dynamic geometry software. Proficient students are sufficiently familiar with tools appropriate for their grade or course to make sound decisions about when each of these tools might be helpful, recognizing both the insight to be gained and their limitations. For example, mathematically proficient high school students analyze graphs of functions and solutions generated using a graphing calculator. They detect possible errors by strategically using estimation and other mathematical knowledge. When making mathematical models, they know that technology can enable them to visualize the results of varying assumptions, explore consequences, and compare predictions with data. Mathematically proficient students at various grade levels are able to identify relevant external mathematical resources, such as digital content located on a website, and use them to pose or solve problems. They are able to use technological tools to explore and deepen their understanding of concepts.

MP6 Attend to precision.

Mathematically proficient students try to communicate precisely to others. They try to use clear definitions in discussion with others and in their own reasoning. They state the meaning of the symbols they choose, including using the equal sign consistently and appropriately. They are careful about specifying units of measure, and labeling axes to clarify the correspondence with quantities in a problem. They calculate accurately and efficiently, and express numerical answers with a degree of precision appropriate for the problem context. In the elementary grades, students give carefully formulated explanations to each other. By the time they reach high school, they have learned to examine claims and make explicit use of definitions.

MP7 Look for and make use of structure.

Mathematically proficient students look closely to discern a pattern or structure. Young students, for example, might notice that three and seven more is the same amount as seven and three more, or they may sort a collection of shapes according to how many sides the shapes have. Later, students will see 7×8 equals the well remembered $7 \times 5 + 7 \times 3$, in preparation for learning about the distributive property. In the expression $x^2 + 9x + 14$, older students can see the 14 as 2×7 and the 9 as $2 + 7$. They recognize the significance of an existing line in a geometric figure and can use the strategy of drawing an auxiliary line for solving problems. They also can step back for an overview and shift perspective. They can see complicated things, such as some algebraic expressions, as single objects or as being composed of several objects. For example, they can see $5 - 3(x - y)^2$ as 5 minus a positive number times a square and use that to realize that its value cannot be more than 5 for any real numbers x and y.

MP8 Look for and express regularity in repeated reasoning.

Mathematically proficient students notice if calculations are repeated, and look both for general methods and for shortcuts. Upper elementary students might notice when dividing 25 by 11 that they are repeating the same calculations over and over again, and conclude they have a repeating decimal. By paying attention to the calculation of slope as they repeatedly check whether points are on the line through (1, 2) with slope 3, middle school students might abstract the equation $(y - 2)/(x - 1) = 3$. Noticing the regularity in the way terms cancel when expanding $(x - 1)(x + 1)$, $(x - 1)(x^2 + x + 1)$, and $(x - 1)(x^3 + x^2 + x + 1)$ might lead them to the general formula for the sum of a geometric series. As they work to solve a problem, mathematically proficient students maintain oversight of the process, while attending to the details. They continually evaluate the reasonableness of their immediate results.

Unpacking a Particular Standard

Standard:	Organize by Nouns and Verbs
Relate to Other Standards	**Vocabulary/Symbols**
How Does This Idea Develop?	**Learning Target Examples:**
Curriculum/Instruction	**Student Friendly Language**

Counting and Cardinality Record Sheet

Student Name:	Date	Number(s)	Comments
Rote counting by ones			
Rote counting by tens			
Rote count by ones from a number other than 1			
Write numbers/write numbers to represent a number of objects			
Assign exactly one number name to each object in a set			
Know that the last number in the count tells the quantity			
Say the number names in the correct order			
Recognize that the counting numbers increase by one			
Count objects arranged in a row, array, or circle			
Recognize changing the arrangement does not change the quantity			
Produce a set with a given number of objects			
Match or count to compare two groups			
Compare two written numerals			

Assessing Understanding of the Meaning of an Operation

Equation:
Drawing or Model:
Word Problem:

Student Work Comments

Name: _____   Date: _____

1. Is the work accurate?

2. If errors are made do they appear to be

   Careless?   Basic fact related?

   Due to a faulty procedure?   From an unknown source?

3. Can I follow the written record? If not, what would make it clearer?

4. How does this work show progress the student is making?

5. What should this student work on next?

Sample Game Observation Summary

Activity:	Date:
Uses number lines to find the sum or difference	Uses drawings to find the sum or difference
Uses abstract reasoning or arithmetic to compute	Computes mentally
Finds accurate sum or difference	Uses estimation and/or number sense to choose numbers that will yield a strategically located sum or difference

Measurement Assessment Checklist

Student Name: _____   Attribute: _____

The student can:

❏ identify this attribute of an object

❏ identify the standard unit to measure this attribute (unit, square unit, or cubic unit)

❏ use multiple copies of same-sized units to measure this attribute

❏ use one copy of a unit to measure this attribute

❏ identify appropriate tools to use to measure this attribute

❏ identify appropriate units to use when measuring this attribute of various sized objects

❏ use tools to measure this object

❏ use formulas to measure this attribute (if appropriate)

❏ recognize the relative sizes of units

❏ estimate the measure of a particular item

❏ solve problems involving this attribute

❏ convert from larger to smaller standard units of this attribute within the same system

❏ convert from smaller to larger standard units of this attribute within the same system

Observation Record

Name: _____   Date: _____

Directions: Note evidence of the different levels of thinking. Include information about the specific shapes the student was considering as you observed as well as whether or not shapes were in traditional or nontraditional positions.

1. The student identifies shapes visually.

2. The student describes attributes and properties of shapes and uses properties to identify shapes.

3. The student identifies categories of shapes, and relationships among them, based on the properties of shapes.

References Cited

Afferbach, Peter, and Summer Clark. 2011. "Diversity and English Language Arts Assessment." In *Handbook of Research on Teaching English Language Arts (3rd Edition),* edited by Dianne Lapp and Douglas Fisher, 307–313. Newark, DE: International Reading Association, 2011.

Alajmi, Amal. 2012. "How Do Elementary Textbooks Address Fractions? A Review of Mathematics Textbooks in the USA, Japan, and Kuwait." *Educational Studies in Mathematics* 79: 239–261.

Alajmi, Amal, and Robert Reys. 2010. "Examining Eighth Grade Students' Recognition and Interpretation of Reasonable Answers." *International Journal of Science and Mathematics Education* 8: 117–139.

Ashlock, Robert B. 2009. *Error Patterns in Computation: Using Error Patterns to Help Each Student Learn*, 2nd edition. New York, NY: Pearson.

Aspinwall, Leslie, and Julie Aspinwall. 2003. "Investigating Mathematical Thinking Using Open Writing Prompts." *Mathematics Teaching in the Middle School* 8: 350–353.

Association of American Colleges and Universities. 2010. *Quantitative Literacy Value Rubric.* Washington, DC.

Atkin, J. Myron, Paul Black, and Janet Coffey. 2001. *Classroom Assessment and the National Science Standards.* Washington, DC: National Academies Press.

Aubach, Susan. 2011. "Bridging Cultures and Building Relationships: Engaging Latino/a Immigrant Parents in Urban Schools." *Educational Leadership.* 68: 16–21.

Barlow, Angela T., and Michael R. McCrory. 2011. "Three Strategies for Promoting Math Disagreements." *Teaching Children Mathematics* 17: 530–539.

Battista, Michael T. 1999. "The Importance of Spatial Structuring in Geometric Reasoning." *Teaching Children Mathematics* 6: 170–177.

Battista, Michael T. 2007. "The Development of Geometric and Spatial Thinking." In *Second Handbook of Research on Mathematics Teaching and Learning*, edited by Frank Lester, 843–908. Reston, VA: National Council of Teachers of Mathematics.

Bay-Williams, Jennifer Livers, and Stefanie Livers. 2009. "Supporting Math Vocabulary Acquisition." *Teaching Children Mathematics* 16: 238–246.

Benson, Christine, C., Jennifer J. Wall, and Cheryl Malm. 2013. "The Distributive Property in Grade 3?" *Teaching Children Mathematics* 19: 498–505.

Bill, Victoria, and Pam Goldman. 2012. "The CSS and the Importance of Assessing the Mathematical Practices." http://ifl.lrdc.pitt.edu/ifl/index. php/blog/index/the_ccss_and_the_importance_of_assessing_students_ mathematical_practices.

Blume, Galindo, and Walcott. 2007.

Bray, Wendy S. 2011. "A Collective Case Study of the Influence of Teachers' Beliefs and Knowledge on Error-Handling Practices during Class Discussion of Mathematics." *Journal for Research in Mathematics Education* 42: 2–38.

Bushaw, William J., and Shane J. Lopez. 2013. "The 45th Annual PDK/ Gallup Poll of the Public's Attitude Toward the Public Schools: Which Way Do We Go?" *Kappan Magazine* 96: 9–17.

Butler, Frances, Susan Miller, Kevin Crehan, Beatrice Babbitt, and Thomas Pierce. 2001. "Fraction Instruction for Students with Mathematics Disabilities: Comparing Two Teaching Sequences." *Learning Disabilities Research & Practice* 18: 99–111.

Carpenter, Thomas P., Megan Loef Franke, and Linda Levi. 2003. *Thinking Mathematically: Integrating Arithmetic and Algebra in Elementary School*. Portsmouth, NH: Heinneman.

Casey, Beth M., Nicole Andrews, Holly Schinder, Joanne E. Kersh, Alexandra Samper, and Juanita Copley. 2008. "The Development of Spatial Skills through Interventions Involving Block Building Activities." *Cognition and Instruction* 26: 269–309.

Cawley, John F., Rene Parmar, Lynn Lucas-Fusco, Joy Kilian, and Teresa Foley. 2007. "Place Value and Mathematics for Students with Mild Disabilities: Data and Suggested Practices." *Learning Disabilities: A Contemporary Journal* 5: 21–39.

Chapin, Suzanne, Catherine O'Connor, and Nancy Anderson. 2009. *Classroom Discussions: Using Math Talk to Help Students Learn.* Sausalito, CA: Math Solutions.

Clarke, Doug, Anne Roche, and Annie Mitchell. 2008. "Ten Practical Tips for Making Fractions Come Alive and Make Sense." *Teaching Mathematics in the Middle School* 13: 373–379.

Clements, Douglas. 1999. "Subitizing: What Is It? Why Teach It?" *Teaching Children Mathematics* 5: 400–405.

Collins, Anne. 2012. *50 Leveled Problems, Level 1.* Huntington Beach, CA: Shell Education.

———. 2012. *50 Leveled Problems, Level 5.* Huntington Beach, CA: Shell Education.

———. 2012. *Using Classroom Assessment to Improve Student Learning: Math Problems Aligned with NCM and Common Core State Standards.* Reston: VA: NCTM.

Colton, Connie. 2010. "Justifying Answers and Providing Explanations for Mathematical Thinking: The Impact on Student Learning in a Middle-School Classroom." *Math in the Middle Institute Partnership Action Research Project Report.* University of Nebraska.

Common Core Standards Writing Team. 2013. "Progressions for the Common Core State Standards in Mathematics: Number and Operations–Fractions, 3–5." http://commoncoretools.me/wp-content/uploads/2011/08/ccss_progression_nf_35_2013_09_19.pdf.

———. 2012a. "Progressions for the Common Core State Standards in Mathematics: K–5, Number and Operations in Base Ten." http://commoncoretools.me/wp-content/uploads/2011/04/ccss_progression_nbt_2011_04_073_corrected2.pdf.

———. 2012b. "Progressions for the Common Core State Standards in Mathematics: K –5, Geometric Measurement." http://commoncoretools.files.wordpress.com/2012/07/ccss_progression_gm_k5_2012_07_21.pdf.

———. 2012c. "Progressions for the Common Core State Standards in Mathematics: K–6, Geometry." 2012c. http://commoncoretools.files.wordpress.com/2012/06/ccss_progression_g_k6_2012_06_27.pdf.

———. 2011a. "Progressions for the Common Core State Standards in Mathematics: K, Counting and Cardinality; K–5, Operations and Algebraic Thinking." http://commoncoretools.files.wordpress.com/2011/05/ccss_progression_cc_oa_k5_2011_05_302.pdf.

———. 2011b. "Progressions for the Common Core State Standards in Mathematics: K–3, Categorical Data; Grades 2–5 Measurement Data." http://commoncoretools.files.wordpress.com/2011/06/ccss_progression_md_k5_2011_06_20.pdf.

Crowe, Marce, and Pokey Stanford. "Question for Quality. *Delta Kappa Gamma Bulletin* Summer, (2010): 36-41.

Dacey, Linda. 2012a. *50 Leveled Problems, Level 1*. Huntington Beach, CA: Shell Education.

———. 2012b. *50 Leveled Problems, Level 2*. Huntington Beach, CA: Shell Education.

———. 2012c. *50 Leveled Problems, Level 4*. Huntington Beach, CA: Shell Education.

Dacey, Linda, and Anne Collins. 2010. *Zeroing in on Number and Operations: Key Ideas and Common Misconceptions.* Portland, ME: Stenhouse Publishers.

Dacey, Linda, and Rebeka Eston. 2002. *Show and Tell.* Sausalito, CA: Math Solutions.

Dacey, Linda, Jayne Bamford Lynch, and Rebeka Eston Salemi. 2013. *How to Differentiate Your Math Instruction: Lessons, Ideas, and Videos with Common Core Support, Grades K–5.* Sausalito, CA: Math Solutions.

Darling-Hammond, Linda. 2012. *Creating a Comprehensive System for Evaluating and Supporting Effective Teaching.* Stanford, CA: Stanford Center for Opportunity Policy in Education.

Delpit, Lisa. 2006. *Other People's Children: Cultural Conflict in the Classroom.* New York, NY: New Press.

Denman, Greg. 2013. *Think It, Show It Mathematics: Strategies for Exploring Thinking.* Huntington Beach, CA: Shell Education.

Diezmann, Carmel M., Tom Lowrie, and Lindy A. Sugars. 2010. "Primary Students' Success on the Structured Number ." *Australian Primary Mathematics Classroom* 15: 24–28.

Dixon, Juli. 2008. "Time: Representing Elapsed Time on an Open-Number Line." *Teaching Children Mathematics* 15: 18–24.

Driscoll, Mark. 1999. *Fostering Mathematical Thinking.* Portsmouth, NH: Heinemann.

Dweck, Carol. 2007. *Mindset: The New Psychology of Success.* New York: Ballantine Books.

Epstein, Joyce, Mavis G. Sanders, Steven Sheldon, and Beth S. Simon. 2009. *School, Family, and Community Partnerships: Your Handbook for Action* (3rd Edition). Thousand Oaks, CA: Corwin Press.

Flanagan, Dawn, Jennifer Mascolo, and Steven Hardy-Braz. 2009. "Standardized Testing." www.education.com/reference/article/standardized-testing.

Frayer, Dorothy, Wayne C. Frederick, and Herbert J. Klausmeier. 1969. *A Schema for Testing the Level of Concept Mastery. Technical Report No. 16.* Madison: University of Wisconsin Research and Development Center for Cognitive Learning.

Ginsberg, Herbert P., and Barbrina Ertle. 2008. "Knowing the Mathematics in Early Childhood Mathematics." In *Contemporary Perspectives on Mathematics in Early Childhood Education,* edited by Olivia N. Saracho and Bernard Spodek, 44–66. New York: Information Age.

Ginsburg, Alan, Steven Leinwand, and Katie Decker. 2009. "Informing Grades 1–6 Mathematics Standards Development: What Can Be Learned from High-Performing Hong Kong, Korea, and Singapore?" *American Institutes for Research*: 1-67. http://www.air.org/files/MathStandards.pdf

Glasglow, Robert, Gay Ragan, Wanda Fields, Robert Reys, and Deanna Wasman. 2000. "The Decimal Dilemma." *Teaching Children Mathematics* 7: 89–93.

Gojak, Linda. 2013. "National Council of Teachers of Mathematics. Partnering with Parents." NCTM. http://www.nctm.org/about/content.aspx?id=39367.

Goodwin, K. Shane, Lee Ostrom, and Karen Wilson Scott. 2009. "Gender Differences in Mathematics Self-Efficacy and Back Substitution Multiple-Choice Assessment." *Journal Of Adult Education* 38: 22–41.

Green, Michael, John A. Piel, and Claudia Flowers. 2008. "Reversing Education Majors' Arithmetic Misconceptions with Short-Term Instruction Using Manipulatives." *Journal of Educational Research* 101: 234–242.

Harries, Tony and Patrick Barmby. 2008. "Representing Multiplication." Mathematics Teaching Incorporating Micromath 206: 37-41.

Hecht, Steven. A., Kevin J. Vagi, and Joseph K. Torgesen. 2007. "Fraction Skills and Proportional Reasoning." In *Why Is Math So Hard for Some Children? The Nature and Origins of Mathematical Learning Difficulties and Disabilities*, edited by Daniel B. Berch and Michele M. Mazzocco, 121–132. Baltimore, MD: Brookes.

Heritage, Margaret. 2008. *Learning Progressions: Supporting Instruction and Formative Assessment*. Washington, DC: Chief Council of State School Officers.

Hufferd-Ackles, Kimberly, Karen Fuson, and Miriam Gamoran Sherin. 2004. "Describing Levels and Components of a Math-Talk Learning Community." *Journal for Research in Mathematics Education* 35: 81–116.

Hull, Ted H., Ruth Harbin Mills, and Dan S. Balka. 2012. *The Common Core Mathematics Standards*. Thousand Oaks, CA: Corwin Press.

Kamii, Constance. 2006. "Measurement in Length: How Can We Teach It Better?" *Teaching Children Mathematics* 133: 154–158.

Kling, Gina. 2011. "Fluency with Basic Addition." *Teaching Children Mathematics* 18: 80–88.

Lamon, Susan. 2012. *Teaching Fractions and Ratios for Understanding: Essential Knowledge and Content Strategies for Teachers*. NY: Routledge.

Larmer, John. 2011. "Debunking Five Myths about Project-Based Learning." http://www.edutopia.org/blog/debunking-five-pbl-myths-john-larmer.

Lesh, Richard and Richard Lehrer. "Models and Modeling Perspectives on the Development of Students and Teachers." Mathematical Thinking and Learning, 5, 2-3, (2003): 109-129.

Lillard, Angeline. 2005. *Montessori: The Science Behind the Genius*. New York, NY: Oxford.

Lionni, Leo. 1995. *Inch by Inch*. New York: Harper Collins.

Locuniak, Maria N., and Nancy C. Jordan. 2008. "Using Kindergarten Number Sense to Predict Calculation Fluency in Second Grade." *Journal of Learning Disabilities* 41: 451–459.

Losq, Christine. 2005. "Number Concepts and Special Needs Students: The Power of Ten-Frame Tiles." *Teaching Children Mathematics* 11: 310–315.

Lutsky, Neil. 2008. "Arguing with Numbers: Teaching Quantitative Reasoning through Argument and Writing." In *Calculation vs. Context: Quantitative Literacy and Its Implications for Teacher Education*, edited by Bernard L. Madison and Lynn Arthur Steen, 59–74, Washington, DC: Mathematical Association of America, 2008.

McCallum, Bill. 2011. "Tools for the Common Core Standards." http://commoncoretools.me/2011/03/10/structuring-the-mathematical-practices

McCool, Jenni and Carol Holland. "Investigating Measurement Knowledge. Teaching Children Mathematics 18, 9 2012): 542-548.

McKenna, Maria K., and Jessica Millen. 2013. "Look! Listen! Parent Narratives and Grounded Theory Models of Parent Voice, Presence, and Engagement in K–12 Education." *School Community Journal* 23: 9–48.

McManus, Sarah. 2008. "Attributes of Effective Formative Assessment." http://www.dpi.state.nc.us/docs/accountability/educators/fastattributes04081.pdf.

Mills, Judith. 2011. "Body Fractions: A Physical Approach to Learning." *Australian Primary Mathematics Classroom* 16: 17–22.

Mitchelmore, Michael, and Paul White. 2000. "Development of Angle Concepts by Progressive Abstraction and Generalization." *Educational Studies in Mathematics* 41: 209–238.

Mullis, Ina V. S., Michael O. Martin, and Pierre Foy. 2008. *TIMSS 2007 International Mathematics Report: Findings from IEA's Trends in International Mathematics and Science Study at the Fourth and Eighth Grades.* Chestnut Hill, MA: TIMSS & PIRLS International Study Center, Boston College.

Murray, Miki. 2004. *Teaching Mathematics Vocabulary in Context: Windows, Doors, and Secret Passageways.* Portsmouth, NH: Heinemann.

National Council of Teachers of Mathematics. 2013. "Position Paper on Formative Assessment." http://www.nctm.org/uploadedFiles/About_NCTM/Position_Statements/Formative%20Assessment1.pdf.

———. 2000. *Principles and Standards for School Mathematics.* Reston, VA: NCTM.

———. 1995. *Assessment Standards for School Mathematics.* Reston, VA: NCTM.

National Governors Association Center for Best Practices, and Council of Chief State School Officers. 2010. "Common Core State Standards." Washington, DC: National Governors Association Center for Best Practices, Council of Chief State School Officers. Accessed January 14, 2014, http://corestandards.org/math.

National Governors Association (NGA) and Council of Chief State School Officers (CCSSO). 2010. *Reaching Higher: The Common Core State Standards Validation Committee—A Report from the National Governors Association Center for Best Practices and the Council of Chief State School Officers.* Washington, DC: NGA Center and CCSSO.

National Mathematics Advisory Panel. 2008. *Foundations for Success: The Final Report of the National Mathematics Advisory Panel.* U.S. Department of Education: Washington, DC.

National Research Council. 2009. *Mathematics Learning In Early Childhood, Paths Toward Excellence and Equity.* Washington, DC: National Academy Press.

———. 2001. *Adding It Up: Helping Children Learn Mathematics.* Washington, DC: National Academy Press.

O'Loughlin, Trisha. 2007. "Using Research to Develop Computational Fluency in Young Mathematicians." *Teaching Children Mathematics* 14, 3: 132–138.

Parker, Frieda, and Jodie Novack. 2012. "Implementing the Common Core Mathematical Practices." http://www.ascd.org/ascd-express/vol8/805-parker.aspx.

Pfotenhauer, Jennifer, Rick Kleine, Yasmin Sitabkhan, and Darrell Earnest. 2013. "Back Talk: Shifting Understanding of Mixed Numbers." *Teaching Children Mathematics* 19: 592–593.

Ramdass, Darshanand, and Barry Zimmerman. 2008. "Effects of Self-Correction Strategy Training on Middle School Students' Self-Efficacy, Self-Evaluation, and Mathematics Division Learning." *Journal of Advanced Academics* Fall: 18–41.

Ray, Max. 2011. "Problem Solving Strategies and the Common Core Practice Standards." http://mathforum.org/blogs/max/problem-solving-strategies-and-the-common-core-practice-standards/.

Rinne, Luke, Emily Gregory, Julia Yarmolinskyay, and Mariale Hardiman. 2001. "Why Arts Integration Improves Long-Term Retention of Content." *Mind, Brain, and Education.* 5: 89–96.

Roberts, Sally. 2007. "Watch What You Say." *Teaching Children Mathematics* 14: 296–301.

Roche, Anne. 2005. "Longer is Larger—or Is It?" *Australian Primary Mathematics Classroom* 10: 11–16.

Roddick, Cheryl, Christina Silvas-Centeno. 2007. "Developing Understanding of Fractions through Pattern Blocks and Fair Trade." *Teaching Children Mathematics* 14: 140–145.

Rowe, Mary Budd. 1986. "Wait Time: Slowing Down May Be a Way of Speeding Up." *Journal of Teacher Education* 37: 43–50.

Rubenstein, Rheta, and Denise Thompson. 2002. "Understanding and Supporting Children's Vocabulary Development." *Teaching Children Mathematics* 17: 107–112.

Russell, Susan Jo. 2000. "Developing Computational Fluency with Whole Numbers." *Teaching Children Mathematics*. 7: 154–58.

———. 2012. "Keeping Teaching and Learning Strong. *Teaching Children Mathematics* 19: 50–56.

Sarama, Julie, and Douglas Clements. 2003. "Early Childhood Corner: Building Blocks of Early Childhood Mathematics." *Teaching Children Mathematics* 9: 480–484.

———. 2009. *Early Childhood Mathematics Education Research: Learning Trajectories for Young Children*. New York, NY: Routledge.

Saunders, Alicia F., Keri S. Bethune, Fred Spooner, and Dianne Browder. 2013. "Solving the Common Core Equation: Teaching Mathematics CCSS to Students with Moderate and Severe Disabilities." *Teaching Exceptional Children* 45: 24–33.

Shaughnessy, Meghan M. 2011. "Identify Fractions and Decimals on a Number Line." *Teaching Children Mathematics,* 17: 428–434.

Siebert, Daniel, and Nicole Gaskin. 2006. "Creating, Naming and Justifying Fractions." *Teaching Children Mathematics*: 394–400.

Siegel, Lee. 2012. "Rise of the Tiger Nation." New York: *The Wall Street Journal.*

Siemon, Dianne, John Izard, Margarita Breed, and Jo Virgona. 2006. "The Derivation of a Learning Assessment Framework for Multiplicative Thinking." *Proceedings of the 30th Annual Conference of the International Group for the Psychology of Mathematics Education*: 113–120.

Silver, Edward. 2010. "Examining What Teachers Do When They Display Their Best Practice: Teaching Mathematics for Understanding." *Journal of Mathematics Education at Teachers College* 1: 1-6. http://journals.tc-library.org/index.php/matheducation/article/viewFile/498/314 .

Smith, Jack, and Funda Gonulates. 2011. "Teacher's Companion to Measurement in the Common Core State Standards I Mathematics (CCSS-M)". https://www.msu.edu/~stemproj/STEM_CommonCoreStandards_Companion%20Document_Draft%20Final_7–11.pdf.

Smith, Margaret, Elizabeth K. Hughes, Randi A. Engle, and Mary Kay Stein. 2009. "Orchestrating Classroom Discussions." *Mathematics Teaching in the Middle School* 14: 548–556.

Steffe, Leslie. P., and John Olive. 2010. *Children's Fractional Knowledge*. New York: NY: Springer.

Stern, Lynn A. 1990. *On the Shoulders of Giants: New Approaches to Numeracy.* Washington, DC: National Academies Press.

Suh, Jennifer M., Chris Johnston, Spencer Jamieson, and Michelle Mills. 2008. "Promoting Decimal Number Sense and Representational Fluency." *Mathematics Teaching in the Middle School* 14: 44–50.

Suh, Jennifer, and Padmanabhan Seshaiyer. 2012. "Technology from the Classroom: Modeling 10–ness Using Tech-Knowledgy." *National Council of Teachers of Mathematics.* 18: 574–578.

Swanson, Kristen. 2013. "5 Tips for Explaining Common Core to Parents." http://thejournal.com/articles/2013/10/01/how-to-explain-common-core-to-parents.aspx.

Thomas, John W. 2000. "A Review of Project-Based Learning." http://www.bie.org/research/study/review_of_project_based_learning_2000.

Thompson, Tony D., and Ronald V. Preston. 2004. "Measurement in the Middle Grades: Insights from NAEP and TIMMS. *Mathematics Teaching in the Middle School.* 9: 514–519.

Tomlinson, Carol, and Marcia Imbeau. 2010. *Leading and Managing a Differentiated Classroom.* Alexandria, VA: ASCD.